Ordinary Girl

Ordinary Girl

My Life in Extraordinary Times

Barbara Wolfe-Johnson

In a few instances, people's names and identifying characteristics have been changed to protect their privacy. Otherwise, everything contained herein is accurate to the best of the author's ability.

In keeping with the author's obligation as a former Central Intelligence Agency employee, this manuscript was submitted to the agency's Prepublication Classification Review Board. The board reviewed it to ensure that no classified information is disclosed herein. The experiences and views expressed here are entirely those of the author and not of the agency.

CR Writers' Publishing
6319 North Louise Avenue
Chicago, Illinois 60646
USA

Ordinary Girl / Barbara Wolfe-Johnson
First paperback edition
ISBN: 978-1-965342-11-4

Dedication

This memoir is dedicated to my sons, Neil and Lee Wolfe, who accompanied me on much of my journey through life and gave me purpose, courage, and patience. We have so many amazing memories to look back on—from sleeping in a jail cell one night in Vicenza, Italy to the many times they got out of the car to put on tire chains for me as we drove to ski resorts in blizzards. Thanks again. I hope you had as much fun as I did.

And I hope that this memoir provides a glimpse into my life, not just as your mother but as an ordinary woman who did her best and lived life to the fullest. My memoir is an emotional reflection of my life. I did not include details of your lives in my book. Your information is private and for only you to write.

❧

The book is also dedicated to my best friend, Ruthie Delaplane. After college, Ruthie became the head of publications for a major firm in Boston. Later, she married and raised kids and racehorses. Fast forward many years later, when she retired in Costa Rica, where we met. When I decided to write my memoir, Ruthie encouraged me and became my mentor, cheerleader, advocate, coach, and loving critic. Ruthie's sight had deteriorated to the point that she could no longer read or drive. So, after writing a few chapters, I would visit her and read my draft aloud while Ruthie occasionally stopped me to make a comment or suggestion. Her support and encouragement culminated in this publication, a joint effort.

It's three days before Christmas, and I'm proofreading my final manuscript one last time before sending it to my publisher. I hear Ruthie in the background encouraging me, "Barbara, it's time to just finish it. It's a good book, and you need to stop editing and get it published. A book is never perfect, but yours is finished."

Bless you, Ruthie.

The purpose of life, after all, is to live it, taste experience to the utmost, to reach out eagerly and without fear for newer and richer experience.

—Eleanor Roosevelt

Prologue

The afternoon of August 19th, 2003, was sunny and hot, as usual. I was driving back home along a quiet road in the Tigoni hills, north of Nairobi, Kenya. My trunk was full of flowers for my new garden.

My husband, Paul, and I had moved to this rural town just a month ago. I was mesmerized by the beauty of endless tea plantations among the gently rolling hills. Nature had painted every hue of green along the hills—a light green when new tea leaves were sprouting, a rich green when leaves matured, and a greenish brown when leaves were harvested. Shadows from puffy cumulus clouds overhead sprinkled darker hues, adding shade here and there across the valley. At sunrise each morning, hard-working Kenyan women with long, deep baskets on their backs picked the tender tea leaves, a section at a time. I could see them from the road in their bright, colorful kangas.

Kenya's siren song had worked its magic on us. We were enchanted by the friendliness of the Kenyans, the vast beauty of nature, and the amazing wild animals.

Suddenly, my cell phone rang. I pulled over to the shoulder, reached for the phone, and said, "Hello?"

Jenny, an American who worked with Paul, urgently asked, "Where are you?"

"I am driving," I replied.

She demanded, "Pull over!" The hair stood up on the back of my neck. I turned off the car.

"What is wrong?" I implored.

"I just heard breaking news on CNN that the United Nations, UN, temporary headquarters located at the Canal Hotel in Baghdad, was just bombed by terrorists. Is that where Paul went on his first consulting assignment?" she asked.

"Yes, it is," I replied.

"I don't know any details, so just stay by the phone. I will update you as soon as I know more news," she offered.

I thanked her, disconnected the call, then sat frozen in the car for what seemed like several minutes, trying to control my initial panic.

Paul was the love of my life. I met him when we were both in our forties. We had been together as friends, lovers, and soulmates for over fourteen years and happily married for nine.

I did not know if Paul was even at the Canal Hotel at the time of the bombing. Perhaps he was having coffee with colleagues at a nearby café, I thought optimistically.

Taking a deep breath, I pushed all emotions aside and searched my heart and my gut for any warning signs. There were none. My focus turned to the Universe to read signs of negative energy.

Whenever a crisis occurs, I go into a controlled, non-emotional, almost clinical, survival mode. I rely on my gut to give me the correct insight during a crisis. Within seconds, I got a strong sense that Paul would be fine, though I did not know if he was "fine" at that moment. I needed to stay focused and wait for more information. Starting the car, I continued toward home. There were no tears because there was no reason to cry.

Paul had been working in Baghdad at the Canal Hotel for only a few days on a two-week security contract for the International Monetary Fund, IMF. A few days ago, he told me that a group of Senior IMF staff members was due to arrive for important meetings. He was looking forward to meeting them.

Unwilling to acknowledge the potential crisis, I reflected on our recent move to Tigon and our goal of continuing humanitarian work in Africa for many years.

❧

Just over a year ago, Paul accepted a one-year contract with the International Rescue Committee, IRC, as deputy director of the mission in Kenya. We both chose to kiss our successful careers goodbye and flew to Africa. That year was amazing, full of adventures and new friends.

We traveled to amazing national wildlife parks, including Amboseli, Tsavo West, Samburu, Masai Mara, Arusha, and Ngorongoro Crater, witnessing wild animals in their natural environment, unencumbered by fences or enclosures. We learned about the tribes of the Masai and Samburu pastoralists.

I volunteered for months at "Save the Elephants," and was lucky enough to witness the elephant GPS collaring, used to monitor their migration.

With his new private pilot license, Paul flew us to an amazing weekend getaway to the Stone Town of Zanzibar on an island off the coast of Tanzania. We were living life to the fullest, and I looked forward to spending many more years in Africa.

Then, without warning, Paul received notice that his IRC contract would not be renewed the following year! International politics had caused enough dissent that the current management staff was being replaced. When Paul told me the news, we were both speechless. Our future livelihood in Kenya was gone.

We both had given up our careers to do humanitarian work. Now, in less than two weeks, Paul had become unemployed. I had taken early retirement so now we were both unemployed.

Our heads swirled with so many questions, issues, and immediate decisions that were forced upon us, it was hard to focus. Could we sustain ourselves on just Paul's Army pension and stay in Kenya? I was sure we could cut back if we were to forgo our favorite restaurants, and instead eat rice and beans, but before long, his work visa would expire. Then, we'd only have limited tourist visas. The clock was ticking.

IRC staff soon arrived at our home, with a big truck to take all the furniture and appliances they had loaned us. I felt angry and helpless until Paul explained, "The staff are not the enemy. These workers are my friends and are just following orders."

I understood but still gritted my teeth as they took our household goods, loaded them on a truck, and left.

Instead of packing up and returning to the U.S., Paul was very optimistic that he could find work with a UN non-governmental organization in the area. Luckily, we still owned our trusty Mitsubishi 4x4. Paul's optimism became contagious. Soon I was looking forward to a new, exciting adventure. After all, we had our health, our zest for life, and confidence in each other.

Our first priority was finding an affordable rental home. We focused our search further north in the more rural areas. We soon found a charming log home among tea plantations in Tigoni. I had never seen a log home in Kenya, since hungry termites will devour it in no time. Nonetheless, it was perfect—isolated, quiet, and secure. This sturdy structure had a nice kitchen, a large living room with a huge fireplace, three bedrooms, and attached guest quarters. It was fenced on one acre and had a lovely sloping lawn that meandered downhill to a creek where white faced monkeys played. It looked magical. We quickly signed the lease and moved in.

After a couple of months of pinching pennies, Paul accepted a two-week security contract to go to Baghdad. I was not thrilled about him going into unstable, war-torn Iraq, but he assured me he'd be fine.

As I turned into our driveway, my mind focused back on reality. The dogs ran up to greet me with enthusiastic, unconditional love and affection.

I rushed into the house and turned on the television. Every channel was covering the terrorist bombing live from Iraq. It showed the UN Canal Hotel in ruins. Rubble lay where the building once stood. I sat stunned, witnessing the unbelievable devastation. Injured staff wandered around in a daze. I became numb, refusing to consider that Paul might be injured.

Thank God, the U.S. military had quickly taken over security at the UN compound. Young soldiers in desert camouflage fatigues were doing their best to maintain order in what was complete chaos.

The only TV channels I could get were in Swahili or Arabic. I couldn't understand any of the news commentary. My frustration became palpable. After several minutes, I had to escape the drone of talking news heads.

Stepping out on the veranda, a welcoming, cool breeze embraced me. The sun was setting, with colorful hues of rose and deep orange, low over the forest. I sighed heavily, realizing the only thing I could do was wait for Paul to call.

Within an hour, I got a call from Wayne, Paul's boss on the contract. I had met Wayne and his wife, Maryanne, a few times socially. Wayne was a tall, broadly built, handsome American in his 60s, with a shock of thick, white hair. His southern accent and cordial manner disarmed his huge physical presence. He was a retired Army special forces officer and also recently retired from a second career with the UN in Nairobi. He had recently recruited Paul for this two-week consultancy in Baghdad.

In a troubled tone, Wayne acknowledged that Paul had been inside the Canal Hotel when the bombing occurred. A personal UN contact at the scene told Wayne that Paul had received a head injury from a piece of metal that lodged in his cheek, but he was conscious and talking.

A wave of relief swept over me like a warm fleece blanket. He was conscious and talking. Thank God! Perhaps he would need plastic surgery to regain his handsome looks, but it didn't sound life-threatening. Now I was sure that Paul would call soon.

After waiting alone by the phone for hours, Jenny called again. I gave her the news I had received from Wayne. A few friends and associates called as well to show solidarity and offer their support and prayers. Still, no word from Paul. I stayed off the phone as much as possible but also wanted to reach out for support from my friends. By evening, I was exhausted, my muscles tied in knots.

Finally, I climbed up on our wrought iron canopy bed, hugging Paul's pillow. His familiar scent relaxed and comforted me.

The next morning, the air was crisp and cold, with a damp fog that had settled in the valley. I massaged my temples, trying to make sense of this nightmare that consumed me. I have always been an analytical person of action, but now I was helpless. Reaching for my sweats, I decided I needed some breakfast.

By late afternoon, I began to worry. I still had no call from Paul. I decided to contact my sons, Neil and Lee, and let them know of Paul's injury. I was a divorced Mom for most of their youth. We're extremely close. My oldest son, Neil, was married, living in Chicago. Lee was also married, living in Mississippi. Neil had a current passport and agreed to come and be with me. Lee's passport had expired, so Neil had the job. What a comfort to know he would soon be by my side.

I picked up the phone again and called Ruby, Paul's oldest daughter. What a surprise when I learned she already knew of his injury. She had recognized her father on a CNN news video and knew of his injury before I did. She described the picture of Paul on a stretcher being carried off by Army personnel in front of the Canal Hotel. She recognized him by his cargo pants and his Kenyan beaded belt. Then, she described the ten-foot metal pole impaled in his left cheek, with a young Army soldier walking beside his stretcher, supporting the pole. It looked like an aluminum rod, she added.

Ruby gleaned more information by watching CNN in the U.S. than Wayne or I had received. She described that the dramatic picture of Paul now appeared in the latest Newsweek magazine. She had picked up several copies. Ruby was a smart, savvy woman who had contacted the IMF in Washington, DC, requesting a flight to see her father.

We agreed to stay in touch. Knowing this new information, I felt even more isolated and helpless. Why had she not called me? I wondered.

After several more hours of silence, I knew, if Paul were conscious, he'd beg or borrow a phone to contact me. My anxiety rose, thinking his injury might be more serious. Perhaps he was not conscious any longer? I tried to remain rooted to the facts, but my mind wandered into the horrible what-ifs.

Al Jazeera continued to report the rescue effort as men, using their hands, dug into the rubble, looking for survivors. The American Coalition Forces in Baghdad, not the Iraqi forces, had taken over the entire rescue effort. I found solace in the fact that Paul's life was now in the hands of the U.S. military.

We were soulmates who supported and encouraged each other. We lived, hiked, scuba-dived, danced, and explored the wonders of the world. Our love was invincible. We would get through this.

After countless hours, Wayne finally called with more news. Paul had been evacuated by helicopter to the nearest military triage site near Baghdad, where he was sedated and intubated. Doctors suspected his head injury could be serious, so they evacuated him again (with the metal pole in situ) to a larger military hospital in Kuwait City, Kuwait. After X-rays, CT scans, and a myriad of other tests, the doctors reported that Paul was in stable but serious condition in the Kuwait Military Neurology ICU, unconscious and fighting for his life!

Oh my God! I ran my hands through my hair, trying to get my head around the fact that he was seriously injured. The news knocked me completely off balance. I finally admitted to myself that I had been naively optimistic about Paul's condition.

Wayne called later that evening to say that Paul had been diagnosed with a skull fracture and traumatic brain injury. I took a deep breath as he continued. Military neurosurgeons performed surgery to repair the damage. He was out of surgery now, in critical condition, with hematomas in both frontal lobes. Wayne's source added that Paul must be in "stable condition" before they would medically transfer him to the closest military hospital in Landstuhl, Germany.

I asked Wayne, "Can you get me a ticket to Kuwait?"

He paused for a moment, then replied, "I advise against that, Barbara. Visas are difficult to get in Arab countries, and you might be in the air to Kuwait when Paul is being flown to Germany."

That all made sense, but it still left me stuck in Kenya, helpless.

I finally had to acknowledge the impossible truth. Paul had sustained a fractured skull in the bombing! The dreadful news forced me to face the grave, life-threatening truth. I did not break down but was frozen in the harsh reality. We were continents apart. I had to be with him. We'd figure everything out from there. I knew his condition was dire, but deep in my heart, I clung to the feeling that Paul could still be okay. My gut had never failed me. But perhaps now I was in denial. Only time would tell.

Not knowing his status was excruciating. For a distraction, I took the dogs, Eiger and Petra, for a walk in the tea plantations nearby, to a small pond in a valley. It was our favorite place to take a walk and throw sticks for the dogs. I gathered sticks along the way so I would be prepared. The dogs loved jumping in and retrieving each stick, then proudly placing it on shore at my feet. I threw sticks until we were all exhausted, then we walked back home. It was much-needed exercise as well as a total distraction.

All I could do now was stay by the phone, clinging to the fact that Paul was extremely healthy and was in the capable hands of the military. I had confidence they would do everything possible for Paul, a retired Army Major, one of their own. I thanked God many times that he was not languishing in a third-world Iraqi hospital, somewhere in the desert.

Critical condition? So many questions came to mind: What was the extent of his brain injury? Could he get worse? Could he be emotionally or physically impaired? When he became conscious, would he recognize me? Could his personality change and become angry, sullen, or deeply depressed? I would not have any answers until they woke him up from his medicated coma. Logic told me to put all my doubts and questions on hold until I could talk to him. But how long would that be?

❧

I began to consider the uncertainty of our future in Africa. Our world was spinning out of control now. Both of us loved Kenya and wanted to stay, but everything was up in the air. Should I make plans to go back to the States and try to get my job back?

Just a month ago, while discussing our unemployment challenge, I shared with Paul that I missed my career after taking early retirement to join him in Kenya. I missed the challenge, social interaction, but most of all, the responsibility, and the fact that I was doing something worthwhile and important. I had been working as a manager for the Central Intelligence Agency, CIA, at the Counter Terrorist Center computer system in McLean, Virginia. I was literally at the top of my game when I decided to retire and follow my love.

I had tried to break into the non-governmental organization, NGO, world in Nairobi, but my expertise in information technology systems for the government did not match. Small NGO missions usually only need a network administrator. I was overqualified! Maybe it was time to go back to the States and rejoin the rat race.

Then, the obvious brought me back to reality, "Oh, yeah," I said to myself, "you are both still unemployed. You'd better make a decision, sooner rather than later. Shit!"

Early the next morning, Wayne called to report that Paul had been taken back into surgery overnight to relieve the hematomas. He was now in stable condition and was scheduled to be medically evacuated to Landstuhl Hospital in Germany early the next morning.

Wayne had already purchased a round-trip ticket for me to fly that evening to Frankfurt, Germany, to be with him.

My heart soared with love and relief. The waiting was finally over. I was going to join my love. I packed some casual clothes, my laptop, a couple of books, and a few things for Paul to wear home, assuming we'd both return to Kenya after he recuperated. Then I made arrangements with my Japanese neighbor to keep an eye on the house and feed the dogs while I was gone.

Wayne arranged for a taxi to pick me up early that evening. I would first meet up with Wayne and Howard, the head of Security Consultants, Inc., and their wives, exchange words of optimism, have a farewell drink, and then go to Nairobi International Airport for my flight.

Riding in the taxi, I looked forward to hugs of comfort and support from our good friends. This was the first step in being reunited with my husband. I could not get there fast enough. I wanted to be there before he arrived at the Landstuhl Hospital.

Part One

1

"Baba too," were my first meaningful words as a toddler. I was declaring from the confines of my playpen that I wanted to play with my sister Veronica. Mother replied, in an authoritative tone, "No, Barbara, play by yourself, honey." Veronica ignored me, shut the door and left to play with her friend, without me. My vocabulary was very limited, but I'm sure I stuck out my bottom lip, pouted, and eventually cried. Life continued with me alone in that playpen. From a very young age, my life was mostly solitary.

❧

My name is Barbara Ann McNeil. I was born just after the end of World War II, the second of three children, and raised in a strict, devout, Irish/German, Catholic family, in the suburbs of Boston, Massachusetts. At just one year old, I had thick, dark-brown hair and dark eyes. I must have been on the small side because my Uncle Jack used to call me "Half Pint." Although I didn't know it yet, I'd become an intelligent, and confident but shy young lady who tried to fit in and always did her very best.

My sister, Veronica, three years older, was a very pretty girl with striking, long,-black hair and dark brown eyes. At five years old, she had already developed a superiority complex and a "holier than thou" attitude. As far back as I can remember, she looked down on me as less than equal.

I have no loving memories of Veronica playing with me or showing me any affection. Even at this young age, I felt rejected. She either ignored me or bullied me. However, Mother never considered her behavior unacceptable toward me, so Veronica continued to show, "I am the superior sister, and you are simply an unfortunate sibling I must endure."

Perhaps I had arrived on her grand stage to compete with her life's performance. After three years of being the only child with her very own bedroom, Veronica was suddenly forced to share life and her bedroom with me. I had never done anything to offend her and just wanted to be loved. We could have had such fun. I will always miss the sister I never got a chance to love.

My brother, Eddie, came along when I started school. He was such a sweet baby. Sometimes Mom let me feed him. I remember sitting outside Eddie's playpen, the same playpen I once occupied. But when Eddie threw out a toy, I would play the game and pick it up and put it back. He loved the attention.

When I started first grade, Mother told Veronica she must walk with me to and from school every day. So, each school day, we went to and from school together. However, she always walked in front of me, chatting away with her girlfriend, while I walked behind, trying to keep up. By this time, I had learned to ignore her behavior.

❧

I grew up in a small, conservative, colonial town, about an hour's drive north of Boston but a world away from the busy capital of Massachusetts. The area was originally settled in 1680 by farmers. It was officially founded as North Reading in 1853.

Our two-story, three-bedroom, wooden, colonial house had a large, attached, barn on a half-acre of land in an older neighborhood. The original house was over one hundred years old. There were rumors that the house was originally bought from a Sears catalog. An old outhouse still stood, unused, behind the barn. Electricity and indoor plumbing had been added years before to make it more comfortable. Let's just say it had no central heat or air conditioning.

A small, wooden ice box in the kitchen required two blocks of ice delivered weekly to keep our food fresh. In the summer, I remember waiting on the front steps for the ice truck to arrive. If I asked politely, he would break off a nice cold chunk of ice for me to suck on.

For communication, we had an old crank phone that was mounted on the wall. It was a "three-party line," which meant we shared the same line with two other families. To use this kind of phone, you would first pick up the receiver and listen. If someone was already talking, you might ask how long they would be, then hang up and wait several minutes, and try again. If the phone was not in use, you would crank the knob on the phone several times, causing an operator's bell to ring. She would ask for the number you wanted to call and then connect the lines at the telephone station. We have come a long way since then. If someone had explained smartphone technology to me in 1950, I would not have believed it.

The stately North Reading Town Hall was our symbol of independence and freedom in America. It stood majestically in the center of town on top of a large hill, which was a great place for sledding during the winter months. Surrounding the town hall were the police and fire stations. A block away was the drug store, with a long, bar-shaped soda fountain, offered root beer floats, my favorite, for fifteen cents, vanilla cokes for ten cents, and scrumptious cheeseburgers, dripping with grease, for twenty-five cents. This place became a teenage after-school hangout. Teenagers parked their hot rods in front, listening to rock and roll from their car radios, smoking cigarettes, and talking for hours. Nearby was my old, red-brick elementary school. The post-World War II baby boomer population grew large enough that the school could no longer accommodate all the children. For three years, we had what they called split sessions, where each child was assigned to either the morning or afternoon session. Luckily, I always got mornings and had the rest of the day to do homework, then I was free to play. After several years, a new high school and elementary school were built, and we went back to full-day sessions.

This quiet, picturesque New England hamlet was my home. It was an ideal, safe place for a young girl to grow up. Large mature oak, elm, and maple trees stretched their long limbs across the narrow roads, providing ample shade. No one ever locked their doors.

Our neighbors, typical New Englanders, were cordial, yet private, and a bit distant. Neighbors waved hello, then just continued with their day not caring how you were. We were newcomers on the street, yet my folks were never invited to a neighbor's home for coffee or an afternoon cookout. They kept to themselves as well. I considered this normal behavior until I left New England.

❧

My mother, Theresa Marie McNeil, nicknamed "Tess," was born in Philadelphia before the Great Depression. She was a devout Catholic of German descent who attended Catholic private schools. After high school, she became a secretary, staying at home to care for her invalid mother until she married. Once married, they moved to Massachusetts after Veronica and I were born. Mom was a slender, lovely woman of about five-feet, eight-inches tall, with striking jet-black hair and hazel eyes. She was intelligent, with a quiet, unassuming demeanor. On a typical Sunday morning in the summer, with the promise that the family could go to the beach for the day, after all the sandwiches and drinks were prepared, we'd all sit waiting, while she finished all her vacuuming and dusting, as if the Pope were coming. She loved music and played the piano. I stood in awe when she played the *Nutcracker Suite* or *Scheherazade.* She encouraged both of her daughters to take lessons, but neither of us was interested in such a strict regimen. Mom was also a good seamstress, making most of our school clothes on her old foot-treadle Singer machine.

I'll always remember her acting like an adult and never displaying childish or playful behavior. Sometimes, I'd watch her get dressed up for Parent-Teacher Association meetings, wearing a stylish dress, high heels, makeup, jewelry, and her special perfume. Dad was dressed up as well, in a suit and tie. Otherwise, they never dressed up to go out as a couple for dinner, a movie, or even to another couple's home for a party. We never had a babysitter.

My dad, Edward James McNeil, nicknamed "Mac," was of Irish descent. He was ten years older than my mother and was an experienced accountant. Dad was a slender, handsome man with short, jet-black hair he combed straight back with a bit of Vaseline to keep his hair in place. He was a gentle, quiet, caring man of few words, but had a spontaneous wit. He was an avid reader of *Reader's Digest* and local newspapers, but I never knew him to check out books at the local library. Every day, he dressed up in a suit and tie and took the train to work in Boston.

Both parents were serious, responsible adults, a common trait in the post-World War II era, since they survived the Depression. Although I knew I was deeply loved, my parents were caring in a distant, non-tactile way. The affection I remember was either a quick hug or a kiss on the cheek. I never observed Mom and Dad laughing, spontaneously dancing, hugging, or having fun together. This seemed like normal behavior for adults of that era. With such wonderful role models, I quickly learned how to be serious and avoid playful, childlike behavior as I grew up. Once I mastered this façade of seriousness, I suppressed any urge to just let go, laugh, and have fun.

I did not hang out with Mom or Veronica. I sought out Dad, following him around every weekend like a puppy dog. He wanted his second-born child to be a son, but I was the next best thing, a tomboy.

We became good buddies. I would help him fix things around the house and he would patiently explain what needed to be done, then show me how to do it properly. He taught me how to paint a room by first putting masking tape around each door and window frame to protect the wood. He then painted around all the window and door frames with a small brush. At the end of the day, he'd thoroughly clean all the brushes. Each summer, Dad and I spent time outside, caring for his vegetable garden of tomatoes, onions, green beans, lettuce, and radishes.

Dad was quiet most of the time, but I always felt his love. Occasionally, I'd tag along with him to the hardware store where he would buy me a handful of penny nails. When we got home, I would hammer them into a spare piece of wood, taking time to keep the nail straight. I'm still working on that. At the age of four or five, I'd pile in the car with Dad on a Saturday morning, and we'd go to his barbershop. I'd sit in the waiting area, listening to the men's conversations, while Dad got his hair cut. One summer day, Dad asked if I wanted my hair cut. "Yes," I said and came home looking like a little boy. Mom was very upset, but I loved it.

My girlfriend Trudy, who lived just up the street, sometimes played together with me after school. But most of the time, I played by myself. I never liked playing with dolls. I preferred collecting different colored rocks and capturing caterpillars of assorted colors. I would use a small glass jar for their house, making small holes in the metal top so they could breathe. Then, I'd feed them leaves every day and patiently watch them turn into cocoons and eventually hatch as beautiful butterflies. Nature was fascinating.

❧

Every Sunday morning, our family would go to Catholic mass, then stay for another hour of catechism study. When it was over, everyone tried to exit the parking lot at once, causing a traffic jam with horns honking and angry looks toward those attempting to cut into the line. It was every man for himself. The priest should have come out and directed traffic, teaching the drivers to be Good Samaritans. Our treat after mass was to stop at the donut store. My favorite was a chocolate frosted or a glazed cruller. There were always evening prayers before bed. Mass was also held on every holy day. Saturday afternoon was reserved for confessions, as needed to confess our sins. This religious upbringing formed a large part of my moral character. Catholics were not allowed to eat meat on Friday.

When I was old enough to go to Ryer's Store, a block away and by myself, I'd go pick up a loaf of white bread for five cents or a quart of milk for Mom for ten cents. In the front by the cash register was a huge, glass-topped, wooden display case full of penny candy. I'd have to get on my tippy-toes to see all the candy. It was difficult to decide how to spend my five-cent allowance. Should I choose a round cow tail of caramel with white sugar in the middle, or a long, white, paper strip filled with rows of small candy discs? The sugar discs always lasted longer but were not as sweet and chewy as a cow tail. This was an introduction to making wise and difficult decisions. I learned that what looked delicious on the outside might be very sour on the inside. It is still true today.

When I was about nine, Dad told me he was building a tree house in the backyard for Veronica. I don't recall any family discussion about a treehouse, but soon, Dad arrived home with lots of lumber and started building. I helped him build it, and when it was completed, Veronica climbed up the ladder, closed the hatch, and refused to let me in.

Without chastising Veronica, Dad resolved the problem by building a separate tree house for me, right next to hers. In a nutshell, that was life for me and my sister, playing in separate tree houses and sleeping in twin beds, two feet apart. However, the emotional distance was vast.

❧

Entertainment in the 1950s consisted of playing cards, board games, or listening to the radio. Most of the time, I was glued to episodes of *The*

Lone Ranger, *Gene Autry*, and *Sky King*. Using my imagination, I'd get a vivid picture of what was happening. Usually, the hero was chasing a villain out of town, or rescuing a damsel in distress, while the radio host colorfully narrated each exciting scene. The adventures of *The Lone Ranger* were my favorites. He was a young, tall, handsome man who wore a tight-fitting white shirt and pants and had a black mask. He rode around the Wild West on his beautiful white horse, Silver, helping ranchers in distress, an early kind of Superman. I was so enthralled that I wanted to be a cowboy when I grew up. Maybe one day, I'd have my very own horse. I asked Santa for a cowboy outfit with a hat, gun, and holster. Santa came through, and I proudly marched around the house looking for a real horse. Then I noticed three horses in the yard next door.

Our neighbors next-door, the Joneses, had three beautiful horses, a sheep, a goat, a couple of cats, and a dog. Jackie, their daughter, was ten years older than Herbie and I, and her brother was my sister's age. After school and during the summer months, I was allowed to visit them and help Jackie clean stalls, the leather tack, and feed and water the horses. Sometimes, we'd give them carrots, apple slices, or sugar cubes as treats. Jackie was a very introverted, frail-looking girl with beautiful strawberry-blonde hair who suffered from chronic asthma that often made her seriously ill. However, she seemed glad to have my company, and we became good friends. Horses were her whole life, and they became mine too. Our best Saturday activity would be joining Mrs. Jones, Jackie, and Herbie when they went to horse shows. Back at home, Mom, Dad, and Veronica usually went to the new shopping mall in a town nearby. Time passed, and the Joneses' barn became my second home. This was a place I could be myself and not be bullied or feel inferior. I was in my element, surrounded by animals. Mrs. Jones and especially Jackie made me feel appreciated and valued. At long last, "Baba" was accepted.

Being around horses, I got to know their nature, personality, and the subtle signals they would convey. I watched the movement of their ears and any sudden body movements. I trusted their instincts and respected their disposition. Being close to a horse was a humbling partnership, one that I cherish to this day. When I entered junior high, the Joneses sold their house and moved away. Jackie went off to college to be a medical technician. We took separate paths. I missed her, but at the same time, I was becoming a teenager, entering an exciting new world, including boys

Looking back:

The Jones family, especially Jackie, made me feel included and valued. The animals taught me a quiet, humble dignity. These relationships served as colorful threads to create the strong, durable fabric of my soul, giving me confidence in myself. I was still shy and remained a loner at heart, but the bedrock of my personality was formed. "Baba Too" could stand on her own, confident in herself and her ability to do her very best.

❧

When I was eleven, Mom decided I should stop acting like a tomboy and start acting like a young lady. She had a talk with Dad and me about me moving out of the tomboy stage, which translated into not hanging out with Dad as much. She probably noticed my small breasts peeking through my shirt, which translated into wearing a bra. Menstruation had already started with the weird napkin paraphernalia held up by uncomfortable belts. I capitulated but was still a tomboy at heart!

2

The prospect of becoming a teenager was exciting. I was ready to move on to high school, with football games, Saturday night dances, Elvis Presley, rock and roll, and, of course, dating. These were happy years, full of school studies and fun with friends.

I became part of a small group of girls who were on the honor roll and did not smoke or drink. We were called "stuck up" by our peers and probably were because we had a clique of our own. We did not fit in with the other groups of girls who were boy-crazy, partying, dating, smoking, drinking, and petting.

The best fun we had on the weekends was to have a pajama party at someone's house. With parents out of sight but still in the house to supervise, we could talk about anything, laugh, and dance to the latest rock and roll tunes on our 45 RPM phonograph record players. We'd stay up all night eating pizza, popcorn, potato chips, and soft drinks. We styled each other's hair and talked about boys until the wee hours of the morning. Then, one by one, we'd crash into our sleeping bags. It was a close sisterhood that remains today, albeit from a distance.

My new friend Marty invited me for a sleepover at her house one weekend. After riding bikes and playing all afternoon, we sat down for dinner with the family. They conversed in a caring and loving manner with interest and without judgment. They talked about their day, asked questions, discussed problems their kids had, and provided advice to each other. There was no comparing Marty to the older brother or vice versa. They were a family unit.

This new view of family life shocked me to my core and crushed the impression that my family life was normal. Dinner at my house was not a time to come together, but for my mother to ask us how our studies were going. Veronica or I might bring up upcoming after-school activities, such as her drama practice or my next basketball game. Mother would probably be disappointed in my latest test results. Dinner was a time to check in but not share feelings, concerns, frustrations, or plans. Dad rarely said anything since Mother ran the house. Compared to the love at my friend's house, my world was like a beautiful vase with lifeless flowers shedding petals onto the floor. I knew I could not do it yet, but I strived to become independent as soon as I could.

Meanwhile, Mother continued to remind me that I should strive to be more like my sister. I see you got two Bs on your report card," Mother remarked. "You also got three As, but I'd like you to strive for all As like Veronica." I sighed. A moment earlier I had been proud of my three As, but now, I just wasn't good enough. Mother made it clear she wanted a carbon copy of her firstborn, and it was clear that I did not measure up. Not wanting to be compared to my sister, I opted for a different, more interesting path.

❧

As a teenager, while I always loved, respected, and obeyed my parents, I now developed a confident sense of myself. I now had a voice and didn't agree with everything my parents told me. My frustrated Mother repeatedly said, "You would argue with the Pope."

"Yes, I would," I replied, "if I did not agree with him." I was not being argumentative; I just wanted to understand their view in order to make a decision, I felt was the right one. Perhaps, there was a touch of assertiveness in my voice. Woops!

I recall two distinct incidents that stand out as an attempt to assert a bit of independence or perhaps even defiance on my part. The first incident occurred when my dog Tippy got into trouble. I don't remember why, but Dad headed after him across the yard with a big stick. I ran ahead, caught the dog, and lay across his body. Dad arrived, furious and yelled, "Get off that dog!"

I turned calmly and said, "No, you will have to beat me instead." He turned and walked away without a word.

The second confrontation was with Mom when I was about thirteen years old. There was a large pine forest across the street from us with a small meandering creek, home to small guppies and frogs. Sometimes, a creepy salamander popped its head up and slithered away. I'd see rabbits and chipmunks, but I never saw a snake. Whenever I had free time as a kid and wanted peace and quiet, I'd go into the woods and spend hours watching nature—raccoons and sometimes deer. The forest was a quiet, peaceful hamlet for me, where I was one with nature. I could relax and clear my head. One summer afternoon, I walked toward the kitchen door and mentioned to Mom, "I'm going into the woods for a while."

She frowned and replied, "That is not a good idea."

"Why, I asked?"

She replied, "You are alone and could be raped.

"That is ridiculous," I said. "After all the years I have spent in the woods, you think that I'm in danger today of being raped? Do you have any evidence that I would be in danger today? If not, I'm going." I slammed the kitchen door as I left, the loud bang echoing my intentions. I would not accept a "do this or do that" just because she said so. I'd argue with her as if she were the Pope.

I was a happy teenager who distinguished herself in her studies and loved sports. I practiced very hard to qualify for the girls' junior varsity basketball team and was proud to make the varsity team in my senior year. I was five-feet, two-inches tall and barely one hundred pounds, so I became a guard, sitting on the bench most of the time. One of my good friends, Nancy, was also on the team, and we hung out together. Our team practiced hard, and then we showered and walked home in the dark, sometimes in the rain or snow.

For away games, we traveled by bus to nearby towns. The entire team had one goal that we worked toward all year. This team building was invaluable later in my career. Mom and Dad never attended any of my basketball games. However, the entire family always dressed up and attended Veronica's plays and other drama events. This was a family event. I just figured they did not like basketball.

❧

A big part of high school dating was going steady. "Casual dating," meaning dating several guys, was fraught with problems and often resulted in not having a date for some important event. However, if you dated a boy for a few months and liked each other, going steady was a way to say we were an "exclusive couple." It eliminated the hassle or fear of being left out. He was your escort to the homecoming dance in the fall and the prom in the spring. You would meet at the football games, then go out on Saturday night after the high school dance. Most importantly, you'd feel like you belonged to someone you cared about. Was it love? Perhaps, but it was a way to explore getting to know potential partners.

❧

In my sophomore year, I met Dave, my first boyfriend. He was a year older than I with curly blonde hair combed like John Travolta's. He was tall, thin, handsome, and a very sweet guy who did not smoke cigarettes or drink. When Dave got his driver's license, he was allowed to borrow his dad's Ford Fairlane. He became my first love. We went steady for over two years. Since there were no movie theaters or bowling alleys in town, after the school dance on Saturday night, we'd get Italian subs with large cherry cokes at a nearby Italian deli, then drive to the state forest where we would eat our subs, listen to music, then make out and steam up the windows.

This was the height of the Cold War with Russia, and students were taught to hide under their desks to protect themselves if a nuclear bomb went off. Everyone knew the shrill sound of the nuclear alert siren. It was tested each Saturday at noon at the nearby fire station. There were also designated nuclear bomb shelters in schools and public buildings. Dave's family took this threat very seriously and built a bomb shelter in their basement, fully stocked with beds for the whole family and enough food and water for months.

I was already fifteen, but my mother never discussed sex with me. To remedy this gap in my education, Dave and I asked our friendly spinster biology teacher if she could provide some material on the subject. She did, and Dave took the book home, read it, and then gave it to me. I was not as clever at concealing my secret because Mother found the book. "Furious" does not describe her reaction. It was more like a nuclear meltdown! She marched into the high school principal's office the next morning and read him the riot act about my teacher sharing this sexual information with her daughter. While Mom was chewing out the principal, Dad was at home reading the book, and he told me later that the information was accurate! The damage was done. Mother never said anything else to me about it, nor asked me if I had any questions. That was the end of it.

❧

We first made love in the back seat of David's Ford Fairlane. Becoming sexually aroused was, well, *wow*. We were both virgins and played around innocently and foolishly. As a devout Catholic, I was guilt-ridden and had to go to confession. Once inside the confessional, I whispered to the priest, "Bless me, Father, for I have sinned. I committed adultery."

The priest hesitated for a moment, then asked in a very low voice, "Have you had sex with a married man?" No! I responded, shocked. "Adultery is having sex with a married person, He continued, "You did not commit adultery. You had intercourse."

I had never heard of intercourse. Intercourse was not mentioned in the Ten Commandments or the Bible that I knew of. However, in my Catholic brain, I knew it was still horribly wrong. I should have asked him if it was a venial sin, but I was too scared.

Dave and I continued our passionate lovemaking while I went to confession much more often. As my coming of age progressed, I was feeling happy and confident.

3

A young woman's career goals in the 1960s were limited by decades of tradition. She was expected to marry and become a homemaker. Television shows portrayed a lovely young wife, devoted to her husband's hopes and dreams, cleaning floors, doing laundry, caring for children, while making fantastic meals from scratch. Popular shows like *I Love Lucy, Father Knows Best*, and *Leave It to Beaver* reflected the societal expectations of the time. One image I recall is a young wife greeting her husband lovingly at the door each evening, smartly dressed in high heels, with polished nails, perfume, perfect hair, and makeup. Dinner was ready and the entire family sat down for a dinner of meat with gravy, potatoes, and a vegetable. I remember Mom changing from her daily housedress to a lovely, pressed dress and heels before Dad arrived home, but after a few years, she stopped dressing up. Our meals were sometimes made from scratch, but frozen fish sticks and canned foods, like peas, lima beans, and creamed corn, were a handy shortcut. Dessert was usually canned fruit cocktail or a fruit-flavored Jell-O.

If a married woman worked to support her family, it was considered secondary income. Single men and women lived at home until they married. A young single woman who started working in the city and rented an apartment were considered "loose" and unchaperoned.

❧

Teachers encouraged the smarter girls to go to college to become teachers, nurses, or secretaries—jobs that could be full-time until marriage. This way, she had a skill to fall back on if her husband became disabled or died. Young women who attended college were not seeking a BA, Bachelor of Arts degree, or BS, Bachelor of Science degree, but an MRS, marriage to a college-educated man who could provide well for her and their family. Typing, shorthand, and accounting courses were available for those who wanted to become secretaries or accountants. Home Economics included cooking, sewing, cleaning, and baby care, a guarantee that young women was ready for her future role.

Our parents and teachers encouraged us to attend college and enrolled in the college-preparatory curriculum. Ours was a typical one-income family. Dad was an accountant and Mom a full-time housewife. We were considered middle class, but she always pinched pennies, and we always had what we needed. My parents never discussed college finances with me, so I assumed it wasn't a problem.

I worked hard in school, earned good grades, played basketball, supported the school newspaper, and the yearbook committee. In my junior year, I was selected to join the prestigious National Honor Society, a nationwide organization based on scholarship, leadership, service, and character.

Veronica became a member three years before. She now attended the prestigious Regis College, a private Catholic all-girls school in Boston, majoring in English. We were on the fast track.

❧

Suddenly, everything changed when Dad had a severe stroke and was hospitalized. He survived without paralysis but was no longer able to perform his accounting duties. He was forced to retire at age fifty-five with only a small Social Security disability income. This was a tremendous blow to him personally, but the entire family was deeply affected. He was a proud man, suddenly confined to the home with no purpose. Depression took over, and before long, he just sank into the background, sitting in his chair in the living room, reading, watching television, or dozing. He no longer participated in any family discussions at dinner. It was hard to witness such a drastic change in him. I missed my buddy and felt powerless but afraid to question him or even bother him. As a result, he was largely ignored. I became fearful of his silent behavior. It was easier to join the rest of the family and leave him in his lonely world, sitting in his chair.

Mom became the breadwinner overnight, a strong matriarch who had experience as a secretary before she married. She took charge and found a job at the elementary school two blocks from home, which enabled her to return home before we got out of school. Mom had always run the household, but now she was responsible for the budget, finances, taxes, and home maintenance. She had total control of the purse strings. Mom said, "Money was going to be tight, so do not expect anything but essentials." I had outgrown my ice skates and needed new ones, but knew they were expensive. What a big surprise when I saw them under the tree on Christmas morning.

❧

My junior year, the guidance counselor announced that if we intended to attend a college or university, we needed to study for the Scholastic Aptitude Tests, SAT, for all students applying for college. We also needed to research colleges or universities that supported our goals and apply to two or three appropriate schools. I came home that day and mentioned all this to Mom, bringing up again the fact that I want to be a doctor.

She looked at me, shook her head without compassion or emotion, and said, "I do not have the money for eight to ten years of college required for medical school. Veronica still has years of college that I must pay for. When she graduates, she has agreed to repay her college debt. I will use that money for your education."

That was news to me! I should have known Dad's retirement would affect my college plans. However, Dad's disability had not affected Veronica one iota. I must now wait at least one year after my graduation before attending college. Stunned and hurt, I went outside and sat for a while on our old metal swing that was now rusting. I felt like Cinderella, left in a cold basement while Veronica, the favorite daughter, continued her education at her expensive, private Catholic college. Mom never told Veronica she must transfer to a more affordable, state-funded college to finish her degree. Mom also never discussed anything with me about college expenses being an issue.

I bit my tongue until it bled. Any attempt to challenge the decision would be fruitless and would result in a deep rift between us. Looking at the glass half full, Mom suggested, "Why don't you look for something more realistic, like teaching or nursing. Being a doctor is not an ideal career for a woman anyway. I am sure you will marry, have children, and stop working while raising a family, perhaps never returning to work. A man who becomes a doctor will be productive for the rest of his life. Do you understand?" Yes, I did, and I wanted to get married someday and have children. Reality hit me like a slap in the face. I needed to pursue other choices. First, I began to investigate scholarships and grants, but was surprised to learn that, even with Mom's part-time income and Dad's disability income, it was just enough to disqualify me from financial assistance. We were not considered a low-income family. Discouraged but determined, I researched the nursing profession, interviewed a nurse, and toured Massachusetts General Hospital, but was not impressed. Becoming a doctor's helper did not appeal to me at all. I even considered becoming a secretary like Mom, but decided I wanted more.

As soon as I turned sixteen, I got a job working after school for a local dentist, making fifty cents an hour, the current babysitting rate. Starting as a receptionist, I called to remind patients of their appointments and did record-keeping. I asked if I could learn dental assisting and soon began training in handling instruments, preparing amalgam fillings, and developing x-rays. I learned to assist the doctor during oral surgery and loved it. I had been dropped down a rabbit hole into a new adult world. I had never conversed with adults except to say hello. This job required me to interact with adults and children. In no time, I was at ease working with patients, scheduling appointments, greeting them, engaging in casual conversations, and even requesting overdue payment. This boosted my confidence. I even learned to carry on a bit of small talk. Cathy, our full-time dental assistant, was a tough, good-looking, blonde in her thirties with a wonderful smile. We bonded quickly. She showed me the ropes and became a mentor, friend, and a great sounding board for this lonely teenager. I thrived in the working world, and my confidence soared. The job also enabled me to save money for college. I was becoming a responsible young adult.

❧

I finally decided on a career as a dental hygienist. It was good money and an excellent option for a married woman with a family. My guidance counselor helped me research the right universities. I could become a certified dental hygienist by completing a two-year program. It was perfect. I applied and was accepted to three schools: Tufts University in Boston, Temple University, and the University of Pennsylvania, both in Philadelphia. Mom was delighted. She even suggested, if I wanted to go to school in Philadelphia, that I could live with her twin sister, Aunt

Gertrude, and her husband Uncle Lynn, both of whom I loved. Mom felt she could manage the tuition for the two-year program if I lived with them. It was a perfect solution! I could attend college, live with family, still have some independence, and experience a new life as a young adult.

4

Life was going great. It was the summer before my senior year, and I was excited about my future and eager for high school to be over. Suddenly, without any warning, my world collapsed. David, my boyfriend of three years, called to tell me he was breaking up with me. He had started dating someone else. I was swept off my feet by a tsunami of emotional pain, struggling to stay afloat. Now I was totally alone and had been rejected. I was not good enough. It was a familiar feeling. I reached out to friends, but they just gave me empty words of support. "You have your life ahead of you. You will find someone at college." They were hollow words I could not grasp. This wave of heartbreak crushed my confidence. Dave was the one person I loved and counted on unconditionally. Now, it was over. I thought we'd get married after college. I was devastated and cried and cried in my room, inconsolable for weeks, moping around the house in the dark fog of despair. I called other friends, but they were all excited about our senior year and did not console me. Veronica gave me looks of disdain and pity. Mother did not understand my overwhelming grief. She said more than once, "Where is your pride?" What did pride have to do with being heartbroken? She was implying that I needed to "suck it up" and pretend I was fine. He broke my young heart into shards of broken glass at my feet. I did not have the strength to walk through it. Nor could I pick up the pieces and go on. I was truly alone, and my confidence took a nose-dive.

❧

My senior year began, but I just wanted the year to be over. Completely miserable, I tried to focus on moving out and going to college. Soon, I'd be free. Days turned into weeks. The Thanksgiving dance was held every year at the private North Reading Country Club. It was a big deal. I had always gone with David. This year, I did not want to attend, but my girlfriends insisted that I get out and have some fun. Snow was falling gently as I walked into the entrance of the country club. The students were all dressed up in their fancy dresses, suits, and ties. As I stood in line waiting to buy my ticket, my friend Christa turned and introduced me to her older brother, Neil Wolfe. She said he was visiting family for the holidays. I turned to greet him and froze. I could hardly speak, except to say, "Nice to meet you, Neil." He looked like a model out of *GQ Magazine*. It's hard to describe how handsome and charismatic he was. I tried to look casual, but my heart was beating out of my chest. I'm sure he could hear it. With broad shoulders and a trim waist, he stood about five feet eight inches tall with a military-style haircut. His hazel eyes sparkled as he held out his hand to greet me. After a few moments of small talk, it dawned on me that he is an adult. He was out of school and had a career working with computers. This charming gentleman oozed confidence. His smile was captivating, and soon we were dancing through the night. He literally swept me off my feet. The night was magical, and I was under his spell. Was he my Prince Charming? As, the night went on, I learned a bit more about him. He lived and worked in Virginia. I knew Christa was Catholic and assumed he was too. His father had graduated from the West Point Academy and served as a colonel during World War II. Neil got to live in England during the war while his dad was stationed in Europe. How exciting. His father was retired from the military and worked for a government contractor. Neil was sophisticated and intelligent. I felt as if I were in a trance. If I blinked my eyes, life could go back to before I ever met him. I was infatuated with this young man. Someone mentioned concern about the rapid accumulation of snow. I remembered I had promised Mom I'd leave early to avoid an impending snowstorm. Over three inches had already accumulated, so I left early. I said goodbye to Neil and wished him a wonderful Thanksgiving with his family. The snowfall continued all night, but I barely slept, thinking of the attractive young man I had just met. He was much more mature than my classmates. Late Sunday morning, after mass, we heard a knock at the front door. Mother opened it to see Neil, smiling, wearing Bermuda shorts, a light jacket, and flip-flops, standing in a foot of snow. I tried to be casual as I introduced him to Mom, who rolled her eyes as if he were crazy and left the room. As I invited him inside, I rolled my eyes as well, thinking, I'm over David!

A few days later, he returned to Virginia. Then he called me long distance, almost every night, and we got to know each other. After a few weeks, he proudly announced that he had been transferred to Boston and was moving into his parents' home, only two miles away. Our relationship then moved very quickly, and we saw each other every weekend. We fell in love quickly and were engaged by Valentine's Day. I showed off my beautiful diamond engagement ring at school, feeling like a princess. I was the only one in my class with an engagement ring, but it felt a bit weird. Sometimes we would double-date with my friends. A couple of my girlfriends complained that Neil had taken their boyfriends to buy liquor, and then they got very drunk. I dismissed it, saying, "If they got drunk, it's their own fault." Mother made it clear she didn't like him at all, saying he was too old for me, but I just ignored her. This mature young man loved me and wanted to marry me. Feeling completely loved and cherished like this was intoxicating.

❧

I was voted "*Most Likely to Succeed*" by my classmat*es*. My picture appeared in the yearbook, climbing the ladder of success. My entire life was ahead of me. At my graduation in June, I was third in my class and was awarded a partial scholarship for the school of my choice—a total surprise. All my hard work had paid off. The valedictorian and salutatorian of the Class of '63 always give commencement addresses. The faculty also asked me to provide a third address. What an honor! I needed to develop a speech that reflected my passion. My most startling and vivid recollection was from research I had done for a term paper on the World War II holocaust. The Nazi systematic slaughter of six million Jews moved me deeply. I could not fathom why any human being would senselessly slaughter other human beings. It was shameful. My commencement address was entitled *Man's Inhumanity toward Man: The Holocaust.* Addressing parents, faculty, and my fellow students, I stood up on graduation day and basically said, "I am ashamed of humanity for allowing the murder of over six million Jews in the holocaust. Humanity must do better. People of the world should care for one another and have the courage to do the right thing." It was not a positive speech about following your dream. It was an important message. One I still live by.

❧

Summer was flying by. Neil and I were both working, and I was making plans to move to Philadelphia with my aunt and uncle in August. Then, Neil dropped a bomb. He told me he was worried that if I were away at college for two years, I'd probably meet a dental student, fall in love, and eventually break our engagement. I passed it off as being jealous for no reason. A week later, I was shocked when he gave me an ultimatum. He firmly stated, "If you attend college in Philadelphia, I will break our engagement. It is too painful for me to sit at home and wait for you to graduate, then get married. I love you so much. Stay here and marry me now!" What? Didn't Neil realize how much I loved him? I would not even date others. I thought he was being selfish. However, I knew he loved me so much that he could not live without me, which made my heart swell. I had to choose between my future college goals and love and marriage. It was very unfair, but he was adamant. What should I do? I knew my true goal was to be married. I was sick of school and loved Neil so much that, after thinking it over for a few days, I chose marriage. He was Catholic, and I did want a family. "Why not start early?" I proclaimed. I returned my scholarship, withdrew from Temple University, and lost my independence. I grabbed the ring on the carousel and chose to grow up immediately. Once I made the decision, I was happy and excited about our future. Feeling overwhelmed with the new expectation of marrying my Prince Charming, I felt like a princess enveloped in a protective sphere of love and acceptance.

It was like Armageddon when I told Mother my decision to marry instead of going to college. She had a fit and said she would not permit me to marry so young. I told her flatly that all I had to do was wait until after September 10th, when I turned eighteen, and she'd have no power to stop me. At last, she acquiesced, knowing how stubborn I could be. Before ending the conversation, she gave me some motherly advice. I will remember her cold words forever as she warned me, "You make your bed, you lie in it. Marriage is forever!" As an afterthought, she added, "He should never physically abuse you. That is wrong and is a reason to leave him."

My parents had no money for the wedding, so we cobbled together a small affair for family and very close friends at the Old Country Inn. My uncle, Father Nick, a Catholic priest, agreed to perform the mass and nuptial ceremony. My wedding dress was a simple, white, full-length satin gown.

Neil was older, so I naturally looked up to him. He already had a career and experience as an adult. He easily took charge of everything we needed, including finding an apartment, turning on electricity and gas, getting a phone, buying furniture, and opening bank accounts. I knew nothing about furniture or anything else, so I just went along while he picked out the Early American furniture he liked. Oh, well, whatever. On the other hand, my mind was a blank slate. I loved and trusted him totally, as a husband who would always love and cherish me and help me become a married woman in a new adult world.

5

Our wedding was held at Saint Theresa's Catholic Church, where I received my first holy communion, confirmation, and numerous acts of contrition to absolve me of my sins. It was a beautiful, sunny autumn day on September 14, four days after my eighteenth birthday. I cannot remember anything significant about the wedding or the reception. Still, I remember us returning home and spending our wedding night on my parents' sofa bed in the living room. It was unbelievably awkward physically and emotionally! The next morning, we self-consciously got dressed, had a quick breakfast, and waved goodbye to set out on our honeymoon. Our destination was a honeymoon resort in the Pocono Mountains for five nights. Although I was young and had lived a sheltered life in a small New England town, I was confident I had done the right thing.

We were eager to start our new life together. Autumn was upon us, and Mother Nature had been using a colorful brush to paint the landscape in various muted shades of yellow, red, orange, and brown. It had been only three months since my high school graduation. I was the only student in my class who had gotten married, except for a girlfriend who had gotten pregnant and had to leave school to get married. It was the first day of my life as a married woman. The luxurious Mount Airy Honeymoon Resort, nestled in the mountains, was filled with young newlyweds just like us—in love and celebrating their new lives together. The resort complex was nestled in a rural, secluded meadow surrounded by colorful autumn trees. Amenities included a large indoor pool, a nine-hole golf course, archery, a tennis court, a large bar, and three fantastic meals a day in the restaurant. The highlight each evening was a delicious dinner, followed by entertainment, partying, and dancing. It was an all-inclusive resort, but I did not ask my new husband how he was paying for it. It was probably a wedding gift from his parents. Most of our mornings began with waking, making love, dozing off, and then showering, dressing, and barely making it to the breakfast buffet before it closed at 11 a.m. In the afternoon, we'd swim, play pool, or walk along the wooded trails, then we'd head back to our room to read, make love again, and snuggle. It was a wonderful beginning to our lives as man and wife. After our first night together, it dawned on me that this was the first time I had been away overnight with him. It was wonderful to share this new beginning.

❧

I did notice a few new aspects of his personality that I had not seen before. He usually drank two to three beers at lunch, then several scotch-on-the-rocks through the evening, while dining and dancing. He also brought a whole bottle of scotch to our room and encouraged me to drink with him, introducing me to scotch, which he drank on the rocks. He never appeared drunk, slurred his words, or was unsteady on his feet, like a few newlywed couples I had seen. Well, it was our honeymoon, after all, a celebration of the beginning of our marriage. We certainly could splurge. Then again, his drinking seemed more than casual. I never drank in high school, so I began to reflect on my parents' and relatives' social drinking habits. They drank on special occasions, when relatives came on vacation. Dad had his cold glass of ale, and Mom had her icy gin and tonic. When I was little, I'd sit on Dad's lap and sip cold, smooth ale. They might also have a highball or two at a summer cookout. Dad usually stopped by the liquor store on the weekend to buy his private pint of whisky and a carton of cigarettes. Drinking was illegal until the age of twenty-one in Massachusetts. I never had the desire to drink and did not hang out with that crowd, although I heard that beer and liquor were present at teenage private parties while parents were away. The only social drinking I could compare this to was movies or television. It was a common practice for a couple to have cocktails before and during dinner at a restaurant, and perhaps a brandy after dinner. "This must just be part of adult social life," I convinced myself. I had a lot to learn about adult married life. Neil could help me understand the difference between being a high school teenager and a newly married adult.

❧

On our third night, after drinks, dinner, and partying with our newlywed friends, we retired to our room. Everyone was in great spirits, and drinks flowed through the night. I was tired, looking forward to a good night's sleep. As I undressed, Neil approached me with a passionate kiss. We had engaged in sex before marriage and were comfortable with intimacy. I gently returned the kiss, softly saying, "I am quite sore from having so much sex in the last few days."

He smiled and responded, "That's okay because I want to try something different." What was this surprise going to be? As he poured himself another scotch on the rocks, he motioned toward the bed and asked me to get down on my knees. I complied, very curious.

"Just relax," he said, then he approached me from behind and attempted to penetrate me. I gasped in pain and pulled away. Something was wrong, but I did not know what!

The tone of his voice changed, now firm and impatient, and, he insisted, louder, "If you just relax, it won't hurt." I felt like a scolded child and tried silently to comply, but as he continued, again I winced, moaning in pain. At that point, he got angry, grabbing more lubricant. He was trying to penetrate my anus. I could not believe this was happening to me. "Why is he doing this to me?" I asked myself.

There I was, totally silent, on my hands and knees in our marital bed, in shock and unbearable pain, unable to move or cry. My mind drifted off as I watched my husband's conquest from the ceiling of the room. I was numb and detached from what he was doing to me. This "*something different*" was very painful, completely humiliating. After what seemed like an eternity, he climaxed and rolled off me, spent.

I lay there silent until I knew he was asleep, then got up, went to the bathroom, and showered for what seemed like forever, trying to wash away what he had done, not just to my body, but to my very soul. He had never explained what he was going to do or why. He just took what he wanted with his repeated instructions to "*just relax*". I felt betrayed by the man I had trusted completely. This was not a loving act of mutual pleasure. Why would he do this to me? I was in total shock. Tears refused to come. Is this what marriage is going to be like? At that moment, my mother's words, repeated in my head, "*You made your bed, now lie in it!*" The message was clear. I was totally alone in a world spinning out of control.

I respected his wisdom and experience, but I did not feel like we were equal partners. From the start, it was clear that he was the leader and I the follower. I was comfortable with that because I had never been in the adult world. I relied on his experience and guidance. I was scared to question him about his sexual proclivities and could never share this horror with anyone. I was alone on an island with a husband I did not recognize. And I had naively agreed to this union. Neil awoke the next day, acting as if nothing had happened. My entire world was shattered. Overwhelming doubt and fear shook me to the core. My love and trust for him had withered to wariness and suspicion. I was not a partner in this marriage; I was subservient and now feared my husband. What would happen if I told him how betrayed and ashamed, I felt? The child in me was too scared and confused. I decided to act as if nothing had happened the night before. My fledgling confidence evaporated overnight, and I put on my happy face and began living under this dark cloud of unthinkable pain.

❧

Young women my age were not encouraged to be assertive. I had never seen a woman confront or challenge a man about an injustice. We were taught to be shy, polite, unassuming, and never to disagree or create dissent over anything except the time supper should be served. Men ruled. They were the leaders, the breadwinners. Wives were there to do what their husbands wanted and be sweet, loving, and always congenial.

❧

After our honeymoon, we returned to our apartment in the small town of Andover, next to North Reading. Our apartment building was an old three-story Victorian home that had been converted into apartments. It stood in a quiet, charming neighborhood with stained-glass windows and a narrow winding staircase. Giant maple trees lined the narrow street, and it was a short walking distance to the shops in town. Our fourth-floor, one-bedroom, unfurnished apartment was small, but adequate for the two of us. Ceilings slanted at odd angles, and two beautiful, antique stained-glass windows allowed colored light to dance along the floor at certain times of the day. I loved it despite the narrow stairs. Autumn had begun painting the bright reds, oranges, and various shades of yellow on all the leaves, but I no longer noticed the wonders of nature as I had before. I tried to put my trauma behind me and look forward to the future. However, the dark cloud had found a home above me and always followed. At any moment, it could turn into a tornado and destroy my physical and emotional strength. Wherever I moved, it followed. Total denial was imperative for me to cope. My role was clear—as a dutiful and subservient wife.

❧

Wedding gifts were stacked up in the living room when we arrived home. Every day, married life commenced with both of us going back to work. Neil drove his car while I carpooled to work with

Cathy, my co-worker, who lived nearby. It was nice to be back in a routine and so good to see her. I told her all about my wonderful honeymoon, blah, blah, blah, too ashamed to tell her the real story.

❧

After a week back home in my new life and another week of what I call *"normal"* sex, my vagina became very sore again. I knew that it would take time to get used to frequent sex, but there was no one I could go to for such intimate advice. I did not have a regular doctor. My close girlfriends were off to college or working full-time. Hopefully, they had not encountered the unusual sexual behavior I had experienced. I could not *Google* it or get advice from *WebMD*, as I could today. Then, one evening, after dinner, Neil became angry when I told him, "We have had so much sex during the week, I am very sore and out of commission." I thought maybe he would take the hint.

Instead, he raised his voice, declaring, "You are my wife, and I have the right as your husband to take what I want." I cringed at his tone of voice! Neil, a voracious reader, picked up a book on his nightstand and flung it across the room towards me. "Take a look at this!" He shouted, "It's *Marquis de Sade*, and describes a variety of weird, sadistic sexual acts and positions. I want to try them all." I had no idea what *sadistic* meant, but it sounded ominous. Neil instructed me to take off my nightgown and lie on my side on the bed. I silently shuddered. He kneeled behind me and masturbated, for what seemed like an eternity, as I lay there naked, getting cold. Then he finally ejaculated all over my back, "How does your vagina feel now?" he said, mockingly. I was unable to move. The sticky substance ran down my back, slowly turning cold. His sadistic ritual continued. I was frozen in this sadistic netherworld, like a scared rabbit, unable to move, speak, or cry out. Why would my husband continue this demeaning, humiliating behavior? Finally, he dozed off, and I took another long, cleansing shower, thinking, "What in God's name have I gotten myself into?" Trying to make sense of it, I looked back at my previous high school love, David. For more than three years, we had gone steady and been intimate, but there was nothing bizarre about it. It was passionate, normal sex—albeit in the back seat of a car—that I enjoyed. As a newlywed, why was I being sexually attacked and made to endure such sick sexual activities? I felt demeaned, confused, and alone.

❧

Part of me thought perhaps I was overreacting to these bizarre sexual incidents. I had no way of knowing what normal, intimate behavior entailed. He had not hit me or beaten me. I had a roof over my head and was fed and clothed. Maybe I should be grateful. No, I could not accept that excuse. My heart was shattered. I was devastated, humiliated, and betrayed. One thing was crystal clear—I could never trust him again. My marriage was now a different ball game, and I was the catcher. I was not a partner, but his sadistic plaything, trapped in a marriage. Mom was right!

❧

Looking back:

As I write this today, I wonder why I never sought help or shared my situation with my friend, Cathy, at work. She was single, over thirty-five, and would have kicked his ass. Or why not go home to my mother and confess my horrible situation? It never entered my mind, even once. I had severed my relationship with my parents. I was alone and trapped. Perhaps I was in denial, but my self-esteem was shredded to a pulp. I had no strength to give up on this forever marriage.

Now, entertaining alternatives, I realize I could have gone back home, continued working for the dentist for another year, and reapplied to Temple University the following year. Why did I not consider that as an option? I have no answer, except to say I felt I was in a permanent, dead-end marriage. In my abused mind, there was no escape. I have never regretted my decision or lack thereof, because I have two incredible sons and three beautiful grandchildren. Despite everything, I have lived an extraordinary life.

❧

On Friday, November 22, 1963, the world stopped when President John F. Kennedy was assassinated in Dallas, Texas. Kennedy was a popular young Democrat from my home state. The entire nation sat in front of their black and white televisions in horrified silence, watching the videos of the shooting. Lee Harvey Oswald had been apprehended, charged, and then was shot by Jack Ruby while in police custody. The First Lady, Jackie Kennedy, stood in her blood-spattered pink suit, a widow. The world was shocked beyond belief! I don't remember much during that period of mourning. Everything shut down, and we huddled at home for several days. Temperatures were freezing with snow, ice, and sleet. The nation grieved, and conspiracy theories emerged. After the funeral march in Washington, a semblance of normalcy returned. However, something was missing. It was trust and hope. The world seemed hollow and without meaning, without Kennedy, our leader.

The Catholic Church prohibited the use of birth control, so we never discussed using it. Since we never talked about anything meaningful, we also never addressed the fact that I might become pregnant. In late November, after Thanksgiving dinner at his parents' house, my breasts began to feel tender. I knew I was pregnant even before I missed my period. I was ecstatic, and Neil was thrilled as well. The best part was that his sexual exploits suddenly stopped. I never had morning sickness, but the pregnancy caused me to be extremely tired all the time. Every night I'd come home from work and go straight to bed. We were now in uncharted territory. I was overwhelmed with fatigue and hardly managed to get through each day. In essence, after only two months of marriage, I became an absent wife. Neil took up the slack, doing chores and cooking dinner, and I soon learned he was an excellent cook! My first visit to an obstetrician revealed I was very anemic. I immediately began taking prenatal vitamins and iron supplements that helped ease the tiredness. I missed my girlfriends, yet realized I no longer had anything in common with them. It was like I was on a different planet. How could I exchange recipes or discuss different sexual positions? I felt very ignorant and alone! While I was off sleeping, Neil took charge of everything in our lives. I had no experience with finances or running a household. He managed finances, bills, rent, investments, insurance, car maintenance, etcetera. I gave him my weekly check of forty-five dollars. He deposited it, giving me money only when I needed it. I was asleep, so I did not notice. The fact that he assumed the household reins was helpful at first, but I started to see him taking control over everything in my life: where I went, what I bought, when I arrived home, and how much cash I had in my wallet. But the weird sex had stopped! But I noticed that Neil was consumed with his job as a computer operator. I admired his passion and dedication, but he was obsessed with reaching a million dollars before he was thirty. He worked long hours and often brought work home while I slept.

6

The following spring, Neil accepted an offer to transfer to a promising position at the new NASA Space Center in Houston, Texas. He was proud and excited about this new career opportunity. I hoped it would be a chance for a new beginning for both of us. I was five months pregnant, moving over two thousand miles away from my family, friends, and everything I had known. Despite the obvious negative indicators, I remained excited about my life. I was looking forward to our future and becoming a mother. The weird sex had stopped now that I was pregnant, so I put the past behind me and looked toward the future. This move would allow me to explore new parts of the country, meet new friends, and experience new things.

The movers came and packed everything. We piled into the car and headed south with our maps in the glove box. It took us over five days to drive from Massachusetts to Texas. After a couple of long days on the road, we reached Biloxi, Mississippi. It was almost midnight, and there were no cars on the road. Perhaps it was under curfew. We continued through the dark, empty streets, when Neil noticed a

Police car following us. The officer did not motion for us to pull over, so we continued. Finally, curiosity got the best of Neil, and he pulled over, got out, and asked, "Good evening, officer, is there a problem?" The officer apologetically replied, "Good evening, sorry for the unusual tail I put on your car. I noticed your Massachusetts license plates. Recently, we have had several racial incidents in the area, involving automobiles from New England. I just wanted to be sure you continued safely through Biloxi and did not stop until you were safely out of the city." We thanked him and got a personal police escort to the city limits. We had been so preoccupied with our pending move and my pregnancy that we did not register the racial problems that had been smoldering in the South. Neil watched television in the evening, so I'm surprised he missed it.

❧

By the time we got to Louisiana, it had become excessively hot and humid. Neil announced that we needed a break in New Orleans for a couple of nights. He wanted to see the French Quarter and Bourbon Street. This beautiful, quaint old city had lots of French character, but the oppressive heat and humidity became unbearable for me. I already felt huge and was not used to such oppressive temperatures. At my height of five feet two inches, there was no place for the baby to grow except horizontally. I looked like a steamroller on roller skates. Neil, of course, wanted to party and try the famous hurricane cocktails on Bourbon Street. I just wanted to sleep in our air-conditioned room. We discussed it, and of course, we partied all night.

❧

After the brief rest, we passed into the East Texas flatland on the final leg of our journey. Neil pulled into a closed gas station in the middle of the night. We had been driving all day, and I really needed to pee. The baby had been pushing on my bladder. There was not even a whiff of a breeze to cool the horrible humidity. Huge pin oaks lined the road on this moonless night. I opened the car door and hesitated. Everything was dead silent. I just wanted to get back inside the car's air conditioning, but my bladder would not allow it. I walked past the gas pumps toward the bathroom in a sleeveless maternity top, shorts, and flip-flops. Slowly opening the heavy metal door, I switched on the light, sat down, and started to relieve my bladder. I just wanted to go back to sleep. Slowly, my head rose to the sink and mirror in front of me. I saw movement! To my horror, I was surrounded by at least forty or fifty, two-inch-long black cockroaches crawling along the floor, up the walls, and across the ceiling. A few flew around, upset by my sudden arrival. I sat frozen on the toilet with my head down to avoid these beasts landing on my head. I freaked out. I bore down hard on my bladder to empty it, then, with lightning speed, not even wiping myself, I pulled up my pants and ran like hell out of the infested room. Once clear of the building, I shook my clothes to be sure none of these prehistoric monsters were hoping to hitch a ride to Houston. Welcome to Texas.

❧

We entered Houston, with its impressive skyline, then took the freeway south toward NASA. Soon, we arrived in the small town of Dickinson, forty-five minutes south of the city. Neil pulled into a cowboy-looking motel just off the highway. It was time to eat and rest. Our priority was finding an affordable apartment. The next day, we dressed like Texans in shorts, tank tops, and flip flops. After a huge southern breakfast of eggs, ham, and grits, we began apartment hunting.

After looking at several apartment complexes, we finally found a new two-bedroom apartment complex, only twenty minutes from NASA. The apartments were in a quiet neighborhood, with giant pin oaks surrounding the complex. We were shown a modern, two-bedroom apartment, fully carpeted, with huge walk-in closets, a nice-sized kitchen with new appliances, and central heating and air conditioning located on the ground floor around a large pool area with several lounge chairs. It became our new home. I was overwhelmed at how modern it was, compared to my parents 'old house. The average temperature was ninety-five degrees in the shade, with eighty percent humidity. We quickly learned the trick of rushing from our air-conditioned apartment to our air-conditioned car to the air-conditioned stores.

❧

New neighbors, with genuine Southern hospitality, welcomed us like we were long-lost relatives. At first, I was uncertain about their overly friendly nature. My experience growing up in New England was that neighbors were private, even stand-offish. My doubts vanished when I realized they had no ulterior motive, and I grew to accept their warm hospitality and caring acceptance. We made friends quickly. There were frequent gatherings around the pool in the evenings and over the weekends. I felt very comfortable in our new home. Things were looking up. In my role as a housewife and expectant mother, I was excited about this new adventure with my husband.

My pregnancy was straightforward and wonderful. I was going to give birth in only four months. A whole new world of motherhood awaited me. I found an excellent young obstetrician named Dr. Riley. He was a tall, slender, very handsome Texan with an easy-going nature and a welcoming smile. His Texas drawl was adorable. I trusted him.

❧

Neil settled into his new work routine as a computer operator and soon became friends with his coworkers. He seemed happy with our new life. He preferred working second or third shifts because of the salary differential. It became a habit for him, after work, late at night, to stop by the nearby Roadhouse Bar & Grill to relax with his buddies. After drinking for a few hours, he'd drive home and wake me up. He'd start ranting and raving for over an hour about how worthless I was and how grateful I should be to be married to him. When he finished his diatribe, I rolled my eyes and went back to sleep. This new pattern of verbal and emotional abuse started eroding the little confidence and self-esteem I had left. I was not even aware it was happening, but I was on a slowly sinking ship, headed for the bottom.

I started to believe that his rants must be true. I was nothing but a high school graduate with no job. I was quiet and socially awkward. Listening to this demeaning attack almost every night began to brainwash me. Perhaps he resented my sleeping at night while he was out slaving away to make a living for us. Maybe he wanted me to stay up until he got home each night, ask about his day, feed him dinner, and finally give him a blow job as a show of gratitude. Well, forget that! I slowly succumbed to the quicksand of emotional abuse until I felt worthless. Why did he tell me that I was worthless? Did he regret being married? He never said so, but never told me he loved me, either. I did not understand his behavior. I was trying to be a good wife, but nothing pleased him. He had succeeded. I was afraid of him and would never dare raise the issue of his verbal attacks. All the while, the nightly verbal and emotional abuse eroded my soul.

A week before I went into labor, Neil had been drinking after work, gone off the road, and totaled the car. He was not seriously hurt, but we now had no transportation. I went into labor a few days later in the middle of the night, and he had to wake up our neighbors to ask for a ride to the hospital. They willingly obliged.

7

My firstborn son came into the world on August 3rd, a month before my nineteenth birthday. Neil insisted on naming the baby after himself, so we started referring to the baby as Little Neil and his father as Big Neil. Little Neil was seven pounds, thirteen ounces, with lots of dark brown hair, deep blue eyes, and very long black eyelashes. I started nursing, and it was very easy. In a week, those little breasts had become DD pumping stations. There was no need to heat a bottle.

Before Neil and I met, he was living with his oldest brother and his family in Virginia. This devout Catholic couple had five kids over the course of seven years of marriage, all babies and toddlers. I was sure Neil had plenty of experience with babies, but this baby business was brand-new to me. I felt self-conscious and unprepared. I had never even fed a baby or changed a diaper. I had read *Dr. Spock's Baby and Child Care*, but I needed on-the-job training. Neil would show me the ropes. Both of our mothers offered to come down to Texas to help. I thanked them, but said no. We needed to do this on our own. After three days in the hospital, we went home in his brand-new, fire-engine red Ford Mustang. I handed Big Neil the baby and slowly tried to get out of the car. Neil turned and took the baby into the house, leaving me to get out of the car, get my luggage, and follow behind. Things were back to normal. Giving birth was nothing special.

❧

I was amazed at how strong Little Neil was as an infant, holding his head up straight, stretching his tiny legs into a standing position on my lap, while tightly holding my hands. I was a proud Mama. I had gained twenty-six pounds during my pregnancy, six pounds over the recommended weight. When I got on the scale at home, I could not believe I had not lost any pregnancy weight. How could that happen? I tried and failed to fit into any of my jeans, so I finally resorted to wearing old maternity clothes. I was devastated by all the extra tummy flab. I had never had a weight problem, so this was yet another reason to feel worthless.

❧

At my six-week check-up, Dr. Riley, who knew I was Catholic, insisted that I go on birth control pills for nine months to get my body back to normal. It was the doctor's orders, so I complied. What he did not bother to tell me was that my milk would dry up. Within a week, it was gone. I was distraught because I had planned to nurse Little Neil for about six months until he could drink from a cup. Well, no use crying over dried milk. We immediately went out to buy bottles, a sterilizer, and other necessary paraphernalia. Little Neil did well on the bottle. Strangers would stop me in the grocery store and tell me how beautiful he was. "Too beautiful to be a boy," many said. I was so proud of my son.

❧

After a couple of months, while Neil was watching the Saturday afternoon football game, I fed Little Neil and put him down for a nap. I told Big Neil I was headed to the nearby mall for an hour or two, to get out of the house. He agreed and went back to his game. The baby usually slept for three to four hours, so I had plenty of time. I never had spending money, but Big Neil gave me cash for groceries, and over time, I was able to put aside a few bucks. When I returned, Big Neil had the sobbing baby in his arms. He explained in a frustrated tone, "The baby woke up right after you left, and cried non-stop for two hours. The same thing happened the other time you left." He said, "Somehow, he knows when you leave and becomes frantic. From now on, you need to take him with you wherever you go." Was it ESP? "That's fine, no problem," I said.

❧

Neil's child-rearing philosophy was, "Do not spoil the child. Follow a strict routine, so he becomes used to eating, bathing, and sleeping at regular intervals." After feeding and changing him, I'd put Little Neil down in his crib without rocking or comforting him. If he cried, I was not allowed to comfort him, even when the crying escalated into sobbing. "You will spoil him. Let him cry himself to sleep," Neil said. Poor baby. I knew he was not sick, but my heart broke listening to him cry on and on.

❧

One morning, I heard on the news that the Houston County Hospital desperately needed volunteers. I had never done any volunteer work, but I wanted to help, so I did. I was excited about the idea of learning something new and having the chance to get out of the house and meet people. I missed the challenge of work. That night over dinner, I explained the program to Neil. "I can take the free course and then do volunteer work at the hospital at least one afternoon a week. You could get a ride to work with coworkers, and I would get a babysitter for a few hours." Without even a pause, he shut me down completely, shouting, "Your job is to be home with our son and be a housewife, not to be a volunteer at some hospital, bringing germs home to our family." Yes, once again, I knew my place—stuck at home serving my husband. My mother's words echoed again, "You made your bed, you still have to lie in it."

❧

The NASA team was full of young, sharp minds just out of college, many married with small children. We were often invited to a coworker's house for a cookout, or we'd have friends over to watch football. If we went to someone's house, we would always take the baby with us. Everyone usually drank beer, but Neil was into the hard stuff, and once he got started, he never wanted to leave. When we finally left, he insisted on driving. About 1:00 a.m., while driving home from a party, he was arrested for Driving Under the Influence, DUI. The police took him to jail, and I was left on the side of the road with Little Neil in the back seat carrier to find my way home. The next morning, I had to borrow money from our neighbor to bail him out.

❧

After nine months, my Catholic guilt took over. I was still using birth control pills. I discontinued them and immediately became pregnant again. This time, I watched my weight, exercised, and only gained nineteen pounds.

Lee Gavin was born on February 24, 1966. He weighed six pounds, seven ounces, with beautiful strawberry blonde hair. Where did that come from, I wondered? Then I remembered one of Neil's brothers had red hair. As soon as I tried to nurse my little infant, he rejected the nipple, and I panicked. Nursing was supposed to be instinctive, so this was not supposed to happen. A kind nurse came in and asked if I had finished feeding him. Over my tears, I told her that I could not get him to nurse. She explained, "It's unusual, but sometimes babies are not born with the suckling instinct. You will need to be quite persistent with him to get him to understand that the breast nipple contains the milk. She showed me by placing the nipple in his mouth, then pumping my breast so the milk would flow into his mouth. After a couple of days, he got the hang of it. My panic was over, and he was nursing like a champ. When we came home from the hospital, Neil and I introduced Lee to Little Neil, who was eighteen months old. He became enchanted with his little brother. He'd sit right next to me whenever I nursed Lee. I became content with life and was delighted that I fit into my jeans.

8

My love and respect for Neil continued to erode, but, as a Catholic, I felt doomed to stay married. I could not confide in anyone about the abuse in my marriage, so I tried to consider the glass half full. Nothing is ever perfect, right? I continued to attend mass every Sunday and prayed that things would work out.

❧

Finally, I admitted to myself that Neil had a serious drinking problem. There had been numerous car accidents and DUIs after unwinding at the local bar with his buddies. Drinking was part of daily life, and it had probably been going on for several years. Upon his arrival in the evening, the first thing he did was go to the kitchen and make himself a scotch on the rocks, even before changing his clothes. Dinner was to be ready by six p.m. When he finally went to bed, he had consumed many drinks. But if I broached the subject, he'd angrily shut me down, and I was afraid his anger could eventually become physical.

❧

Neil always saved and invested his money, even getting into the stock market. At last, we were able to kiss apartment life goodbye and buy our first house for twenty-four thousand dollars. This new brick ranch-style home had three bedrooms, a large great room, a two-car garage, and a nice, fenced backyard. We were both excited to have our own home. Neil was very proud. This new subdivision in South Houston was a small community of young families, all with husbands who worked at NASA. I must admit that I watched soap operas when the boys were down for a nap. My favorite was *General Hospital*. Most soap opera plots were very dramatic, portraying powerful, controlling, abusive men with beautiful wives, cheating on each other, their teenagers getting pregnant or running away, while devious friends and relatives interfered. I considered it so unrealistic until I grew older and realized the show reflected everyday life. After settling into our new home, we became friends with several couples in the subdivision. Socializing on the weekend, centered around weekend football games or a barbecue on Saturday night. Of course, Neil always drank to excess.

❧

Our next-door neighbors were a lovely couple with two toddlers. They both worked full-time. Lee was about six months old, and Neil about two, when I offered to babysit their two young children. They agreed. It gave the boys playmates and gave me something productive to do at home. The extra money was a blessing. Oddly enough, Neil never asked me to turn my money over to him.

❧

Little Neil and Lee became inseparable. When they were a bit older, I branched out and was allowed to join a women's sorority in the neighborhood. It gave stay-at-home spouses the chance to have lunch while participating in community charity projects. Life was much better, and I had a little more freedom. However, our marriage continued to deteriorate, and the nightly tirades continued. My children were my only reason to continue, but eventually, even with a new house, my self-esteem sank into the gutter. I became a shell of my former self, living day to day. The boys were my only joy.

❧

When the holidays arrived, we celebrated our first Christmas in our new home. Our Christmas tree was decorated, and Santa Claus delivered lots of toys for the boys. However, there were no other gifts under the tree because Neil said, "It is a luxury we can do without." Nevertheless, he indulged in shotguns and rifles to use on his hunting trips with the guys.

❧

On New Year's Eve, we were invited to a party at Jeffrey and Cindy's house, a few blocks away. Jeff worked with Neil, and Cindy and I were sorority sisters. I was excited to dress up, put on make-up, and go to a real party. It was a nice change for me with lots of fun, great food, drinks, and dancing through the night. Their house was packed with local neighbors and friends. As the evening wore on, Jeff asked me to dance. He was a tall, handsome, charismatic man, about thirty with blonde hair. His career was in computer marketing, and he was very outgoing. After our third dance, he said he'd like to see me again. I was shocked by his request, and all I could think was that someone found me attractive. After all, I was nothing. I replied, "I'm flattered by your interest, but no, I am married and not interested." He smiled and wished me a wonderful New Year, telling me again how lovely I looked. I had the feeling that this was not the first time he had hit on someone's wife. I felt weird that his wife was a friend of mine.

❧

After ringing in the New Year, we arrived home, and Neil drove the babysitter home. When he returned, I said, "We need to talk." He looked at me curiously. I told him that Jeff had tried to hit on me and asked me out on a date. I waited for his reaction, thinking he'd be furious. After a long pause, he casually said, "Well, I'm busy with my career, so if you want company, go ahead."

I turned on my heel and left the room in tears. I was beyond furious and devastated by his casual, cold willingness to share me sexually with his friend. His tone was as casual as "Pass the milk, please." I stood in the bedroom, heartbroken and enraged. It was clear that he didn't love or value me in any way. I was consumed by anger, which quickly turned to an intense hatred. My subconscious confronted me, snickering, "So now, what are you going to do about it, Barbara?" I sobbed until I fell asleep. I could not reconcile Neil's cold, unforgivable response. Should I ignore him, like I usually did? No, this time he had gone too far, farming me out like a prostitute. Something in the back of my mind told me to do exactly what he suggested. My anger morphed into overwhelming revenge. The next day, I called Jeff and asked him to visit me that night after 8 p.m. He was delighted and agreed. That evening Jeff knocked on the door, looking very sharp. The boys were asleep, and Neil was on shift work until midnight. I was not sure how to handle this, but I invited him into the kitchen. I didn't even offer him a drink. We stood in the kitchen as I explained that when we got home after his party, I told Neil about Jeff's interest in seeing me again. Neil said, "Go ahead." Jeff was delighted, saying, "We should plan to go out in the evening to the Ellington Officers' Club, nearby, where we can have a drink, listen to music, and dance." We agreed. He kissed me briefly on the cheek and left. A few days later, I hired a babysitter and started a torrid affair that lasted over nine months. Jeff picked me up in his red Mustang convertible, and we went to the officers' club or a piano bar. He introduced me to his friends as his date. Sometimes we saw each other twice a week. Finally, I was having fun for a change. Jeff and his friends enjoyed my company. The sex was amazing, and my suppressed sexuality blossomed. I was amazed that life could be fun.

☙

Over time, I shed my battered shell to realize "I am OK. There is nothing wrong with me." My husband had intentionally destroyed my confidence and self-esteem. My resentment had turned to disgust and hate after all the years I had been under Neil's abuse. Jeff and I continued to see each other as often as we could. The sex was addictive, and I was hooked on feeling liked and appreciated. My confidence slowly returned. But my Catholic guilt haunted me. This time, I was committing adultery and could not stop. It felt so good to feel alive once again and have a great evening. I was finally feeling good about myself, almost back to normal. However, it was a Catch-22. I knew I didn't love Jeff, nor did he love me, but we were obsessed with each other. I was hooked on the euphoric feelings. We never got a hotel room, so our sexual encounters were in the backseat of his Mustang convertible. Jeff is a tall, large man, and I could not tell you how we did that.

❧

Once my battered haze lifted, I realized I was a shy but fun-loving young woman. My confidence grew, and within a few months, I crawled out of my insecure shell into the real world. The by-product of my newfound confidence was a deep hatred for Neil, for all the years I had suffered. However, I continued to carry a constant guilt about the affair and sought the advice of a Catholic priest. He discouraged my behavior but always emphasized that I should never tell my husband. I went back several times but got no useful guidance. After all, he was not married. How could he know the complexity of marriage? I continued confessing my sexual obsession, and the affair continued.

After nine months of engaging in a double life, I knew was morally wrong, I decided I could not continue. Finally, my confidence was back. The affair was tearing me up inside, and it went against everything I had learned. I was a married woman with children. The affair had to stop. But I was too weak. I tried many times to stop seeing Jeff, but we always ended up back together. If I told Neil the truth, I would be forced to end the affair. I had no idea what the outcome would be, but I knew I had to tell him the truth, finally. Would my marriage last? I did not know, but I knew I had to be prepared to be on my own. At the age of twenty-two, I had grown confident, assertive, and a force to be reckoned with! I needed to carefully plan my confession and determine all contingencies before I admitted my affair to Neil. I was putting myself in a vulnerable position, but I felt strong and confident.

Part Two

9

I told Neil I wanted to go back to work. He said, "No." I told him I needed a car because I was going back to work. He said, "No." Then on Saturday, he took me to a nearby Toyota dealer and bought me a new Toyota compact. Wow, I should have done this years ago, but I knew I was not strong enough then. I applied for a dental assistant position through newspaper ads. After a couple of interviews, I got an offer for a full-time job and accepted it. Then I found an excellent childcare facility nearby. I was all set.

❧

After working full-time for a couple of months, with fresh courage and resolve, I sat Neil down and told him the truth about the affair with Jeff. He went ballistic and got out his shotgun, threatening to kill Jeff, me, and then himself, leaving our children orphans. I reminded him that he had suggested it, but he told me he never thought I would do it. I knew I had shamed and hurt him terribly, but I had to clean the slate if we were to continue as man and wife. In one of his rants, he threatened to take the children away if I left. After a couple of very tense days, he became enraged again, pushed me against the wall, and started pounding my head against the wall. At that moment, I remembered what Mom had said, "You don't have to tolerate physical abuse. You can leave him if he becomes abusive." I think I was smiling when he whacked my head one last time against the wall. Our marriage was over. I had had enough. A surge of relief swept over me. I would finally be free. After deciding to leave, I kept my plans secret until I could arrange my exit. First, I needed to find a place to live and an attorney, then I'd be ready.

I was making only forty-five dollars a week, with major expenses of rent, car payment, daycare, food, and clothes. It greatly limited the places I could afford. I checked out classified rentals in the newspaper for a week. The only place within my budget was a very old, dilapidated, two-bedroom, furnished duplex across the street from Houston Hobby Airport, in South Houston. The owner, an old widow, agreed to show the boys and me the place one day after work. I met her in front of the property. It certainly was very shabby looking, but beggars cannot be choosers. As we approached the house, a huge jet suddenly appeared forty feet above our heads, directly towards us. It was on final approach to the Hobby Airport runway, just across the street. The noise was deafening. Little Lee looked up and started screaming, then began sobbing at the top of his lungs, thinking the monstrous jet was going to crash into us. I hugged him tightly and covered his little ears as the huge airline passed overhead. It seemed low enough to touch. Immediately, I took Lee's hands and covered his ears with mine, making a game of it. I reassured him he did not need to be afraid, because the jet was passing low, ready to land across the street. He calmed down, and we continued the game whenever we heard a jet approaching. Finally, the crisis was over, so we went inside to a small living room with a window air conditioner that hopefully would cool the entire place, a kitchen with an eating area, and one bedroom with a dresser, a double bed, and a small bath. There was an unused room behind the kitchen that could be the boys' room but had no furniture. The backyard was small but had a couple of large, lazy old shade trees. It was quiet and peaceful, most of the time. Rent was sixty-five dollars a month with utilities, and roaches included. I snatched it up. It would become our new home. It looked like a castle to me, a castle of freedom.

❧

I told Neil I had found a place to live and was leaving with the boys. He again ranted and raved about killing us all or going to court and taking the boys away from me. I ignored him. The only things he allowed me to take were our clothes, toys, the Electrolux vacuum cleaner, and, of course, my new car. When he finally finished his tirade, I was totally drained, and my only emotion toward him was pity. He had caused this. I had once been in love with him, but he had destroyed it, day by day and year by year. He had taken away the core of my being, trampled my heart, and my confidence, too many times. I had lost all love and any respect for him.

❧

The affair, although wrong, became my lifeline back to normalcy. My self-esteem returned. I had finally overcome the feeling of worthlessness and being unlovable. I was now powerful and unstoppable. I loved my new home. It meant freedom and triumph against all odds. In truth, it was a rundown dump, but it was all mine. I painted the kitchen a bright yellow to brighten up the place. I even got used to the front headlights of jets beaming in my window at night as they approached the runway. After being married for four long years, I was going to be free. I could smell my freedom in the breeze and was excited to be on my own with my sons for the first time in my life. I had become a powerful force and was determined to be a successful, professional woman, but more importantly, a successful, loving, understanding mother. I had no idea what the real world would be like, but I was jubilant and even a bit giddy to begin my life.

10

Without further procrastination, I called Mom to tell her about the situation at home and my decision to leave. I was shocked when she told me that she already knew all about it. Neil had been calling her in the middle of the night for months, very drunk. He told her all about my affair, too. Oh shit! I was a sinner in her eyes, but she never chastised or blamed me for my sins. With true love in her heart, she chose to support and encourage me rather than chastise me. She implored me to move back home so that the family could help, and I could go to college. I refused. I thanked her for her offer but explained that I had my own family now and needed to try to do this on my own. Mom understood but said the offer was always open. In my mind, going home would be a failure. In fact, I did not want my sons raised by my mother. I loved my sons more than anything, and they came first. We could do this together. She agreed, but told me I must have a phone in case of an emergency and so she could talk to me regularly. I got the phone installed, and she sent me a check every month for five dollars. We talked every Sunday evening. She never again compared me to Veronica, as she could have so easily. Veronica had successfully graduated from college with honors and soon after married the only fellow she had ever dated.

❧

I needed a good lawyer but did not want to ask any of my neighborhood friends. The headhunter who hired me knew my circumstances, so I asked him for advice. He referred me to an attorney he knew personally in the city. I made an appointment, drove into the city after work, parked the car in a nearby lot, and found the attorney's huge, high-rise office building. There I was, in my white dental assistant uniform and matching shoes. Up to the twenty-first floor, into the luxurious office of Bennett Nichols, Attorney at Law. His office overlooked the entire city. He was of medium height, not someone you would call handsome, but he had a warm, friendly air about him. He was successful, judging by his high-rise office. He greeted me with a warm Texas accent. We sat down, and he asked me how he could help. Without tears, I told him the whole story—the abuse, the affair, my boys, and finally, the fact that I was now back to work but had no savings. He described the risk of losing the children because of my affair, but said he would take the case. His estimate for the divorce was one thousand, two hundred dollars, but he agreed to receive ten dollars monthly, which meant I'd be paying forever, but that did not matter. Perhaps he considered it a pro bono case. I could sense that he wanted to help me, and he did, without any sexual overtones or advances. Once outside the high-rise, I heaved a sigh of relief. I was on my way to freedom. Two months later, the December divorce was final. I was awarded primary custody of the children, and Big Neil was granted normal visitation privileges, and I was awarded monthly child support for both boys of one hundred dollars.

❧

I was the first Catholic in the family to get a divorce, yet in the eyes of the church, I was still married. I began my own spiritual path. I continued to attend Sunday mass with the boys and take them to Sunday school when they reached school age. Big Neil no longer communicated with his sons or me, claiming that it was too painful for him. Little Neil missed his Daddy now, but Big Neil did not bother to consider how his sons felt. His feelings were the important ones. Little Neil was also upset about the massive change in our lives, but I comforted him and tried to explain that everything would be better. We soon got into a routine. I was comfortable in my new job, and the boys had the consistency of a wonderful, small childcare home, located in a small house with a fenced yard and about twenty children of all ages. It felt like a home with lots of kids. I had lucked out. The owner, Miss Cathy, was a sweet, caring older woman. I instantly liked her and soon grew to love and depend on her. The boys were happy to be with new friends and had fun while I worked. They soon loved Miss Cathy like a grandmother. I was so grateful to have a positive childcare environment for my boys. It was so important to me.

Without their father in their lives, I took on the role of both Mom and Dad. Every morning on the way to Miss Cathy's daycare, we'd drive by Big Neil's apartment, and Little Neil would point over and say, "That is where Daddy lives. Can we go see Daddy?" Daddy was very busy working, but perhaps one day they could. I never said anything bad about him. I kept all my feelings to myself and felt it was vital for them to have a father, even though he was absent, no phone calls, no visits, no birthday cards, nothing! Lee was probably too young to remember his dad, since he was only one and a half years old when we left. Soon, the monthly child support checks started arriving, and I needed every penny.

When Little Neil first learned to talk, he often stuttered. I had asked the doctor about it, but he said not to worry, that he'd grow out of it. The boys had been going to Miss Cathy's for about two months when she took me aside and said, very proudly and with a smug smile, "Neil does not stutter anymore." "*Oh, my God*," I said. It was true. The strain in my marriage had contributed to my son's speech difficulties. Thank God. It was clear that I had done the right thing by leaving.

❧

My boys were my entire life. I was so happy to be on my own. I felt as though I had been freed from an emotional prison. I had learned to budget while working part-time in high school and somehow managed to live within my means in that quaint old duplex, with jets on final approach. I was free, alive, and in charge of my destiny. I was blessed with a home in the suburbs, a Toyota with air conditioning, and a good job as a dental assistant. Life was perfect!

I took my responsibility as a parent very seriously and wanted my sons to know they were always loved and cared for, without favorites. I never compared one to the other, as my mother had done with my sister and me. Loving, hugging, kissing, and even sometimes tickling my kids, I told them how much I loved them and that I would never leave them or let them down. I showed them that love, consistent parenting, and fair discipline were important. They knew the boundaries of right and wrong, but, as kids, they sometimes pushed or bent the limits.

Looking back:

Even today, during visits to my sons and their families, sitting around a festive Thanksgiving or Christmas dinner table, when there was a lull in the conversation, one son would inquire with a sheepish grin, "Remember that Christmas in Houston when the next-door neighbor accused us of breaking all his outdoor Christmas lights? Well, we did do it! Just wanted you to know."

"You both vowed that you did not do it," I said, incredulously. "I refused to replace the bulbs, because you both swore you did not do it, even when the neighbor said he caught you doing it." I leaned back in my chair and said, "I always stood by you, sons. Now, where is my hairbrush? I owe you both a twenty-year-old spanking." We all laughed.

❧

Life was going along very well. The boys had adjusted, and I enjoyed my work. Then one morning, Little Neil came into my room and said he could not find his panties. Oh, shit, what have I done! I almost laughed, but needed to cry, when I realized what I had innocently done. What a wake-up call! I was very conscious that my boys should grow up without too much feminine influence, but they were not exposed to any male influence.

❧

Summer weekends, our duplex became so hot and humid that we could not stand being inside. The solution was perfect. I packed a picnic lunch of peanut butter and jelly sandwiches, cookies, lots of Kool-Aid, and then we jumped in the car and drove to Galveston Bay. Sometimes we went to the beach, but often we'd go crabbing at Port Bolivar, a long, narrow peninsula that was usually deserted. I enjoyed walking along the surf, hunting for shells, hoping to find a Spanish doubloon. One day, the entire island was full of beautiful orange and black monarch butterflies, flying in swarms along the shoreline and then resting on the sand. It was their migration stopover on the way to Mexico. What a magical day. The boys and I were captivated. I always loved the ocean. It was so relaxing. I found a few channels on the bay side that had been dredged out and were easily accessible. It was a perfect place for crabbing. I showed the boys how to tie a chicken neck to a string and slowly lower it into the water. They learned to watch the bait below the surface until a crab started feeding, then quickly scoop the net and catch the crab. It was always a fun and relaxing day. The boys became excellent crabbers using this technique. By mid-afternoon, we'd have a trash can full of blue crabs that we'd bring home, and I'd boil them for dinner. Picking crabs is a lot of work, but I managed to get enough to make Miss Cathy's gumbo during the week. After such a long, hot day in the sun, we went to bed early, with a bit of tender sunburn on our shoulders. Crabbing became a tradition and an inexpensive way to have fun.

❧

As the boys grew, I realized they needed to learn more boy things. So, Santa Claus brought them fishing poles with tackle boxes filled with hooks, weights, slimy worms, etc. I paid for a one-year family pass to the Galveston Fishing Pier, and the boys soon learned how to fish. I knew nothing about fishing, but there were plenty of experienced Texans on the pier every weekend. I just suggested that the boys ask the fisherman right there what he was catching and what bait he was using. Those old boys always enjoyed helping my sons bait a hook or add more weight. I'd watch as the boys went up and down the pier, watching men cast their rods. Once, Lee came to me and said, "Next time, we need to make bait out of cotton and cheese. Okay, great tip. In the meantime, I just sat in my folding lounge chair reading a novel and watching them out of the corner of my eye. They never caught anything worth taking home, but that was not the point. My boys were getting some real male bonding time. Lee loves fishing to this day. He often enters kayak fishing tournaments in the Gulf of Mexico. Neil now calls his underpants jockey shorts. What a relief!

❧

I met two young, divorced women who both had young kids. We'd get together, share a sitter, and go to happy hour on Friday nights at the Ellington Officers Club. Soon, we met some officers stationed at the base. I started dating Mel, a Second Lieutenant, who was just out of college. We saw each other almost every day for a couple of months, and he was great with the boys. I started dreaming of marrying him and moving all over the world. One day, he went home on leave. When he returned, he was engaged to his college sweetheart. I was hurt, but I realized we had never expressed any love or commitment to each other. He was barely twenty-two. I was the same age, with two children. The fantasy was all in my head, but the pain was real. I could not blame him. I just picked myself up, wished him well, and moved on. I was learning that the dating game was more difficult because I had two young sons.

11

With only a high school diploma, my career choices were limited. I worked extra hard and did my very best as a dental assistant, but I realized there was no room for advancement in that career. I searched for a more challenging career. The Houston Police Department advertised that it was looking to add women to its ranks. That would be an exciting job. I applied and filled out the eight-page application, but I was not qualified. If I were single, great, but since I was a single mom with two dependents, they said no. Next, I visited military recruiters and asked if I would qualify to join the service. The answer was the same. They were not recruiting single moms with dependents. I could not blame them.

❧

My life changed the day a friend came into the office for an appointment. She took me aside and mentioned that her company, TRW Systems Corporation, was looking for math aides for the NASA program and asked if I was good at math so I applied for the job. I interviewed with this global aerospace company and accepted a position at NASA. It's true, my title was "*computress,* a bit sexist, but I didn't care. I was a female math aide. It was a dream come true. I never imagined I would qualify for an hourly position with a starting salary of one hundred dollars a week. Previously, I had no benefits, so these benefits were excellent: medical and life insurance, a pension plan, a 401 (k), and stock options. I was ecstatic! My salary had doubled overnight. At last, I could afford to move from the old duplex by the airport runway to a two-bedroom apartment with air conditioning and a swimming pool. After two weeks' notice with the dentist, I traded my dental uniform for everyday work attire, quickly turning out a few comfortable A-line dresses or the popular polyester pant suits.

❧

The nineteen sixties were a pivotal moment in history. I felt honored to be a part of it. In 1962, President Kennedy set a bold goal for America with his famous words: "We choose to go to the moon, not because it is easy, but because it is hard." Sending a man to the Moon and bringing him safely back to Earth was an unprecedented challenge for America. Kennedy united the nation in the race against the Soviet Union to achieve this monumental feat. NASA engineers and scientists were pushed to make the impossible a reality, and I had the privilege of supporting and witnessing this incredible triumph.

The Apollo Program offered me a once-in-a-lifetime opportunity to take part in a technological challenge. The entire world was watching. The Russians were already ahead of us, having already put Yuri Gagarin into orbit in 1961.

My type A personality and thirst for knowledge paid off. I was working in the space race with several young, dedicated, enthusiastic aerospace engineers. It was a pivotal point in my life. Little did I know it would launch my career into orbit.

❧

Computer technology was in its infancy compared to today's technological advances. The few existing computers were as big as a large room, requiring an equally large room to house the huge, water-cooled air conditioner needed to keep them cool. Trained computer operators like Neil managed these enormous computers. The programmers who had computer tasks to perform had to create a set of keypunch instruction cards that enabled the computer to read each punched card, follow the instruction, then go on to the next punched card, and so on until the machine read all the cards. These computer "*jobs*" would be submitted to run overnight, and the results, called printouts, were picked up the following morning. It was an exacting process. If there were a typo on a punched card, the job would fail. Once corrected on the punched card, the job would be rerun the following night. The system was in its infancy, but it worked. Back in those days, all engineering documents were produced using manual typewriters. Diagrams for those documents and formal presentations were done by hand with special ink pens using various rulers and drafting curves. My initial responsibility was to create these pen-and-ink drawings from hand-drawn sketches for use in engineering documents. It took me a while to become proficient in making these diagrams of flow charts, rockets, orbits, and other complex figures, without any mistakes, or at least hiding my mistakes with a trusty bottle of white-out.

I hated being idle and never wanted to be seen as a slacker. So, during slow times, I would ask math aides in other sections if they needed help. They always appreciated my help, and soon management noticed. My boss announced that I was being promoted to a department-level position, supporting all sections. It was amazing. My efforts had paid off.

During the holidays, I was invited to the department Christmas party. I got a date with a young, handsome engineer from New York, bought an inexpensive black evening dress, and found myself among all the department management staff and their wives at a party. "*Baba*" had come a long way.

I loved my job and enjoyed working with the staff. I had become confident that my career could flourish with more hard work. Being young and cute did not hurt either.

The young aerospace engineers I worked with were male, except for a few fully qualified women engineers. The female support staff held jobs as secretaries, admin assistants, or keypunch operators. I was not a secretary or an admin assistant. I was not an engineer or computer programmer. Instead, I was a math aide, supporting the work of the highly skilled aerospace engineers who were reaching for the Moon. It was a unique position.

Looking back:

After my career of over the years, I recall how professionally and respectfully I was treated as a young, divorced woman. I never encountered harassing remarks, leering looks, or inappropriate behavior. The engineers were always very respectful gentlemen who would smile and say hello as I passed.

No one ever fathomed that sixty years later everyone would have a smart mobile phone, make calls around the world, be connected to the Internet, do online banking, watch a movie, or listen to music. I was a witness to the birth of these tremendous advancements, but I still have trouble using my smart mobile phone, which is smarter than I am.

❧

When I joined NASA, I did not realize the complexity of such a challenge. Once scientists determined the engineering requirements and developed detailed procedures for getting a man to the Moon and back, a primary backup system had to be developed for every contingency, in case the onboard computer, electrical, communications systems, or any other unexpected failure occurred during the flight. A secondary backup system was also developed in case of secondary failure, and ultimately, the third backup consisted of manual procedures, published in spiral-bound notebooks and placed onboard in case communication was lost. Each new Apollo mission put us a step closer to landing on the Moon and returning safely to Earth. It was an enormous challenge, and everyone working on the program felt the pressure to meet the launch deadline.

I will never forget the Apollo 11 Moon landing on July 20, 1969. I gathered around a black-and-white television with my kids, my boyfriend, and his friends to watch the Moon landing. We won the race to the Moon, and the entire world cheered! Apollo 11

Astronauts, Neil Armstrong and Buzz Aldrin, successfully landed the Lunar Module on the surface of the Moon. Next, they stepped onto the lunar surface and planted an American Flag. What a fantastic accomplishment. In a small way, I had been part of it.

After Apollo 11's successful splashdown, there were endless splashdown parties, night after night. Then the euphoria of success grew dim. Work on the next mission, Apollo 12, lacked momentum. I found that I had no new work to do. I couldn't sit at my desk and do nothing while others socialized or read books. I tried to wait out the lull but became miserable. Although I loved working at NASA, I was bored, and as far as I was concerned, I was wasting time that could be spent learning something and furthering my career. So I decided to take a night course in engineering drafting at the University of Houston, thinking I could use it with all the ink drawings. Then looked for and found a job as a draftsman at a manufacturing company near Hobby Airport, drafting engineering drawings of rivets, yes, rivets. This work was far from exciting, but it came with a small pay increase. I submitted my resignation with TRW and started work in a large aircraft hangar. It was a noisy, dirty factory setting. On the first day, I realized that a shirt and jeans would have been adequate attire. My office was a cubbyhole at the edge of the factory. This company made custom rivets for strollers, bicycles, and car seats. It was a niche market. I had to draft an accurate drawing of a specific rivet requested by the customer. It sure was not rocket science. Within two months, I cleared their huge backlog of drawings and then developed a new filing system. Once again, I found myself completely bored.

Eventually, I found an interesting job as a photo interpreter with Lockheed Corporation. Once again, my so-called career was heading in a completely new direction, but I was open to the change. I had to get out of the rivet business. Although I became a good draftswoman, there was no room for advancement in rivets. Honestly, how hard is it to draw a rivet? But I digress. This new job with Lockheed had nothing to do with the space program but was still under NASA's umbrella. Special government aircraft were used to fly missions to photograph a specific target area on the ground. The mission could be a hurricane disaster area, a particular coastline with erosion concerns, or a corn field with insect infestation. The aircraft shot row after row of photos over a target area grid to create a mosaic map. It was much like mowing a lawn, back and forth with overlapping rows. My job was to take an assigned mission, with the associated maps and all exposed rolls of film, and use a spectrometer, a device I could look through at each photo frame to get a three-dimensional projection, to determine each frame's location, and record the frames on a detailed map. Private Investigators, i.e., scientists and engineers, could request access to this data, analyze the photos, and estimate the extent of potential hurricane damage, coastline erosion, or corn crop damage. My coworkers were a couple of guys with some military experience as cartographers. It wasn't very challenging, but it felt like solving a puzzle, and it paid the bills.

❧

I had been at this job for less than a year when my former boss at TRW called me to request a meeting. They wanted me back and offered me a professional position with a higher salary. My work had paid off. I immediately accepted. I was now a Member of the Technical Staff, MTS, a significant advancement that only professionals received. I was no longer an hourly employee, but a salaried professional. It was a dream come true. Very few hourly employees had been promoted to MTS. Why was I different? I was hardworking and dedicated, and I always did my best at my job. I had confidence and was eager to learn new things. It was the work ethic I learned as a child. It was not anything special, just important. It was sure paying off. I was now a valued professional.

❧

I will never forget the Apollo 13 flight emergency. "Houston, we have a problem!" Everyone in the entire space program was glued to the voice transmissions after the explosion, praying the engineers would find a way to return the capsule safely to Earth. Aerospace engineers in different specialties worked in teams, around the clock. The biggest challenge was to produce enough oxygen for the astronauts to breathe until they returned to Earth. Carbon dioxide was building up rapidly. A young aerospace engineer who worked in flight control and human factors told me many years later how they figured it out. Over dinner one night, he described the event. He was pulled into a conference room with all the other human factors engineers. Before them was a large conference room table, piled high with extraneous parts from the wounded spacecraft. He said they were locked in the room and told to come up with a solution to the oxygen problem. It may not have been duct-tape and baling wire that were used, but engineers improvised and brought our Apollo thirteen crew home safely. We all had tears in our eyes upon a successful splashdown. Everyone cheered when the astronauts emerged from the capsule alive.

❧

Later, I was assigned to work on the Contingency Navigation and Return-to-Earth Procedures. If communication or navigation problems occurred during an Apollo flight, the astronauts would be forced to use contingency navigation. This navigation device was the trusted sextant, used for centuries to navigate the globe by sea. An astronaut would take readings from the brightest stars that he could see from their position in space. Once he had several readings, he would manually calculate the trajectory required to return the capsule to Earth. After checking and rechecking the numbers, the pilot would initiate slow burns to realign the craft onto the trajectory needed to get home.

My job was to select the brightest stars at intervals throughout each flight and submit a report. I reviewed computer printouts containing the mission trajectory and selected the brightest stars available. My supervisor, an experienced aerospace engineer, always checked my work before submitting the data to Mission Control.

I was selected for the NASA Snoopy Award for outstanding achievement. The award included a small, sterling silver tie tack with Snoopy in an astronaut outfit. Since I never wore a tie, I had a replica cast in fourteen karat gold and wore it on my gold charm bracelet. I was the only woman that day recognized for outstanding achievement, along with five other men.

The Feminist Movement was sprouting wings, and companies were encouraged to hire and promote women. I rode those warm thermals for years, knocking down obstacles along the way. I had a remarkable career and was not even thirty years old.

12

It had been three years since the divorce. I had dated occasionally, but there was no one special. Then, Miss Cathy, my daycare provider, and her daughter fixed me up on a blind date. I had heard great things about Dennis, so I met him at her house for dinner. He was a tall, good-looking man, nine years older. He had been divorced for several years and had two kids in Florida. He was a gentle, caring man. We started dating, and he grew to love my kids, and they loved him. He was a father without a family, and I was a family without a father. What a great match. Neil was in first grade and had joined the neighborhood t-ball team. When he wanted to join football, Dennis became a lifesaver, helping me figure out how to fit the different pads into his football uniform.

Dennis worked for Lockheed Corporation as a cartographer. However, he eventually told me he was also a covert operative for the Defense Intelligence Agency, DIA, working in the war-torn country of Vietnam. I had never heard of such a thing. But as he predicted, one day he would get a call from Washington, DC, pack his bags, and leave for a few days up to a few weeks. During that time, I had no communication from him nor any way to reach him. Then he'd return home, freshen up, and continue his job as cartographer. He seemed just like Clark Kent, the reporter who turned into Superman when needed to save the world. He explained he had been a prisoner of war in Vietnam for eighteen months. I saw his scars to prove it.

Trying to explain his job in an unclassified way, he said, "I have a knack with explosives," meaning he was a covert demolitions expert. As Dennis explained, the explosive fuse they used to detonate the C4 explosive was not reliable "down to the second". Given that the covert team was in the middle of hostile territory, blowing up bridges, he improvised by holding the fuse with his fingers until it started burning his fingers, then he'd let go and run like hell. As a result, his thumbs and index fingers had scars on the fingertips, so instead of fingerprints, he had scar tissue and deformed

fingernails. Dennis gave me some advice regarding his specific military training. He trained in hand-to-hand combat, he warned me, "Don't ever walk up behind me, surprise me, or wake me out of a sound sleep, or I might react by hitting you." I had never been around anything military, but I said OK.

We dated for several months, fell in love, and when he asked me to marry him, I said, "Yes." Our wedding took place in a protestant church in Clear Lake City. My wedding ring was a jade band wrapped in gold that he had specially made for me in Vietnam and fit perfectly. The boys attended the service too. As we drove from the church, a dark cloud descended over me. I froze in the front seat. I felt as if I had just been captured and caged, like an animal. After several minutes, I was able to dismiss the feelings, but they remained in my subconscious. To me, marriage equaled control. I was imprisoned. This negative feeling surfaced from time to time, trying to convince me that I should not be married.

❧

With my frugal savings, I was able to put down a deposit on a three-bedroom house in Kirkwood, South Houston. Our happy family moved right in. We settled into married life, and, as he'd described, he'd come home to say, "I am going on a mission." After packing a few essentials, we would hug goodbye. A week or two later, he'd suddenly show up, ragged and exhausted. He never discussed his work, but one time he said I'd know what he was involved in by watching the news. The news broke several days later, reporting that a prisoner of war camp in North Vietnam had been attacked by the U.S. military and all the prisoners had been rescued. I was so proud of him. He was a silent patriot!

13

After Dennis and I married, Big Neil also remarried. His wife had a little girl, Heather, from a previous marriage. They lived nearby in Clear Lake City. Four years after our divorce, Big Neil finally reached out to say he wanted to see the boys. We arranged visits every other weekend, and the boys seemed to enjoy them, adjusting to the new stepmom and Heather.

Eventually, Big Neil accepted a new job and moved to Kansas City. When he called to ask if the boys could visit him in for a week that summer, I readily agreed. The boys were very excited about their plane trip. Neil had everything arranged, and soon they departed, on their own, flying from Houston to Kansas City. It was strange not having the boys around. We had never been apart before, and I missed them all the time. I was looking forward to picking them up at the end of the week and learn all the things they had done with their new family. After a very long, lonely week, Dennis and I picked them up at the airport. I hugged them, got their luggage, and we headed home.

❧

Finally on the road home, I turned around and asked them how their trip was going. Neil said, “It wass finnne,” in a soft, mumbling tone. I knew immediately something was wrong. Turning around in my seat with a smile, I asked, "Honey, why are you talking differently?" He said, "Theerr was an acssaadent." I could see his swollen face, and it was clear he was unable to speak clearly. When Neil said, "There was an accident," my heart sank. I knew their father had coached him. He never used those words. With my stomach churning, I asked, "What happened?" Lee explained that they had been playing ball outside with Heather when she ran inside to tell her mom that Neil had taken her ball. Big Neil had not arrived home yet. After dinner, Heather told the boys to go to bed. When Big Neil finally came home, he stormed into the boy's dark bedroom, grabbed Little Neil by his pajama bottoms with one hand, and began spanking him on the buttocks with the other hand, yelling and accusing him of taking Heather's ball. According to Lee, the loud, angry tirade continued in the darkness until Big Neil accidentally dropped Little Neil on his face. According to Lee, "*there was blood everywhere*." I surmised that once they got the bleeding under control, his dad explained to them that it was just an accident. Little Neil's front teeth were loose, wobbling in his swollen mouth. Big Neil failed to take him to an emergency room or a dentist, and he didn't call me to report the accident. He minimized the incident and prepped both boys on what to say to me when I picked them up. He was such a coward. I was beyond furious, on the verge of going ballistic.

Taking a deep breath, I said as calmly as I could, "Let's wait until we get home, and I will take a look at your face." Then I changed the subject and told them how much the dogs had missed them.

Why had Neil not called to inform me of this accident? I am his mother! It was not that I would never find out. My poor little son had a violent, traumatic accident on his first trip away from home to see his dad, and his little brother witnessed everything. They must have been so terrified and confused, being so far away from home in a strange place. My heart went out to them both. My fury was palpable. My son had been accused, beaten, and then dropped on his face. I tried desperately to control my anger and appear normal.

At home, I examined his mouth. It was still very swollen some four days after the accident, and I'm sure it was excruciating. The two upper, permanent front teeth were loose, wobbling back and forth. He could not speak clearly due to swelling in his mouth and could only eat soft foods and liquids because of loose front teeth. I hugged him for a long time and told him that I was so sorry it had happened and that it was not his fault at all. I wanted him to share how he felt, but he never did. I wanted so much to take his trauma and pain away, but he was silent, probably obeying orders. Lee was also very upset about everything. I hugged him next and comforted him as well. What a trauma to live through, seeing your father act so violently and then try to cover it up.

I was so enraged at the violence Little Neil had endured that, if I had had access to a gun, I might have gotten in the car, driven to Kansas City, and shot their father dead. It was a powerful, visceral need for justice. No one hurts my sons! I knew it was a wild idea, so I focused on how I would ensure that this never happened again.

The next day, I consulted a dentist, a few doors down from where I had worked. I explained the situation and asked him if he would be willing to examine Neil and have him explain what had happened. I needed a deposition I could use in court to restrict further visitation rights. I told Little Neil that he needed to see a dentist, and he agreed. The dentist was very gentle with Neil when he briefly examined his face and mouth and asked questions. "I am puzzled about your injury and would like to know how the accident occurred." Neil sat in the dental chair and told everything that had occurred, answering all his questions. At the end of the exam, the doctor told me there was no treatment for the two upper front teeth, which were severely damaged. The front teeth might stabilize, but if not, they must be extracted. If they did stabilize in his mouth, they would eventually die from the trauma, becoming brittle and discolored. When he became an adult, he would need root canals and crowns on both teeth. The dentist agreed to make a formal deposition about his examination and what Neil had told him about the accident.

With the dentist's written deposition, I contacted a lawyer who filed a motion in family court, not to remove Neil's visitation rights, but to insist that all future visitations be in my presence until the boys were eighteen years old. I wanted the boys to keep seeing their dad. Still, I needed to eliminate any chance of another "accident" in the future. Big Neil called, furious that I was taking him to court for a change in visitation, because of just a little accident. He complained several times over the phone that he did not have the money to drive back to Texas to appear in court. I was not sympathetic. That made no sense to me. He and his wife were both working. How important were his two boys to him if he chose not to appear to defend himself? He could have easily borrowed money from his parents, his source of extra cash whenever he needed it.

The court was uneventful. Big Neil never showed up in court, and there was no attorney to represent him. The judge was not impressed by Neil's absence. Based on the dentist's deposition, he granted the change in visitation to protect the boys, and I must be present at all future visitations. What a relief! My boys would be safe. After the court ruling, Big Neil disappeared from their lives. He never made any attempt to contact his sons by phone or to celebrate birthdays or Christmas for years.

❧

After their graduation from high school, I invited Big Neil to both boys 'graduation parties in Virginia, and he attended both. At that point, he started a relationship with them. I figured they were adults and could handle themselves. Until his death, Big Neil complained often and bitterly to his sons, saying, "It was your mother who kept me from seeing you. It was all her fault. I wanted to see you." This mantra continued every time they saw him.

14

The boys loved Dennis. He was a very caring stepdad and an ideal male figure. He left the disciplining to me but occasionally resorted to a truly unique form of punishment. Neil never put his bike away in the garage. We reminded him constantly, but it was still left on the front lawn. One day, Dennis brought the bike into his bedroom and put it on his bed. He told Neil he'd have to sleep with it. The same thing happened when he forgot to take out the trash. Neil still tells that story at family occasions, about how he was forced to sleep with his failure to respect the rules. It made a lasting impression and was brilliant. No restriction or other forms of punishment were needed! Lee wisely watched his older brother screw up and always had a clean, spacious bed for himself.

After six months, the honeymoon was over. It was just the day-to-day routine of married life, and I became bored and discontent. I refused to think I had sabotaged the marriage, but the undertow made me restless and unhappy. With Dennis's covert job, he'd disappear for an unknown period and suddenly reappear, after I had been managing without him. I resented his being gone and realized that he was married to America, and not to me. Things continued to deteriorate until one day everything changed in an instant. It was a sunny weekend, and all four of us were in the front yard. Dennis and I were gardening while the boys played on their bikes. A heated discussion ensued. I don't even remember what it was about, but I was livid and turned to him and said, "That is not true. You are lying," He turned around, slapped me across the face with such force, I went flying across the yard, landing on my butt. Both boys had seen it and ran over to me to ask if I was okay. I stood, dusted myself off, looked at Dennis, and said, "Get out!" That was it! I had had enough and would not tolerate violence.

To be fair, Dennis was a great guy. But our marriage was built on sand from my past. To this day, I have a lot of respect and admiration for his ethics and his sense of duty to his country. I knew our marriage would never work. I did love Dennis, but one of the reasons I married him was to give the boys a father figure.

❧

The fallout from our separation and divorce was that Little Neil was devastated at losing another father figure he had grown to love and admire. Lee, two years younger, did not show that the separation impacted him. Little Neil became an angry little boy when Dennis packed up and left. His grades began to fall. Then I had reports from teachers that he had started fighting in school. I was asked to meet with his teacher and a guidance counselor. I explained the reason for his anger. Neil had lost the father figure he loved. First, they wanted to perform a series of aptitude and personality tests. They also recommended he see a psychologist to enable him to talk about his feelings. I had no money for that kind of treatment, but they had a child psychologist who was part of the Harris County School System, in downtown Houston, that I could use and pay on a sliding scale. Once a week, for the next several months, after work, I would pick up the boys and drive into Houston. Lee and I would wait outside in the garden while Little Neil spent an hour talking to the male psychologist. He never complained and went willingly. He never told me anything about their discussion, and I never asked. Slowly, he started to improve at school and at home. Little Neil gradually became my happy kid again.

15

Most of TRW's contracts in Houston were for the Apollo and Skylab. The next big contract was the huge Shuttle contract. All the top government contractors bid on the contract, but TRW lost. It was an enormous loss to everyone involved, leaving many of us feeling uncertain and vulnerable. Our staff totaled four hundred professionals. Apollo was over, and Skylab was phasing down. Our facility was suddenly required to downsize fifty percent of the staff in the next two to three months.

Since I had been promoted to MTS, I had the opportunity to interview and transfer within the company gave me hope and a sense of possibility for my future.

With the help of a couple of my engineering buddies I updated my meager resume. Maybe I should have taken out the part about my rivet drafting job. I was concerned but not panicked, hoping that since I was not highly paid, I could stay to support the remaining contracts. I did not want to leave Houston, my only home as a single adult.

Management held an all-hands meeting, explaining the situation and telling us they would do their best to find jobs for the two hundred professional staff scheduled to be laid off in two months. TRW Corporate then organized an internal company job fair in Houston. Managers from all locations around the country who needed additional staff were asked to post the job openings and attend the job fair. At the fair, I interviewed for jobs located in Los Angeles, San Bernardino, California, and McLean, Virginia. I was invited to fly to California for in-depth interviews. Los Angeles was well known for its horrible drug problem. I did not want to expose my boys to that environment, but that might be my only offer. So I might have to consider it.

❧

I will never forget the feeling I had while driving my rental car from Los Angeles to San Bernardino for an interview supporting a missile defense system. The sun was out, the windows were down, and the radio was blasting *Aquarius*, by the Bee Gees. I sang along, high on life, seeing California for the first time. I was proud of my incredible career. My hard work had paid off, providing me with new opportunities.

My first choice was a position in McLean, Virginia, near Washington, DC. It would give me new experience in computer software and database technology used across the entire U.S. Army. The position required a Department of Defense, DOD, top-secret security clearance that would provide more opportunities in the classified field of intelligence. There was also the possibility of an overseas assignment. I carefully weighed the risks and benefits, and it became clear that accepting this role was the best way to advance my career and secure my family's future. It was a no-brainer. I accepted the job in McLean, Virginia, and things started happening very fast. The company bought my house, packed all my household goods, and moved me to Virginia. I felt like a princess packing the Pinto wagon with suitcases for the boys and me. I was very sad to leave Texas, but also excited about my new position in Virginia. As I pulled away, I realized how much my life had changed and how well I was doing as a single parent. I loved the Texans and would miss my friends, but I leaned into the wind of opportunity. It was also a plus that I'd be closer to family. The company paid for my relocation trip, so I decided to splurge. We spent two nights at the Holiday Inn at Navarre Beach, on Florida's Gulf Coast. It was our first real vacation where we were not sleeping in a tent. After relaxing and swimming in the clear Gulf water, we drove on toward the Appalachian Mountains. It was the start of a new adventure together, and I could not be happier. It was a dream come true.

The boys were sad to leave their only home and all their friends, but they were excited about the future. Luckily, they did not give me a hard time. Upon arrival in McLean, Virginia, we checked into a hotel. Before I could start work, I had to find a place for us to live.

The planned community of Reston was recommended, only thirty minutes from work. I got a realtor, and we took off to see what a planned community looked like. Boy, I was very impressed. The design combined commercial offices with nearby residential areas, including apartment clusters, condominiums next to shopping and restaurant areas, and secluded pockets of tree-friendly townhouse and single-family homes. I fell in love with it. It looked like everyone rode their bikes. I quickly realized I could not afford to buy any of the single-family homes, but I could rent a charming townhouse for a reasonable price. I signed the lease and enrolled the boys in an elementary school within walking distance. We could move in as soon as the household goods arrived, but before I could start working, I also needed a sitter for after school. I called Mom, thinking she could keep the boys for a week while I got settled and found a sitter. I was not expecting her answer. She told me she really was not able, but recommended my sister, Veronica. Fuck! She was the last person I ever wanted to see, let alone ask her for a favor. But without other options, I called her, and she agreed.

❧

Saturday morning, the kids and I drove over three hundred and forty miles to my sister's house in Connecticut. It took all day on the turnpikes. By late afternoon, we were approaching the turnoff. I started to get a migraine and popped two Excedrin. Suddenly, the sky opened, and the rains came pounding down on my little Pinto wagon. In such a downpour, it was almost impossible to read the signs, but with only a map and some directions, I took the correct turn off the turnpike. Now in suburbia, it was impossible to read the street signs in the downpour. I got lost more times than I can count and was exasperated with a horrible migraine headache that would not stop pounding. After a stop at a gas station and a call to get clear directions, I trudged on into the night. At last, I made it to Veronica's house. We were welcomed into her home. Veronica said she had dinner ready, but I explained about my terrible migraine, that I could not eat anything, and I went straight to bed. On Sunday morning, I felt fine but had to return to McLean immediately to start my new job the next day. I hugged the boys fiercely, told them to behave, and drove back to Virginia. Picking them up the following weekend.

❧

It was a turning point in my life. After years of just getting by and working so hard to prove myself, I had finally been recognized as a professional with an exciting future. My confidence and drive to succeed at this new job were unstoppable. Virginia is a beautiful state with endless wooded rolling hills. The boys and I loved living there. I had to work very hard to learn the database systems software. When I needed to work on the weekends, the kids and I would drive to Tysons Corner, in McLean, which was within walking distance of my office. The boys would go to the mall to see a movie, have lunch, then walk back to my office. The TRW four-story building sat on the top of a large hill, so on snowy weekends, the kids brought their sleds and spent hours sledding while I worked. We were a team. In the meantime, I was learning about emerging database technologies.

❧

I became fast friends with a co-worker named Gloria, a short, bubbly Italian from Rhode Island with a New England accent I loved. She was married with a son in high school. Although she was fifteen years older than I, she took me under her wing, calling me *"Baabra"* and became my best friend. She was full of fun and knew no strangers. We talked about everything, shared secrets, and stayed close over the years.

On my first day on the new job, I was welcomed by the manager of the McLean office and the employees in my new section. I immediately started classes on the new database software developed by the company. This system was already operational in many government offices, including the FAA and CIA. The army system was under development at our office.

Database software was a new, important technology that organized and stored large amounts of structured data, such as Name, Address, Phone number, City, State, and Zip code. Any or all of these terms could be searched, for example, "Name=Barbara and City=Reston," and the software would search all the records in the database and only return the records that contained Barbara and McLean. It was not the Google of today, but it was revolutionary back in 1974.

This TRW office had a different social dynamic than the Houston office, which was staffed mainly by male aerospace engineers. I found myself among professional men and women, married and single, which made it more fun. My section would sometimes go out to lunch, have a birthday cake at work, or organize a cookout at someone's house. We had never done that in Houston.

The office manager had recently formed the TRW Women's Committee. The purpose of the committee was to address professional women's issues and gain points for being politically responsive to the growing women's movement. I was the new kid, so I ran for president and won. We had enough women members to fill the auditorium and organized speakers to discuss a range of topics relevant to women, including legal rights, personal safety, and estate planning.

16

I was content in Virginia and was happy with my job change. The kids made new friends at school, and I dated occasionally. Dennis made a surprise visit and said he wanted me back.

"No," I said, "I have moved on."

After a year, I realized the cost of living in the Washington, DC area was more than I could afford. I saw no immediate solution and did not want to go into debt, so I called my boss, the person who had hired me, and set up a meeting. He began by saying how well I was doing. I thanked him, said I loved the work, and then explained my problem. He listened patiently, then paused and said, "There might be another option." My hopes rose as I took a deep breath. He continued, "Once your top-secret clearance is approved and you have learned the new Army database system, you could go on a temporary duty, TDY assignment for a year or more and work on the database system at a military site, such as Fort Bragg, North Carolina, or Fort Hood, Texas. Since it is a temporary assignment, you would receive an allowance of about twenty-five dollars per day. Your household goods would be shipped as well." He looked directly toward me with a crooked smile on his face, asking, "Does that appeal to you?"

My mind raced as I imagined this exciting adventure: being on-site, assisting the army in using our system. I would be a co-consultant working on an operational database system. I had the biggest smile on my face when I told him, "Yes, this will solve my financial problem and provide me a focus to learn the system in depth. It will also be an amazing adventure. When can I start?"

I began daydreaming. I could leave the expensive Washington area behind, move to a much more affordable location in North Carolina, and start saving the TDY money toward the boy's college fund or a down payment on a house. This opportunity was the answer to my prayers. My boss went on to say that the Army intelligence project had another site in Heidelberg, Germany, and if I did well at Fort Bragg, then Heidelberg was a possibility. "Yes, yes, yes!"

❧

With his direction, I was quickly reassigned to learn the specific army intelligence system. Within a few months, I accepted a consulting position at Fort Bragg, in Fayetteville, North Carolina. Movers packed us up once more, and the kids and I drove the old Pinto to Fort Bragg. The boys did not seem to object, as they had only been at Reston school for about a year. Bless their hearts, we had become nomads.

❧

My boss, Howard, was a friendly, down-to-earth man in his early sixties who had started his career as a dairy farmer in New Jersey. After a serious back injury, he had to switch to a desk job and went back to school to learn about computer software. He was a true tech wizard. We became close colleagues. Howard was like a father figure, teaching me far more than I could ever learn from a textbook. He was fun to be with and had so many stories about his dairy farm.

I rented a three-bedroom ranch house in a small neighborhood near Fort Bragg. The entire neighborhood was made up of active-duty military, except for me, and this military mindset was new to me. I found myself embedded in the military community and soon learned that the neighborhood was ruled by the highest-ranking military person on the block. Everyone fell in line under Brad, but I was a different duck.

After six months, my top-secret/sci security clearance was approved, and I was formally briefed by security personnel on the new top-secret compartments, i.e., the specific classified data that I would be exposed to as part of my work.

❧

I met David, a young, handsome Army Staff Sergeant with a wonderful smile and great sense of humor. On our first date, he drove over an hour to Raleigh, North Carolina, to see a play. I was impressed and felt a mix of excitement and nervousness as I embraced this new chapter. We started dating regularly. He grew to love the boys, and I included him in soccer practice and our activities. I was not the typical professional government contractor. I was a twenty-nine-year-old divorcee with long, dark brown hair, a career, and two kids. I was now swimming in their pond, so I tried to conform. David tried his best to teach me how to navigate the military and build a new life here.

❧

I became friends with my neighbors, and many kids my sons ' ages started playing at our house. The house soon became the hangout for the young boys. Over a holiday, I took the boys and their friends camping at Nags Head, North Carolina, home of the giant dunes. We ate lots of pizza, swam in the ocean, and had a great time.

Our home was only one block from the huge army installation that covered over two hundred and fifty square miles of tank trails used for military exercises. The area was unfenced, so the boys and their friends often explored along the tank trails. A few of their friends had dirt bikes that they were allowed to ride on the dirt trails. Naturally, the boys asked me for a dirt bike and said they would share it. For Christmas, I bought them a used Honda xr150, and they loved riding all over the forest and willingly took turns. After several months, the bike broke down, and I took it to the Honda dealer. The mechanic said it was a broken timing belt. I asked him if I could fix it. He smirked and gave me diagrams to follow. I could do that. After all, I had learned to change the oil in my Pinto. When we returned home, I set up shop. I only had a carport, so I put the Honda on a big plastic tarp in the spare bedroom. As I disassembled it, I noted where each part or nut/bolt was from and put them in order in cupcake tins along the tarp. Finally, I reached the timing belt and replaced it. Using my notes, I reassembled the bike. Now that it was ready to try, we took it outside, but the engine refused to turn over. Damn, maybe I ruined something trying to save money. I dragged the bike to the Honda mechanic, explained my sad story, and asked him to check it out. He called a couple of days later and said it was ready. When we arrived, he explained that I had done everything correctly, except that I had not aligned the timing belt properly. The instructions had not told me to do that. A man would already know something like that. Then he smiled and said, “You’d make a great mechanic with a little more effort. No charge.” Yes! I am a woman, hear me roar! A cute smile helped!

❧

I became friends with Jane, the young wife of a West Point graduate named Captain Brad. They lived in my cul-de-sac, only two doors down. She was a beautiful, sweet young woman from Pennsylvania with two preschool-age girls. Over time, I began to sense that she was having marital problems when loud fights were heard through all our open windows. Eventually, she admitted that Brad was abusing her. She felt trapped. He would not let her leave and had threatened her. She wanted to go back home to her family in Pennsylvania, and I encouraged her to plan her departure and offered to help in any way I could. She’d sock away some cash from grocery money and hand it to me to keep safe. After a few months, she finally had three hundred dollars, and she said she was ready. She wanted her daughters out of this abusive environment. Things had deteriorated, and he had threatened her again.

❧

On a day when she knew Brad would not be in town, I drove her to a U-Haul store where she rented a big truck. We returned to her house, and the two of us moved her furniture and household goods into the van. Once we packed up, she put the girls in the front seat with her and headed to Pennsylvania. I followed her for several miles to make sure she was okay and not being followed. She called to thank me after she was settled in Pennsylvania and was welcomed by her family. Months later, I visited Jane on one of my trips to see my mom and found her happy and relieved. My heart swelled with pride. She had moved on with her life. I admired her guts for leaving the asshole. Brad learned immediately from neighbors that I had helped his wife. He banged on the door one night, furious and threatened me. It really scared me. No telling what he would do to get even. His entire army Company knew his wife had packed up and left him. I immediately contacted his Commanding Officer, CO, and filed a complaint about his threat.

17

After working for the Fort Bragg Army Intelligence Office for two years, I had the opportunity to serve at Army Europe Headquarters in Heidelberg, Germany. This three-year assignment felt like a milestone, and reflecting on my career, I felt proud of what I had achieved since starting on my own. I was flying high and enjoying life. Most of our household goods went into storage, and we packed only clothes and other essentials. We boarded a Pan American flight to Frankfurt International Airport in Germany. There we were met by a coworker. TRW had booked a rental car for me, and I followed them south on the autobahn, about an hour to Heidelberg. We stopped at the quaint, old *Gästehaus Zum Löwen*, where we would stay until I got an apartment. Our room included three beds, each with an old-fashioned featherbed and a huge, puffy pillow, like a duvet filled with goose down. It was truly heaven in the wintertime—so toasty warm when you snuggled underneath. The bathroom, or water closet, had a toilet with a pull chain high on the wall, for water pressure. While staying at the hotel, I observed the local Germans as they entered the restaurant. They seemed courteous but reserved until the evening began and the beer started flowing. Then they really let their hair down and partied long into the night.

❧

My sons and I were the Three Musketeers in a wonderful Old-World environment. My contract enabled each of us to get a Department of Defense, DOD identification card, with privileges that included the use of the post exchange, PX, commissary, and recreation center facilities, not just in Heidelberg, but at any other Allied military base in Europe. Since we were civilian contractors, we could not live in the military housing. That was an advantage because we were now immersed in the German community and could pick up basic German. *Guten Tag*! Good day!

I found an affordable, fully furnished two-bedroom rental in the small town of Mönchzell, a rural farming area thirty minutes from Heidelberg. Our flat was on a quiet, dead-end road on the edge of town near a forest. The village was only two blocks long, with a *bäckerei,* bakery, a *metzgerei,* butcher shop, and a great German restaurant we frequented for delicious *Wiener Schnitze*l with mushroom gravy. I enrolled the boys in the DOD school, and the contract fully paid the tuition. A DOD bus transported the boys to and from school each day. We immediately started learning German.

❧

My commute to and from work each day was a scenic drive through a lovely countryside with gentle rolling hills and fields of wheat, mustard, and sugar beets, displaying vibrant colors from nature's palette. I fell in love with Germany. It was so quaint. Now I knew where my mother learned to clean until she dropped. There was. I think there was a law that each home or shop owner had to scrub their front steps each morning. The *hausfraus* were always busy.

The boys were enthralled with the historical surroundings. It was as if we had been transported back in time. Heidelberg had been founded in 1386 as a university town, before Christopher Columbus discovered America in 1492. Now I understood that America was a very young country compared to it. European history goes back over two thousand years. Roman castle ruins dotted the landscape. Quaint, old towns like Heidelberg—the city of Romanticism—were settled in the tenth century. Walled towns, old churches, cobblestone streets, and quaint shops provided a sense of history dating back hundreds of years. The Old City, home to Heidelberg Castle, built in the 1200s, is still probably the most popular castle ruin in Germany. This majestic castle sat prominently on the side of a hill overlooking the historic town along the shore of the Neckar River.

Army headquarters had been a military post occupied by the Nazi's in World War II. Swastikas had been replaced by the U.S. Army insignia at the stone entrance. There was a cafeteria, gym, laundry, and a parade field where I used to go jogging at lunchtime. The Intelligence building was in a small, secure facility near the rear of the compound. The year was 1977, and the Cold War was ongoing. But here the Soviet military was only two hours away, traveling in tanks on the autobahn from the Czech border to the old city. We were issued orders for an evacuation of all civilian personnel if Germany became unstable. All DOD civilians were told to have a *"Go Bag"* including passports, important papers, prescription drugs, a jacket, water, and other essentials in case of an evacuation order. I took it seriously, and each of us had a Go Bag at home, but I never felt we were in imminent danger because there were no serious tensions between the U.S. and Russia.

❧

The military took its mission in Europe very seriously. They held war game exercises with their partners in the North Atlantic Treaty Organization, NATO. I was invited to participate in a NATO exercise at a large, old Hitler bunker near the French border. Our tactical intelligence system would be used during this exercise. I was pleased to participate and worked a twelve-hour shift in the bunker during the day, and hot-bunked in a nearby tent outside the bunker for female military personnel at night. There was also a canteen outside the bunker where meals were available at all hours. I pinched myself again. Was I really in the Hitler bunker playing war games?

It was a five-day exercise. My job as a private consultant was to perform user training and ensure the intelligence system remained operational. Our intel unit had a small room in the bunker where our staff, mostly corporals, worked twelve-hour shifts. I worked the twelve-hour day shift. I had no idea how a real- life war scenario worked, but I figured there would be more activity and tension for officers in charge of the exercise as the war game progressed. However, the reality in our little room was just the opposite. By day four, most of the team members were bored to death, endlessly playing cards, taking smoke breaks outside, and complaining. When new position data came in from the field, it needed to be entered into the system immediately. After hours of waiting, we received new enemy position coordinates. However, the young corporals decided they would not jump to attention, so they continued playing cards and taking smoke and coffee breaks. It was only an exercise, but I was disappointed in the *laissez-faire* insubordination. I suggested they enter the data, and I was told, "Don't worry about it." After an hour, they still refused. I was not in charge of these men, but I was associated with their unit, and it certainly reflected on the new tactical computer system I was supporting.

I took my job very seriously, and as a result, I became more frustrated. I knew Russians could attack from the Czech border at any time and drive their tanks on the autobahn in and be in Heidelberg within two hours. That was a fact I did not take lightly. I was stuck in the middle as the soldiers continued wasting time.

As a government contractor representative, I did not want to be associated with the failure to keep the system up to date. Anyone could query the info and receive inaccurate information. Yet, I had no authority over these soldiers and was unable to inform our military supervisor, outside our secure bunker, of what was happening. I was in a bunker with no commercial phone service. Stuck, I finally made my decision. I packed up and left the exercise. It was a difficult decision, but my gut told me to be true to myself and my job. I did not know what the fallout would be. During the three-hour drive back on the autobahn to Heidelberg, I thought through my position and why I had decided to leave. The CO could have fired me on the spot, and I'd have packed up and returned to the U.S., but orders are orders, and I would not stand by and let the system be misused. I was representing TRW, the company I worked for, and the success or failure of its tactical intelligence system could have been compromised because of a couple of lazy corporals. As soon as I got back to Heidelberg, I went to the office and called the CO. It was late Sunday morning. He was at home and agreed to meet me later that afternoon. I was apprehensive when I walked into his office. I had no idea how he would react to my decision. At 3 p.m., he opened his door and offered me a seat. As the CO in charge of the entire intel unit, I knew he probably didn't know who I was or what my assignment was during the exercise, so I gave him a short background on who I was and what my job was at the exercise. Then I described the incident involving his staff's refusal to update his intel system, which other military units in the exercise expected to be up to date and correct. I added that I took the matter very seriously and decided to step back to protect my integrity and the reputation of the TRW intel system. If the data were challenged and determined to be incorrect, a complaint was lodged. He asked me no questions, made no comments, thanked me for the information, and then dismissed me. I heard nothing more of the incident. My job and integrity remained intact.

❧

Another bizarre incident occurred while under the umbrella of the DOD. I got a call at work from the Provost Marshall, requesting my presence in his office. I quickly determined that the Provost Marshal was responsible for the military police and base security, among other responsibilities. When I arrived, the Provost Marshall described the incident involving my sons. He explained, "I was jogging this afternoon along a road in the army housing area, and saw my sons playing frisbee in a nearby grassy area. As I approached, one of them threw the frisbee, hitting me in the head as he jogged past."

Oh, my God, is this really an issue? I bit my tongue to keep a straight face.

Then he demanded, "Who is your sponsor?" In other words, who is your military husband?

I gave him a smug smile and confidently told him, "I am the sponsor." I handed him my civilian identification, ID card, which indicated that I was the sponsor of my two sons. He assumed I must be a military wife, i.e., a dependent. Then he would have the power to call my military husband and make trouble for him. Sorry, dude, no military husband needed. I'm the new female career woman with the contract authority to be here and use your facilities. I am on my own and do not need to be married to a soldier! I briefly spoke to the boys, who said, "Mom, why would we try something like that? That would be crazy."

After a few flustered moments, I offered, "This was an unfortunate incident that occurred on a beautiful afternoon while playing in the sun. I apologize for my son's error in judgment in this matter." He returned my ID card. I turned, and under my breath, I softly spat, "Kiss my ass," as I walked out of his office. What a dick.

❧

During the summer, there were always fairs and fests, with beer halls, and the Oktoberfest was the most popular. *Fasching,* Ash Wednesday parade in the sleet and freezing rain before Lent near Wiesbaden. The famous *Christkindlmarkt,* Christmas market, was always a must-see, with *Glühwein*, a delicious, piping hot, spicy red wine, and hot cider for the kids that warmed our gloved hands as we strolled past each chalet filled with handmade Christmas ornaments as well as the many tasty delights.

❧

On an Easter trip to Venice, Italy, my water pump broke in my old Fiat, stranding me in Vicenza, at the Italian NATO Military Base, not far from Venice. I walked to the military police office and explained my dilemma to the Italian Carabinieri, Officer in Charge. It was Good Friday afternoon. He explained that all repair shops would be closed for the entire weekend. He invited us into his office and tried to get us a hotel, *Zimmer Fre*i, room for rent, nearby, but everything was full. I had packed our four-person tent and sleeping bags. Perhaps we could pitch our tent inside the police compound for the night. The next morning, we could take the train to Venice for the weekend and get the car fixed on Monday. Perhaps he didn't the idea of us pitching a tent in front of the military police station.

"I think I have a better idea," he said. He seemed hesitant for a moment and said, "At least you will be out of the cold and safe here." We walked to another building that contained prisoner holding cells, each containing four bunk beds. He gestured to the cell. "It is perfect and completely safe," I told him. I was delighted with this solution, and the kids loved it. We could say we spent Easter weekend in an Italian jail. He showed us the cantina, and we ate sandwiches for dinner, then retired. I was exhausted after a long day. We had two days in beautiful Venice, got our car fixed, and said *Arrivederci* to our wonderful host.

The boys wanted to learn how to ski so we joined the popular Heidelberg Ski Club, learned how to ski, and went on great, affordable ski trips to Italy, Austria, Switzerland, and France. Our favorite was the Christmas-week ski trip to the Italian Alps, with long, gentle slopes and good snow. After a day on the slopes, we'd ski back to the lodge and relax in the indoor pool and sauna. Dinner was a wonderful five-course Italian meal with delicious Italian table wine.

Another adventure was a weekend in September to Turin, Italy, to see the famous Shroud of Turin, said to be the image of Jesus Christ on his burial shroud when he was entombed two thousand years ago. My Catholic curiosity got the best of me. It was a chance to see the shroud. It was a last-minute trip, and I knew we could not get hotel reservations. Crowds had waited in lines to see the shroud all summer long. This was the last weekend. I hoped we could get there, see the shroud, then head home and find a hotel on the way. Just in case, we had our trusty tent and sleeping bags.

The three of us set off in the early morning, stopping for hard rolls, *brotchen*, butter, and salami for a typical breakfast, and maybe even lunch. The route through Germany to the mountains of Austria was breathtaking, and then across into Italy was uneventful but took hours. We arrived in Turin in mid-afternoon and drove directly to the church. The line wasn't that long, so I parked the car, and we got in line. After only a couple of hours, we entered the church to see the shroud. Still in my heart a dyed-in-the-wool Catholic, I wondered if I'd feel something different once I was close to it. The shroud was encased in glass and hung on the wall for all to see. Fire had caused some scorched areas along the fold of the fabric, but you could distinguish the likeness of Christ's face, the blood from the wound in his side, and the crown of thorns. Was it the authentic shroud of Jesus Christ? Unless they get the real DNA from Jesus Christ, we will never know. The shroud has been analyzed by scientists and historians over the years, and they had only proven that the cloth was of that period.

❧

It was getting dark when we exited the church. I checked some hotels, but all the managers said everything was booked, so we headed north on the Autostrada. We stopped for a pizza dinner, but no rooms were available. I drove on until about 11 p.m., when I was too tired to continue. I pulled off in a forested area not far from the highway. We got our sleeping bags, some water, and settled in a nearby grassy field. Unknown to us, we had settled right next to a busy railroad track. Trains came barreling through all night long. It must have been the express lane. It was hard to fall asleep, but eventually we dozed off. Early next morning, I awoke and looked around the field. Off in the distance, a few cows were grazing. Then I spotted four men approaching from a distance, rifles slung over their shoulders. I quietly woke the boys, gathered our belongings, climbed over the barbed-wire fence, and we performed a stealthy retreat without incident.

❧

After three years living a dream in Heidelberg, my contract was ending, and I needed to return to the office in McLean, Virginia. Since this was our *"Last Hurrah"* in Europe, I had an idea. If the kids, my boyfriend, and I drove my old Fiat to Italy, we would take the ferry to Greece. We could charter a sailboat and sail the Adriatic Sea for a week, then take a road trip across northern Greece to all the famous Greek ruins—Epidaurus, the Meteora, Delphi—then to Athens, the Parthenon, Mt. Olympus, and the national museums. It was an incredible adventure full of ancient Greek history.

We took off in June. The weather was sunny, hot, and clear. We drove to Italy, took the ferry from Brindisi to Greece, and met our sailboat Captain Jan, a charming, tall, Swiss bloke with blond hair. For a fantastic week, we sailed the warm Adriatic Sea, stopping at remote ports along the way. We grew fond of moussaka, beef in sauce, green beans, and my favorite, the Greek salad with lots of olives. It was the custom to go into a restaurant's kitchen and choose your meal from the steaming pots on the stove, typically for only two dollars. The local Greek wine was made with pine resin and tasted like gasoline. I preferred a French table wine.

I calculated that I could have a fantastic vacation, and once we got to Athens, the boys and I would fly back to Virginia. My boyfriend bought my car and returned to his army base in Germany. The flight from Athens to Virginia was cheaper than the flight from Germany to Virginia. What a grand exodus from Europe.

18

Upon returning to Virginia, I was placed in a job I was not suited for, but it was the only position available at the time. I was feeling unsettled and alone. Except for Gloria and a few others, I was an unknown, someone who had worked overseas doing who knows what, for five years. It was like, out of sight, out of mind. Only my project managers understood the unique, valuable experience I had gained at the customer sites. But it felt like I was starting over. There were so many new faces in the office. I did not know them, and they did not know me. I felt completely out of place. Had I wasted all that time having an adventure? I did have my two project managers who had looked after me. However, I never learned I should develop a network of mentors, i.e., respected managers who could foster my growth, and ultimately have my back, if I screwed up.

For five years, I had been saving my per-diem money, and I finally had enough to buy a house. I found a one-year-old, three-bedroom townhouse in a quiet neighborhood in Burke, Virginia. The kids were growing up fast, both attending Springfield High School. Lee was chosen for the soccer team and became an excellent varsity player.

They both adjusted to repatriation and made lots of new friends at school, integrating back into society without missing a beat. I was proud of them.

After a few months, I felt more at home, but was not dating or socializing. My job still sucked. On Friday nights, I'd go to an antique auction and watch the antique furniture from England go up for sale. It was good entertainment. I had hot dogs for dinner and watched people bid on antiques while my kids went to football games with their friends. I bid on and bought a few lovely antiques, including two identical, beautiful stained-glass windows from someone's front doors and a carved walnut drop-leaf desk to mix modern with a few antique pieces. It was fun.

❧

For several months, I was assigned to a Navy "*Black*" project at the Naval Research Lab across the Potomac River in Maryland. I considered it only temporary because I had applied for a CIA security clearance and was waiting for that to be approved. In the meantime, I was miserable, surrounded by Navy men in a windowless building, being asked to write Fortran. But I was not a programmer; I was a consultant. To put the icing on the cake, my project boss sexually harassed me, and I immediately reported the incident to personnel. The offenders were counseled, and I became a pariah, looking for another position.

When my clearance came through, I found an internal posting for an excellent job with a promotion to task manager of a group of six programmers, working for the CIA and DIA on a joint National Intelligence System. I passed the required polygraph and joined a large team developing a new generation of intelligence systems. It was the perfect niche for me, fascinating and challenging. I worked on this huge project for over eight years, working in a secure vault. Gradually, I was promoted from task manager to assistant project manager. Finally, my experience was valued and rewarded. The promotion into management was challenging, so I took some in-house courses to learn to manage others. I had always relied on myself, so delegating was a new ball game. At the end of the project, all our software was delivered without error. The entire team was very proud.

❧

Neil and Lee were fully occupied with soccer, friends, school activities, and girlfriends. Some of the boys had cars, so the kids had wheels. At sixteen years old, Neil got his first job at a nearby Roy Rogers Restaurant and rode his bike to and from work while saving for a car. Lee followed in his footsteps, earning his own money.

The boys were very independent now, and I had extra time on my hands. I had never had time to do volunteer work, but I looked at county programs for women and found a fascinating program, Fairfax County Victims Assistance Network, VAN. They accepted me, provided extensive counseling training, and then signed a contract to work four hours a week for 1 year. My first job was working a four-hour shift on the VAN telephone hotline. The best part was that I could work from home because VAN switched my phone to the VAN line for 4 hours. I usually signed up for Friday or Saturday night, when the house was quiet. If the boys were home, I told them they could not answer the phone for the next four hours. I'd stay by the phone, reading or watching television in my bedroom, waiting for the phone to ring.

I was apprehensive, wondering how I would handle a person in distress. After a few awkward calls, I became calm and went with the flow of the conversation. We learned specific counseling techniques that I incorporated into the conversation, but the most critical part was listening to their story and getting the facts. I took notes, but only first names were used. A woman calling back probably would not get the same counselor. We were forbidden to give out our private line. After perhaps spending two hours on the phone with a very distraught, scared victim, they would hang up, and I would never know what happened. Most of these women were stuck in a relationship or marriage to an abuser, with several kids and no job skills. Did she go to a women's shelter? Did she leave her boyfriend or husband and return to her parents for protection? Or was she still in the same situation? Many were frightened they would be killed if they tried to leave. It was like being on a tightrope, trying to give women encouragement and courage, without endangering them. Fairfax County is a fast-growing middle-class suburb just outside Washington, DC. My clients were mostly non-working housewives with several children who lacked the proper training or experience to get a decent-paying job and ditch their husbands. However, one was an attorney and another a successful businesswoman. More than once, the abuser was her husband, a local police officer. After the shift, I was emotionally exhausted.

In a small way, I felt that I was helping these women. Sometimes I wondered why I chose this type of volunteer program, but it was a very satisfying effort and different from my technical career. I worked the hotline for two years. Then, I was invited to join a weekly support group meeting that met every Monday evening for two hours. Several women, many regulars, would gather to discuss and listen to the abuse issues of others. Having abused women listen to other women struggling with domestic violence of a physical or emotional nature was powerful. I continued the support group work for several years. In a small way, I felt I was giving back to the sisterhood.

❧

My sons graduated from high school a year apart, then headed off to college. They both attended Northern Virginia Community College for a year, improved their grade point average, and then applied to a university. Lee chose Texas Tech University in Lubbock, Texas, and Neil was accepted at George Mason University in nearby Fairfax. I was able to manage their college tuition expenses with my savings.

❧

In 1989, the vast intelligence System was delivered to the CIA and DIA. The team started packing up all the documentation we had produced to turn over all official records to the government. Each of us was looking for our next job opportunity. The contracting business does not guarantee each employee will always have a job. My managers were actively looking at what was available for me and about thirty others on the project. Meanwhile, I was preoccupied with project closure and had not yet thought about my next job. I felt confident I'd have no problem.

Then, I got a call from my old boss, Larry, the manager who sent me to Heidelberg thirteen years ago. He told me I was wanted back in Heidelberg and explained he got a call from my old army boss, Cpt. Bill Wilson—now Lieutenant Colonel, Ltc. Wilson—who requested me by name to work on his new logistics contract in Heidelberg, Germany, again. Wow, what an honor. I was speechless, so I just listened. He described the contract briefly and suggested we talk in person. It seemed incredible to me that Ltc. Wilson would ask for me by name. He had not even asked for my résumé. I had not seen or heard from him since I left Germany. I tried to comprehend the magnitude of this offer. Cpt. Wilson was my army supervisor. We had become professional colleagues, but never personal friends, and we had never gone out to lunch. It was strictly business, and he always treated me professionally. I must have done something right. My work and moral ethics have reaped valuable dividends. Management was happy for me.

The timing was perfect. Both sons were in college and encouraged me to accept the position, saying they would visit me during the summer. I had just sold my old townhouse in Burke, Virginia, and bought a beautiful, new, larger townhouse in Fairfax, closer to work. The closing on the new property was still pending. What was I to do? Neil said he could rent out rooms in the new townhouse to his fraternity brothers. He promised no wild parties. That would take care of the mortgage, but I had been planning to move into my beautiful four-bedroom townhouse with a lovely fireplace and a finished basement. I thought long and hard about it, but still could not decide.

My sons, both in college, were now very independent, and I was not worried about them, but I could not decide on another overseas assignment away from everything I had built here, including my close friends. The weekend came, and I had still not committed to accepting the position. Saturday was a beautiful, warm, sunny day, but I was restless with indecision. As a true Virgo with a type A personality, my analytical mind and my heart could not agree. My boss was expecting my decision on Monday. So, I got on my bike and went for a ride to get some fresh air and weigh both options. As I rode along the bike path to Arlington, then along the Potomac River, I weighed the pros and cons. I was wrestling with two opposing forces, the appeal of a new adventure and practicality of remaining home. When I got to Reagan National Airport in Arlington, I stopped along the bike path and watched the jets take off every three minutes to parts unknown. That visual was all it took! I thought to myself, "Yes, I'm going back to Heidelberg.

Part Three

19

It was a cold, rainy Saturday morning in November 1989 when I drove into the familiar army headquarters in Heidelberg, Germany. I was meeting my old colleague, Ltc. Wilson and his project team for my new one-year assignment. This weekend meeting was unusual, but I had arrived the day before and had nothing else to do except get over jet lag.

❧

As I parked my rental car, I saw a very handsome army officer dressed in his camouflage uniform. He was slim, about six feet tall, with very light brown, almost blonde, curly hair, clear blue eyes, and a cute smile. I was wearing jeans and my special flight jacket I'd received on my last tour in Heidelberg. Maybe I looked like a fighter pilot. Well, probably not. He approached me and said, "I'll bet you're Barbara Wolfe. Welcome to Heidelberg. I heard you were coming."

I smiled and replied, "Yes, I am, thank you."

We shook hands as he replied, "Paul Johnson, at your service, Ma'am." I noticed the gold cluster insignia on his shoulder, indicating the rank of major. A glance at his left hand revealed no wedding ring. This assignment might be fun after all, I thought to myself. He led me into the conference room. Ltc. Bill Wilson welcomed me warmly, thanking me for coming back. After a meet-and-greet with the team, Bill provided an overview of the logistical effort. It involved a logistical, tactical system for troop readiness and tracking of nuclear, biological, and chemical attacks during wartime. I had to get up to speed quickly, understand the contract requirements, and understand what my task contract entailed. We agreed to meet on Monday morning in the conference room to get started.

I saw Paul frequently. He was always pleasant to everyone, smiling and with a cute swagger in his step. He was a career officer who had enlisted and worked his way up to an officer rank. He had a master's degree in foreign affairs and had served as an intelligence attaché in Moscow. He was separated from his second wife and living on post in the Bachelor Officers Quarters. Since he had no car, he rode his bike everywhere.

❧

Over the next two months, Paul's flirtation grew, and I found myself looking forward to our interactions, feeling a mix of excitement and uncertainty. Then he started leaving funny cards on my desk. That went on for a few weeks, until one day, I stopped him and whispered, 'Are you going to ask me out or not?' His surprised smile made my heart flutter. He nodded and said, 'Yes, of course.' We went to dinner a few days later, marking a turning point in our connection. We were walking down the cobblestone *Haupstrasse*, the main pedestrian street in the old city, on our way to the restaurant, when we encountered crowds celebrating *Fasching*, Ash Wednesday. One of the groups in front of us was a group of contractors who worked in the same building as Paul and me. Our cover was blown on our first date. Shit! We stopped to talk to them, trying to be casual. After a few minutes, Paul slipped behind me, lifted me by the waist, spun me around, and said to the group, "Got to go!" He touched me! He had the guts to lift me physically up on our first date, without asking. Boy, that broke the ice! He obviously was not afraid of me. That began chipping away at my heart. We laughed all the way to the restaurant. It seemed like we were old friends. The dinner was wonderful. We enjoyed a bottle of Italian wine and laughed and talked through the entire evening. Electric and effortless, the chemistry lit up the room. I began to realize there was something very special between us.

❧

On the downside, this budding romance could cost me my job. A similar incident happened several years ago in Heidelberg. A female coworker I knew started dating her married but separated army boss in Heidelberg. That was a classic case of conflict of interest. Someone, most likely a competing contractor, complained to the CO. He resolved the problem by immediately removing her from the position and sending her back to the States. She took the blame, and the incident left a mark on her professional reputation. The military man walked away unscathed—his only loss, perhaps, was that he lost his new girlfriend.

As experienced government consultants, we develop a professional rapport with the customer, but the lines of professionalism and friendship are clearly defined. I was not going to take any chances. My professional reputation for the past twenty years was my "*Gold Standard*," and I would not allow it to be tarnished. Paul was scheduled to retire next summer, after completing his twenty-year career. I didn't think he would object to being moved to another assignment if he wanted to continue our relationship.

One evening, I sat down with Paul, feeling a knot of anxiety in my stomach. I needed to be honest about my feelings and the professional risks. I put my cards on the table and said, 'I really enjoy your company and want to continue to date you, but I cannot, under the current circumstances.' My voice trembled slightly, knowing that this decision could change everything between us, and I hoped he understood the gravity of the situation. He frowned, puzzled. I explained, "Our relationship poses a professional conflict of interest because you are my supervisor." "This is a dilemma that could jeopardize my career," I explained. "I cannot continue to date you unless you are removed as my supervisor. The contractors saw us in public and know we are dating. Any of those contractors could lodge a complaint against us for a conflict of interest". With a huge grin on his face, he slowly exhaled, saying, "Is that all it is? No problem! I'll talk to Cpt. Bill tomorrow. He'll be really tickled to reassign me." I told you that he kept telling me, "You wait until Barbara Wolfe comes here. You just wait! She is coming. You just wait." Had he set us up, I wondered? Problem solved. He went to Bill, described the situation, and was reassigned that day. The CO heard about it and wished us luck, saying we made a cute couple.

❧

Once I moved into my small apartment in the old city, I asked Neil to ship my Doberman, Brutus, to Germany. I was a dog lover, and Brutus, my male, red Doberman, was about four years old and fully trained. He was my buddy and protector. The three of us started walking along the Neckar River every evening. Crowds would part as we approached, moving to the other side of the street. Bob, a talented programmer on my team from New Jersey, asked me if Paul and I would like to take a day trip to the Czech Republic border with him and his wife to visit the crystal and porcelain outlets. Sounded like fun. That Saturday morning, Paul and I piled into the back of Bob's small Fiat and off we went. Bob had been in Germany for years, and once we hit the autobahn, he accelerated to at least one hundred kilometers an hour. I had driven the autobahn years ago and didn't mind the speed. We passed tiny, picturesque villages snuggled within valleys. Stately Roman castle ruins continued to claim the top of a prominent escarpment on distant hills. We could see church steeples peeking out of small villages. It was late spring, and the weather was sunny and warm. Forests were vibrant green with trees in neat rows. The forest floor was immaculately groomed without even a pine needle out of place. Interspersed flowering trees added bright yellows and soft pinks to the scenery. We relaxed and enjoyed the view. It took almost three hours to reach the border town where the shops were, so we stopped along the way to get snacks and stretch our legs. It was our third date, and we were still getting to know each other. It was fun to have another couple with us.

Once we got to the shops, Bob parked the car and pointed out the shops we should look at first. Then he took off with his wife and said, "We need to pick up a few things we have ordered." Paul and I first entered the crystal shop. Everywhere you looked, crystal sparkled in countless shapes and sizes, including chandeliers, bowls, vases, and sets of crystal glasses for every occasion. I love cut flowers, and soon found a beautiful, large crystal vase I fell in love with, so I bought it that day. There was a Saturday farmers' market in the old city near my apartment, where I could get a variety of beautiful flowers year-round. We joined Bob for lunch, then they went to check out the porcelain shops. We took a cursory look around, then decided to have a cappuccino at a nearby café and wait for Bob.

Bob finally approached and apologized, saying, "We picked up a few things we needed, and I filled the small trunk, but had to put the fragile boxes in the back seat. Hope you have enough room back there." We looked at the overflowing back seat and just smiled. Good luck, I thought to myself. Paul got in first and sat against the side door, then I got in and moved sideways to find a small space to sit. We were jammed in like sardines, so close together, he put his arm around me, and we almost had to spoon together in a sitting position all the way home. Did Bob do this on purpose? Where did all these Matchmakers come from?

I smiled, realizing it was going to be so nice being close to Paul for hours. Yummy! Our closeness could not be avoided, so we made the best of it. Once the sun went down, he kissed me several times. Oh boy! We did not steam up the windows, but at the end of the trip, we both felt closer to each other, emotionally and physically. Our relationship had moved to the next level.

☙

Languages were Paul's forte, with fluency in Russian, Spanish, and German. He was intelligent, outgoing, and loved music, especially classical. He even enjoyed operas and ballet during his time in Moscow. We went to wonderful concerts in the area. Fitness was essential to him, and he ran marathons. Most importantly, he was fun to be around and, at least on the surface, enjoyed life.

We continued to date, and our closeness grew. He was different from other men I had dated. He was not intimidated by this assertive, intelligent, professional woman. That was huge! He slowly tore down my protective façade and showed me how to loosen up, laugh, and have fun. As a single Mom, I always felt I needed to be in charge and serious like my parents had been. But now, with my sons on their own at college, I was away from them for the first time. Slowly, I began to relax and just be me. One night, we were kissing when he stopped, pushed me back to arm's length, and told me he did not want us to make love until we got to really know each other, after maybe a month. Was this reverse psychology? Maybe. It was a difficult month, but in the end, he could truthfully say, "I did not have sex with that woman."

He had divorced his Mormon wife, and the church after fourteen years of marriage. With the responsibility of six children, he was paying lots of child support, so we always split expenses. He had remarried on the rebound to a woman who had two daughters. Now, he was separated from his second wife, whom he had married only three years earlier. On the other hand, I was free as a bird, but this bird also had an abysmal marriage history. Paul and I were both in our early forties and felt we had something together so special that it should not be compromised.

After a few months, I felt uncomfortable getting serious with a married man, even though he was separated. He had not started any divorce proceedings, so after about three months of dating, I said, "If you and I are serious about our relationship, I think you should take steps to get a divorce." He agreed, soon traveled to the States, spoke with his wife, retained an attorney, and began the divorce process.

❧

Our entire time in Germany felt like an enchanting dream. Heidelberg is a quaint old Roman town on the Neckar River in central Germany. I knew it well. My small apartment in the *Altstad*t, the old city, was located on the river with a magnificent view of the old Roman Heidelberg Castle. Paul and I often sat on the balcony in the evening with a glass of wine, gazing up at the magically lit castle, sharing our thoughts and dreams. After dark, we'd climb into my king-size and make love. Saturday morning, after sleeping late, we'd walk down to Le Journal for a decadent brunch. In the evening, we'd take Brutus for a walk along the river, and then to the *Hauptstrasse*, the main walking street, to enjoy a delicious souvlaki sandwich from a nearby Greek carry-out. I hardly ever cooked.

Heidelberg was an ideal departure point for our trips to Amsterdam during tulip season, Luxembourg, Brussels, and Paris in the springtime, and south to Switzerland for summer hiking around Lauterbrunnen. Our final trip before leaving Germany was to Greece, island-hopping by ferry to Santorini, Delphi, Ios, Mykonos, and Naxos on the Adriatic Sea. However, our time together was finite. I had a one-year contract, which would expire the following November. Paul was due to retire from the army in August. Our planets had converged for a splendid moment, but we realized it would take effort and commitment to stay in an orbit of our own making.

❧

Hiking in the Swiss Alps in the summer was our long weekend favorite getaway. Both of us were fit and loved hiking and exploring. We would take any weekend we could and drive down to the Interlaken area, stay in a rustic old chalet in the beautiful valley of Lauterbrunnen, with the three famous Swiss Alps, Eiger, Jungfrau, and Joch, reaching high above us into the heavens. Brutus often joined us. Switzerland was beautiful beyond words, with clear, cold lakes and streams of ice-cold meltwater rushing down majestic, snow-topped mountains to quaint villages nestled in the valleys. Lazy milk cows, with a bell around their neck, grazed along the hillsides. Rustic chalets sported vibrant flower boxes at each window. Wildflowers, glinting in the sun, painted the fields in bright colors of blue, pink, yellow, and white. Hiking trails were everywhere. We would hike until we dropped and then take a tram down to the chalet.

After a restful sleep, a hearty breakfast—strong coffee, a boiled egg, hard rolls with a variety of deli meats and cheeses, we would set out for the day to hike from the valley to the small alpine villages of Mürren or Wengen. It felt like stepping into *The Sound of Music*, to experience the extraordinary beauty of the Alps as fat, dairy cows meandered across the mountain pastures, indifferent to our presence. Other weekend activities included biking along the river to nearby castle ruins, or to the ancient, walled town of Ladenburg, which claims to be the first town in Germany on the bank of the Rhine River, settled nearly five thousand years ago. Everything was new and exciting and each weekend a new adventure. In the fresh air, and with exercise, fun, and great food in this beautiful, tranquil place, our love blossomed. Over many weeks, we shared everything: our lives, our families, our careers, our problems, our triumphs, and, especially, our hopes and dreams.

20

Early in our dating, I told Paul, in a serious but joking tone, "I am allergic to marriage!" Due to my divorce history, I felt cursed, like many who fear commitment after past heartbreaks. I'd fall in love, then, after vows were exchanged, I felt caged. Then I would slowly undermine the relationship, finding flaws and problems, and finally end it. After several months, I knew our relationship was becoming serious, so I mentioned my allergy to marriage again. Paul smiled, kissed me, then, in a serious yet mindful tone, said, "You know I love you, and if our relationship continues, I will definitely want to marry you, so you better get over it." I kissed him back, realizing I was behind a protective wall I had carefully built. After taking a long look inside myself, I knew he was the love of my life, and I could not let this special love fail because of my hangups. I decided to invest in psychological counseling to confront and understand my hidden fears and past traumas. This step was crucial for my healing journey, as I wanted to break free from the emotional barriers that kept me from trusting again. Paul was very supportive of my endeavor. We both knew this was important to our future. I found a qualified American clinical psychologist who had a practice in family counseling. Let's call him Dr. Phil. He was a tall, unassuming, almost compassionate man, a bit older than I. With his shaved head, he looked like Dr. Phil of the *Dr. Phil Show*. During my first visit, Dr. Phil described how the counseling would work. I told him my goal of resolving the issues concerning my first marriage, which had prevented me from becoming a happily married woman. He gave me a battery of personality tests, including the Minnesota Multiphasic Personality Inventory. I looked forward to the next session, finding the test results, and getting started. On the second visit, he reported candidly, "Your results were not completely valid or conclusive."

"That is not possible," I responded defensively. "I answered each question truthfully, without any agenda."

He suggested, "Perhaps you are unconsciously hiding a past trauma in your life."

I insisted, "No, I am being completely honest."

After a few moments, he finally said, "Okay, let's get started."

Opening Barbara's Pandora's box during each session—exploring my childhood and two marriages—was often painful, but very revealing. It was vital for me to understand what trauma had caused such an overwhelming unconscious aversion to marriage. The doctor asked me to describe specific periods of my early life. After I described my childhood and the resentment between my sister and me, he revealed that he thought I felt shut out of my family, that my sister was the center of attention, and I was almost treated like a stepchild. He was right. I looked back on my childhood as a happy time and held no resentment toward my parents, now deceased. Then he pointed out the favoritism and how I was marginalized. The bottom line was that it made me who I am now: a solitary woman, confident, assertive, dedicated, and compassionate, with many barriers in place to ensure no one ever marginalizes me again. He asked, "Did you escape your family situation by getting married?" He was right again. Circumstances had pushed me toward an early marriage, while I was very naive and unprepared for marriage. Then he asked about my high school years, dating, going steady, meeting

Neil, our quick romance, and marriage. I went on to describe our honeymoon resort in the Poconos with frequent partying and drinking. Having mentally prepared myself, I recalled the traumatic sexual event when Neil subjected me to "*something different*," anal sex. Then there was the Marquis de Sade episode.

I went on to explain that, after only eight months of marriage, we moved to Texas, a pregnant new wife alone. Neil became very controlling over all the money and my time with my few new friends. Then the emotional abuse began. He'd wake me up in the middle of the night, ranting and raving about how useless I was, that I should be glad he married me. I tried to minimize the reality of my life with a controlling, abusive husband. I explained, "He only hit me once. I had a roof over my head. It was not that bad." Or was It? Did I not feel the pain of being controlled and emotionally abused for years?

After I finished the story of my marriage, the affair, and the divorce, Dr. Jim took a few moments, then described, with genuine compassion, "It must have been devastating for you at such a young, naive age". But I denied being impacted long-term at all. My life went on. Finally, he described how, as a young adult, I would have reacted to this cruelty from my husband. He explained, the "*vulnerable inner child*" within you, who had put all her love and trust in Neil. After a few moments of silence, Dr. Phil said, "It's no wonder you cannot trust men!" That hit me like a ton of bricks! He described me as the battered wife. Even though I was not physically abused over a long period, I was verbally and emotionally abused throughout your entire marriage. I had been stripped of all confidence and self-esteem and believed in my heart that I was worth nothing. At last, I understood the hold he had on me and how the affair had freed me, but even when I was happy with my new freedom, I carried the trauma I had endured, like an albatross around my neck. Without knowing, I had unconsciously undermined all future relationships to stay safe. What a breakthrough!

The sessions continued every week for a year and helped me work through the trauma I had suffered as a young child, and especially as a young woman. When the therapy ended, I felt the dark clouds that had followed me all those years had finally dispersed. I was back in the sun, a mature and capable woman who could make wise choices, with a new slate, understanding the past, but no longer allowing it to control my future. I loved and trusted Paul completely. If I loved him enough and wanted a future with him, I needed to be willing to shed the old skin of early trauma and create a new, bright future, full of love, trust, and hope. Old habits are hard to break, but I knew I must do it if I ever wanted to be truly happy.

21

We were both caught up in the enchantment of being deeply in love while an uncharted future was just around the corner. I'd be returning to Virginia to find my next assignment. Paul would retire in August after twenty years of service, then would have to find work in the private sector, I hoped in the Northern Virginia area. We enjoyed every moment we had in Heidelberg, knowing the clock was ticking. By this time, Paul and I were deeply in love, planning a life together, including marriage.

Paul polished his very first résumé for the private sector and began contacting information technology companies in the Heidelberg area, but without success. His retirement ceremony that August was well attended. Overnight, he became an unemployed civilian with only tourist status in Germany. By the fall of 1990, with no promising leads in Germany, Paul realized he needed to return to the States to find a job. He was still paying child support for his six children. The pressure was high. My contract was up in just three months, and I would relocate back to Fairfax to find my next assignment.

☙

I contacted my best friend, Gloria, whom I had known for the past fifteen years. Gloria was now retired from TRW, divorced, and living in a large home in Vienna, Virginia. She had met Paul during a trip to Germany to visit us. She said she'd love to have Paul become her house guest for as long as he needed. Before I knew it, Paul and I hugged and kissed, and hugged some more, as I dropped him off at the Frankfurt Airport for a flight to Dulles Airport in Virginia.

❧

I remained in Heidelberg, pining for my love. The cost of phoning each other even once a week was prohibitive. The internet and email had not become a reality, and a smartphone was just a gleam in Steve Jobs' eye. Letters would take at least two to three weeks. How could we stay connected? The answer was using two mini-cassette recorders. Using a U.S. Express Mail envelope, we could mail mini tapes to each other for only ten dollars. Express mail was fast, usually two or three days. I bought a recorder and a package of mini-cassette tapes. I started recording conversations that we would typically have after work, during dinner, and even later. He did the same, and soon we were hearing each other's voices.

It was a lifesaver. I could hear Paul's voice and tell by his tone whether he was happy, excited, or frustrated. Listening to the tapes was like having him in the room with me, expressing how much he loved and missed me.

❧

Paul had extensive experience in IT communications, plus an up-to-date secret security clearance. After several interviews with numerous military contractors, he received an offer to serve as a communications consultant at Booz Allen for one year. The downside was that the job was in Panama City, Panama. He had been stationed with the army in Panama and enjoyed the tropical Latin environment. He accepted. I was excited for him and knew he would be very comfortable in the military environment, and now he is a well-paid contractor. It was not an ideal situation for us, but it provided him with a place to start, much-needed income, and a new experience as a civilian. He packed up his few things, hugged Gloria, and said, "*Hasta Luego.*"

❧

The Gulf War was heating up after Saddam Hussein ordered the invasion and annexation of Kuwait. The U.S. responded quickly with what became the Gulf War. The army unit I was working for was expected to deploy its tactical system to assist its military garrison in the region. Saudi Arabia raised its hand and welcomed U.S. forces to Riyadh, where some military units were already stationed. My bosses were trying to recruit experienced contractors to go to Saudi Arabia for a six-month TDY to support the operational system and provide training to the military. It was an excellent opportunity for me to support a wartime system in the field, but this time it was a real war. I was excited about the opportunity to support the system and extend my contract overseas. After all, the love of my life was now in Central America, an ocean away. However, my boss in the States said no women employees were permitted to go to Saudi Arabia on contract. I knew they could not discriminate against me and prohibit me from being selected, so I pushed the issue. Female soldiers in headscarves were already working in Saudi Arabia. The Saudi government demanded that women soldiers always wear a headscarf and be escorted by a male while in public. However, management determined it would be too risky to send a woman, and the special escort requirements would drain vital resources on the ground. They refused even to consider me. I was distraught but knew I could not fight it from afar.

❧

Upon returning to Virginia in the Fall of 1990, I focused my career within the intelligence community. I loved working with their professionals and had great respect for the CIA employees. They considered their job a patriotic one, not just an 8:00 to 4:30 workday. We had worked some long hours together. I received a well-earned promotion to Senior IT Systems Engineer, with a focus on computer systems development. I loved my work and was recognized by professionals within my company and the government. My dream of having a successful career had come true, and I had done it with only my high school diploma. Thank God for on-the-job training. I had become a confident, assertive professional known for my hard work, dedication, and especially my integrity and candor. The customer valued my directness. If I thought a design was poor, I'd suggest it could be improved, and work offline with engineers and developers to produce a better product. As a result, I was asked to manage a CIA system that was in trouble and behind schedule. I did, and at the end of my review, I told the customer the project was beyond saving. It didn't earn me any points with my TRW boss, but I did the right thing. I was finally acknowledged for my extensive experience and outstanding performance. The best part was that everyone on the project assumed I had a college degree. My government counterparts held mid-level management positions. I felt confident in my abilities to hold my own and challenged any engineering plan if it should be handled differently.

❧

Time passed, and Paul received another offer from a contractor in McLean, Virginia, only a few miles from my home in Fairfax. When his contract was up in August, he accepted the offer and flew back to Dulles Airport, where I was waiting with bells on. Finally, we would be back together, living in the real world.

Part Four

22

Life together as government contractors in Northern Virginia was very fulfilling. Our jobs were challenging and demanding, often requiring long hours and months without a break. Luckily, we were able to schedule a getaway for a vacation in Roatan, Honduras, an island surrounded by a breathtaking coral reef, with a shocking precipice that dropped to a depth of six thousand feet.

We had two days of relaxing, snorkeling in the shallow water, and eating lobster for dinner, and we realized we were in diving paradise. With a hundred-foot visibility, Roatan had the clearest, bluest waters I had ever seen. An abundance of brightly colored tropical fish swam peacefully against the deep blue underwater landscape. As we snorkeled, large, colorful parrot fish would sometimes come up close to check us out. Beautiful black and yellow striped angel fish always swam in pairs, mated for life. An unusual-looking spotted beige puffer fish would blow up like a balloon with little spines all over its body when threatened. Large, ugly grouper hung out at a distance in deeper water. White and pink-tipped anemones, with tentacles swaying in the current, sought protection in the coral. Enormous brain corals and a variety of other luxuriant corals formed stunning underwater gardens.

❧

After watching all the divers walking up and down the dirt road, Paul suggested we could complete a scuba diving course while we were here. With a glance at our schedule, we decided we could complete the five-day open-water basic diving course if we used our remaining vacation time. Paul was excited, but I was apprehensive. Diving is physically and psychologically challenging. At depths of over thirty feet, scuba equipment is needed to breathe. You must have an experienced buddy diver whom you trust with your life to help you if something goes wrong. In comparison, if your car breaks down, you can get out and walk or call a tow truck. You are not in danger of drowning. Not so if something about your air supply suddenly fails at depth.

I was reminded of a life-threatening experience when I almost drowned off the coast of North Carolina years earlier. The memory is still vividly terrifying. I had taken the diving course while working at Fort Bragg. I had completed my first qualification dive in a cold quarry and was scheduled for my final open water dive, a shipwreck dive five miles off the coast of Wilmington, North Carolina. Due to a sinus infection, I missed the open-water dive with my class and the experienced dive instructor. Once I recovered, I was assigned to an open-water qualification dive boat with about twenty young, macho Army soldiers, barely twenty years old, and a dive instructor I had never seen. Not a comforting thought, but I was willing to try. It was a cloudy, windy day as I drove over an hour from Fort Bragg to the Wilmington departure point along the coast and finally arrived at the dock. The dive instructor gathered us together and warned us that there were five-foot swells on the surface, but we could still dive.

Off we went, traveling on a small open boat five miles off the coast in five-foot swells. I was hanging on to the side of the boat for dear life. Finally, the captain anchored on the wreck. I could not see land. The instructor shouted the dive briefing to us as we readied our dive gear. "The visibility underwater is very poor due to the high waves, so you need to hold on to the anchor line as you descend. Go slowly and equalize. You will reach the wreck at a depth of seventy feet. Another dive master will be at the wreck to guide you through the steel structure." I'm thinking, "So, we are not going to just swim around it? Shit!"

He emphasized, "Hold on to each doorway as you enter, because the swells are so powerful they could slam you against the doorway or across the deck." I pondered, "Do I really want to do this?"

❧

With great enthusiasm, the young soldiers jumped into the ocean and went down, one by one, holding onto the anchor line. Then it was my turn. I entered the water and swam around to the front anchor line. The boat was pitching violently in the five-foot swells, with the bow coming crashing down as the waves passed. The instructor yelled to me, "Stay away from the front of the boat so it does not hit you in the head." I grabbed the anchor line for dear life and saw less than one foot of visibility before the anchor line disappeared into a murky abyss. Here I was five miles offshore, next to a small boat, in five-foot swells, with an instructor I did not know, telling me to deflate my buoyancy-control vest, BC, a life jacket, and go down to the wreck surrounded by treacherous currents. By this time, I realized "I don't want to do this." I wanted out, as I yelled to him, "No!" very loudly, but with the boat crashing up and down against the anchor line and the wind, he did not hear me. I kept yelling, "NO!" Next thing I knew, without saying anything, he grabbed my BC to deflate my vest himself. Reality hit, and I felt like I was going to drown, right there. So, I panicked and kicked him with all my strength in his crotch. Maybe he would listen now. After my assault on his groin, he got the idea, and he shouted, "Get back in the boat!"

At this point, I was exhausted. I was hyperventilating from the terror I had experienced. Slowly, in the huge waves, I managed to swim around the bow to the stern and reach the boat ladder. The captain pulled me into the boat. When I sat down, I realized my hands were partially paralyzed. If that was not enough, I had to sit in the pitching boat for thirty minutes, crashing up and crashing down, until the remaining divers surfaced. Heading back to shore took an hour, followed by my exhausting hour-long drive home. I was wiped out, physically and emotionally, but glad to be still alive. That close call made me realize the importance of safety, perseverance, and trusting my instincts-lessons I carry into all areas of my life, including my current diving adventures and personal growth journey.

❧

The clear, warm waters of Roatan were nothing like my near-death experience in the choppy Atlantic. I was eager to learn how to dive with Paul, so I decided to give it another try. We took classes in the morning, watched countless videos, and downed a quick lunch. In the afternoon, we had practice time in the shallows. Later, we studied the dive books into the night after an exquisite fresh fish dinner. We passed all the chapter exams and our quarter-mile surface swim. It was time for our qualification dive. This test included essential emergency procedures you may need if something goes wrong underwater. I was still very nervous. Eight of us from our class sat in full dive gear on the gunwale of the Boston Whaler, at a depth of only forty feet. We could see the bottom clearly. Holding our masks firmly in place with our left hand, we each performed a backward somersault out of the boat into the ocean, quickly surfacing by the boat.

It was a beautiful sunny day. I could see the sandy bottom clearly. We had a qualified, young German woman, a dive instructor. She instructed everyone to swim down to the bottom and form a circle on their knees in the sand next to their buddy. Everyone went down except me. Still holding onto the boat, I suddenly went into complete panic and told her, "I can't do it!" The night before, I had explained my fear and my experience of almost drowning.

Patiently, she replied, "Please go ahead and try. Just take it slow, step by step. You have performed so well in class and the water. You know how to do this, and I'm sure you will be fine. But, if at any time you want to surface, signal me, and you can return to the surface and discontinue the test." Those were the magic words. She gave me confidence in myself. It calmed me to know that I had her permission and acceptance if I panicked. I descended, kneeled next to Paul, my trusted buddy, and completed each test with renewed confidence. I was in control. The tests were easy. We had practiced them all many times, and the test was over before I knew it. We both became certified Open water basic divers. Wow! I could not believe I had done it. Our vacation was over, and the next day we boarded a plane back to Virginia. I wished we could have stayed for a few more days to go on some real dives together on the beautiful reef.

It took me some time to become a confident diver, but Paul was very patient. After several dives, including a scary night dive when my night light quit, I became more confident in my ability to react appropriately, always factoring in the currents, visibility, depth, and, most importantly, our air consumption. We eventually returned to Roatán and became certified advanced open-water divers. As divers, we now share a mutual passion. Over the years, we continued to plan diving vacations to the Roatan Islands, Cayman Islands, Hawaii, Bermuda, and then often to the Red Sea in Jordan, and finally a week in the Maldives, in the middle of the Indian Ocean.

23

In 1989, Paul came home one night to tell me he had been offered a TDY assignment to Heidelberg, Germany, as a project manager for six months. He was excited about the chance to return to Germany as a well-paid contractor. It was an opportunity for us to return to beautiful Heidelberg, where we met and fell in love. My current assignment was not challenging to say the least, so I decided to join him. I requested leave without pay. I would remain an active employee, with the understanding that, upon my return, the company could not guarantee me an open position.

We were excited to have another adventure. Paul departed first and found a cute apartment above an Italian café in the old Roman-walled town of Ladenburg, just downriver from Heidelberg. We had shipped some furniture, our SUV, Eiger, our new German shepherd, and all the parrots we had accumulated, when we thought we would never be going overseas again.

I arrived in November to wet, frigid weather of snow and sleet. Paul worked all day, and I was a stay-at-home *hausfrau*. What was I thinking? I fixed up the apartment and then was totally bored. My only activities were walking Eiger through the old village or cooking dinner. Paul made several friends at work, while I was stuck at home. We did socialize, but I was still a duck out of water. I expressed my boredom and frustration to Paul, and after some thought, he suggested that I plan our Christmas vacation. The government civilians were all taking leave over Christmas, so we could get away.

I jumped at the opportunity to do something different. We were now relying solely on Paul's income, so I had to plan carefully. I wanted to go somewhere new, where the weather was warm. Before long, I found the Last-Minute Tour Agency advertising a ten-day trip to a beach resort in Mombasa, Kenya, with all meals and round-trip airfare for only five hundred dollars each. What a deal! It would get us to Kenya, but that was not our real destination. Our idea of fun was renting a car and going on safari to the national game parks. I was so excited. Both of us had always wanted to see Africa, but never had the opportunity. It was our chance to explore Kenya for ten days. I was psyched!

I checked safari package tours online and realized they were too expensive. We always preferred to use our own transportation, rather than be bused like cattle from site to site. Then I found an old English-language *Lonely Planet Guide to Kenya* at a used bookstore in town. Using that and the internet, I planned a general driving route from our resort in Mombasa to the nearest Tsavo East National Park, then on to the more popular Tsavo West National Park. If time allowed, we'd drive south to Amboseli National Park, near Mt. Kilimanjaro, then to Nairobi for a couple of days, and finally return to Mombasa for our return flight to Germany. We could adjust our plan, based on the reality on the ground, and stay at one park longer if we wanted. It was impossible to determine how long it would take to drive from one place to another, and the national park's dirt roads would be even sketchier, so we had to be flexible.

We booked our ten-day trip to Kenya. My research indicated that a four-wheel drive vehicle, costing about sixty dollars a day, was not required if we stayed on major roads in the game parks. An economical sedan with necessary air conditioning would be sufficient. After I explained the route to Paul, he called Hertz, using his best German to rent a car in Mombasa, which would be delivered to the resort the morning after we arrived. It was all uncharted territory, and we were eager to explore it. I could not wait to see the elephants.

❧

After a long, full, overnight charter flight from Basel, Germany, with very little sleep, we landed at the Mombasa Airport in the early afternoon. Oppressive heat and humidity assaulted our senses as we emerged from the plane. After passing through passport control, our tour guide led us to the transport vehicle, which drove us through the crowded city of Mombasa and along the coast to the resort.

Being in Kenya rallied our spirits. Tall concrete security walls surrounded all the luxury resorts along the coastal road, with ornate wrought-iron gates guarded by uniformed security guards. Our resort was a private, tropical paradise with lush gardens, a large swimming pool, and beach access on the Indian Ocean. Vibrant splashes of red, orange, yellow, and green bougainvillea welcomed us to this new tropical environment. The hotel staff, in crisply ironed uniforms, greeted us with *Jambo*, the Swahili hello. After a welcome fruit drink, we were briefed by the hotel staff in German, then in English, about the hotel's amenities and meals. After standing in a long line to check in, our luggage was taken to our small but comfortable ground-floor room. There was no need to unpack because we were leaving early the next morning on safari. Kenyans use the term safari to mean a journey, trip, or vacation. *Nzuri safari* means good journey.

We changed into our bathing suits and set out to explore the pool and beach area, hoping to catch a quick nap in a shaded lounge chair. The resort was full of older German couples, many in friendly groups, lounging by the pool and drinking lots of beer and fruity cocktails. I felt a bit out of place. Each woman wore a colorful bikini while their husband sported tiny thongs. They were having fun working on their suntans without a care about displaying their extended belly or thigh fat. I wondered how they could be so casual with their imperfect bodies. Americans are so hung up on their body image. Most cover up with a large wrap to hide any bulge or overhanging flab. Europeans, on the other hand, were completely at ease with their bodies, regardless of shape or size. I applauded them silently, but sometimes could not watch as they stretched their ample bodies on lounge chairs to pay tribute to the sun god. I did have to admit a few younger bathers were tan and lovely to watch. But I digress.

❧

Around 6 p.m., a loud bell rang to announce the dinner buffet. Both of us had traveled enough to know not to eat fresh salad, drink the water, or even use ice in drinks. Soup and cooked food were usually safe. The buffet included lots of luscious fruit salads, various hot and cold casseroles, and a variety of what I call filler foods, rice, potatoes, and a variety of breads. As the sun slowly set, the music and partying began. We took that as our cue to retreat to our room, but first, Paul used the office phone to confirm the arrival of our Hertz rental car at 7 a.m. the next morning. We were so excited to be going on an adventure in the African bush.

After a leisurely breakfast, Paul met the Hertz representative in front of the resort and signed the rental agreement for a used, four-door sedan. He chatted with the Hertz guy about our visit to Tsavo East Game Park. Our safari luggage included hiking clothes, good hiking boots, socks, a small tent, a box of granola bars, and two bottles of water. Other essentials included money belts, sun block, bug spray, backpacks, and, of course, cameras. I had forgotten hats.

With full stomachs, we started through Mombasa during rush hour, driving south toward Voi. One of the first things we needed was to buy more bottled water and a detailed road map at a petrol station. It was fascinating to watch the many locals waiting in long lines for buses along the road. Women were dressed in colorful *kanga*, a meter of brightly colored batik cotton fabric wrapped around their waist, then another piece for the upper body. A few locals were dressed in second-hand Western clothes. They were all spotless and looked sharp. Men were showered, shaved, and outfitted in perfectly ironed shirts and trousers with firm creases. Their brightly polished shoes were already full of road dust. I was intrigued by this new Kenyan culture. They were joyful and light-hearted, talking and laughing as they waited for transport in the hot sun. It almost seemed like a reunion of these neighbors and friends enjoying each other's company. What a stark difference from Americans riding on a metro, bus, or elevator, each looking down, keeping to himself, without any expression or even a slight smile. I wondered what we Americans were missing. How could this poor, humble culture be so happy and carefree? What were we missing?

Obviously, we were the minority, the only whites in a sea of blacks, so we assumed a low profile as we drove along, or at least tried. Once we were out of the stop-and-go traffic, the roads quickly deteriorated with potholes that could consume a tire or even a motorcycle. Paul was a very skilled driver, adept at avoiding potholes, bicycles, and people suddenly darting across the street. After a couple of hours driving south, we arrived in the small town of Voi. We were getting hungry and decided to stop for an early lunch of fried chicken and a soda, something safe to eat. After a filling meal, we made a stop at the water closet, bathroom. It was a single stall with no door. On the floor in front of me were two large footprints embossed into the concrete, with a sizable hole in the middle to eliminate waste. There was no seat, so I tried my best to squat and balance, while demurely peeing into the hole. Since women cannot effectively shake their genitals like men, I made a mental note to carry ample tissues with me. Before continuing, we stopped at a petrol station, filled up the tank, and checked the water and oil. There were no maps for sale. They could not understand why we needed one.

By 11 a.m., it was getting very hot, so we rolled up the windows and turned on the air conditioner. We continued our journey northwest, through a rural town. Homes were poorly constructed shacks with rusted tin roofs, wet clothes hung on a line, and very emaciated dogs lying in whatever shade they could find. A few young barefoot children played in the dirt nearby. Scrawny chickens grazed in the yard, and a goat was tied to a nearby tree with no water. We were headed toward the Tsavo East southern Voi Gate entrance on this small, unnamed dirt road. We had no way of knowing at the time, but tourists rarely use the Voi Gate. The Tsavo West National Park, next to Nairobi, the capital of Kenya, is a more popular destination. Live and learn!

Suddenly, steam came rolling out of the hood. "Oh, shit, what now?" I thought. The radiator had overheated in the ninety-degree heat! Perhaps it was too optimistic to run the air conditioner on high. Paul stopped, raised the hood. The road had become more desolate with no other cars in sight and no gas stations for miles. A few curious children surrounded our vehicle as we waited for the radiator to cool down. They were smiling and staring at these silly *Mzungus,* Caucasians. Many years ago, I remember having a similar situation. My friend, Gloria, and I were on a summer trip when her car overheated. She confidently explained, "Just open all the windows and put the heater on high. That will cool the engine. Then, we can get the car fixed at our destination." I explained my remedy to Paul. He was skeptical but willing to try anything. With all the windows open, we started the engine with the heater turned on full blast. The radiator temperature quickly dropped back to normal. We were able to buy an extra gallon of water from a nearby shack to refill the radiator. Then we jumped back into the hot car, relieved that we had overcome our first obstacle.

❧

I planned for us to reach the Tsavo East gate by 1 or 2 p.m., then drive north to the popular *Kiliguni Lodge* in Tsavo West, which looked luxurious online. I hoped we could get a room for one hundred fifty dollars a night, but I did not make a reservation for the first night, because I was not sure if we would arrive in time. I read that there were a few camping areas in the park, so I packed our trusty tent. We were flexible and adventurous. The southern Tsavo East gate turned out to be a truly arid, desolate area, with no hotels, restaurants, or even a souvenir shop. We arrived after 3:30 p.m., two hours later than planned. The only park ranger at the gate was a robust Kenyan woman in her thirties in an olive-green uniform, a bit too small for her ample body. She spoke English well, with the distinct British accent adopted by locals during Kenya's British colonial period. She was very friendly and chatted with us as we paid for a three-day pass in the park. I asked her if our sedan would be sufficient in the park. She replied, "As long as you stay on the main dirt roads, you will be fine. It is not the rainy season, so the roads are dry." She thought we could get to *Kiliguni Lodge* in about two to three hours, have a refreshing shower, and enjoy a delicious dinner. I was looking forward to the luxury of Egyptian cotton bed linens, perhaps with a 700-thread-count. She wished us a *nzuri safari, good travels* as we drove through the gates into the game park.

Many years ago, I became intrigued by elephants after reading *Ralph Helfer's The True Story of the Greatest Elephant that Ever Lived*. I was fascinated by their intelligence, their close, caring family bonds, and human-like emotions of love, compassion, and the gentle nurturing of their young, not only by the mother but also by other female aunties in their group. It is well documented that elephants shed tears and have a ritual of burying their dead by covering them with branches. These gentle giants are wise and humble, yet humans often kill them for their ivory tusks. Although elephants are now protected under CITES, Convention on International Trade in Endangered Species) as an endangered species, poaching continues. CITES is an agreement between governments to ensure that international trade in wild animals and plants does not threaten their survival. My elephant passion continued, and I read as many non-fiction books as I could find, including *Among the Elephants* by Ian Douglas Hamilton, *Silent Thunder* by Katy Payne, and *Coming of Age with Elephants* by Dr. Joyce Poole, each about African elephants. This trip was the culmination of my dream to finally see them living free.

❧

The afternoon sky was clear as we drove into the park. Paul slowed down to ten kilometers per hour along the winding, narrow dirt road to make sure we would not miss anything. The heater was still on full blast to cool the engine. It was working well, but Paul, the driver, could not escape the heat. I tried to catch a slight breeze by perching myself with my butt on the passenger windowsill and my head out the window. At last, there was a slight breeze in my hair. Smiling to myself, I am getting the real feel of the African bush. The roadsides were wooded, with thick clusters of thin trees surrounded by tall, dry acacia thorn bushes. As we continued north, the landscape grew more barren, dry, and dusty, with only a few dwarf acacias scattered across the vista. Our eyes searched for wild animals, but it seemed as if we were the only animals in the park. Wild animals obviously avoided the gate. As we came around a corner, we saw two magnificent giraffes feeding on the thin leaves of the tall acacia trees. We stopped to watch while they continued eating without a care. These animals were used to safari vehicles in the park. Further on, we passed a couple of watering holes the size of small swimming pools. The edges were covered in dried mud, with many animal footprints as evidence of their visits. Only a bit of mud was left in the center, and there was no visible water for animals to drink.

The park was an arid, desolate place where wild animals roamed freely. Tsavo East was over 13,747 square kilometers, almost the size of Connecticut. The vast area was unfenced, and the animals usually stayed within the safe perimeters, rarely venturing into nearby villages unless in search of food or water. A couple of times, we glimpsed what we later learned were dik-diks, miniature antelopes the size of raccoons. When startled by our car, they'd hop like rabbits to a nearby hiding place.

Around 5 p.m., the air cooled as we drove out of the dense bush to slightly higher ground, leaving the woods behind. We were now on a breathtaking, vast, arid plain. I had seen similar views on television documentaries of the African bush. The vast landscape was devoid of rocks and trees, except for a few stunted, dry acacia bushes, and other short green bushes were sparsely dotted across it. The rust-colored red dirt was a stark contrast to the colorless dry vista. Not a blade of grass was in sight. As the car crested a small hill, it died in the middle of the road. We looked at each other, thinking, "What now?" We had not encountered any vehicles since our radiator overheated.

I, on the other hand, became mesmerized by the jaw-dropping vista around us! About three to four kilometers down a gently sloping hill, a long tree line snaked across the lower savannah. The map told me it was the Tsavo River. Now we understood approximately where we were within the park. Still, there was not a single animal or bird in sight. There was no place for them to hide and no place for us to hide either! Voi gate had a large sign to warn visitors, "All visitors are prohibited from exiting their vehicle inside the park." We felt confident that no wild animals were near, so we got out of the car, and Paul tinkered with the engine.

I stood there inhaling this magnificent raw beauty. To the southwest, I could see the snow-capped Mt. Kilimanjaro, rising majestically out of the plain. "Kili," as it is called, is a dormant volcano along the northeast border of Tanzania, with an elevation of 5,862 meters. In my euphoria, I reflected, "I'm finally here in Africa. It is a dream come true." The flat tire seemed like an unavoidable time delay. We would soon be on our way and could perhaps still arrive at Kiliguni in time for dinner and a blissful night's sleep. I wandered a few meters from the car to the top of the small hill, immersed in the wild bush. We encouraged each other, saying that surely a vehicle would come by soon that could give us some help. Paul continued in vain to get the engine to start. Fearing that we needed a plan B, I dragged the tent up the hill just a bit, saying, "It's getting dark, and we may have to camp out for the night, unless you want to sleep in the car." There was no answer from Paul. In no time at all, I had the tent in place, only twenty meters from the car. We needed to be close enough to hear any vehicle approaching. I put the backpacks, granola bars, snacks, a couple of liters of water, and sunblock in the tent. What else did we need? A flashlight would have been nice, but I had not thought to pack one. As dusk fell, we climbed into the tent and sat at the entrance looking across the plains. We munched on granola and discussed our situation.

❧

No one knew where we were on our vacation. We had not provided Paul's office or any family members with our itinerary. We were winging it, as we usually did on vacations in other parts of the world. We never thought of contingencies, but of course, we had communications. We also deliberately did not inform the front desk at the Mombasa Beach Resort that we were leaving on a safari because we wanted to keep our room until we returned for our flight back. Bottom line, no one would miss us for nine days when the hotel in Mombasa realized we had not checked out of the resort. Even then, no one would have a clue where we had gone. On the bright side, we were intelligent, strong, capable adventurers. Neither of us discussed the apparent danger or what might happen if we encountered aggressive animals like lions. Hopefully, there will be a car, sooner rather than later. Darkness fell over our little tent, and a vast, magical, full moon appeared, rising slowly into the night sky. Soon, thick, dark clouds rolled in, obscuring the moon, turning the bush into total darkness. A powerful wind began slapping the thin nylon sides of the tent against the aluminum frame. It was futile to get any sleep with such a racket. We tossed and turned, trying to get comfortable on the hard ground. After about an hour, we heard the distinct sound of a group of wild animals approaching our tent. They meandered, grazing, toward us. I tried to visualize these creatures rooting at the base of bushes, foraging for dry roots since there was no grass. Listening closely, I estimated there were at least twenty good-sized animals among us, although there could have been more in the distance.

The good news was that carnivores usually don't eat roots, so we were imagining antelopes, wild boars, hippos, giraffes, wildebeests, or maybe elephants. Our tent was zipped up tight, and I could not see anything. We silently listened to the subtle breathing and occasional grunts and farts as they came close without ever touching the tent. Our little tent was now surrounded by gentle wild animals, ignoring our bright-blue nylon tent in the middle of the bush. Then I became very nervous. If something startled them, perhaps an involuntary sneeze, they could suddenly stampede. I did not want to get trampled inside the small, zipped-up tent. I whispered my fear to Paul, and he slowly unzipped the entrance. We peered outside, seeing total blackness, not even a silhouette of the animals. Our sudden unzipping of the door did not startle the herd, as they continued grazing slowly up the hill and beyond.

Later that night, there was still no way to sleep with the wind constantly flapping the sides of the tent. We dozed, on and off, through the night. I woke up around six a.m. Paul was already dressed, outside, drinking water, looking at the Kenya guidebook.

It was a beautiful, cool, clear morning, with a temperature around sixty-five degrees. The fierce wind had subsided. The ground around the tent was dry and dusty. There were no visible tracks or spoor in the loose dirt left by our mysterious visitors. It was also clear that no vehicle had passed during the night. We were stranded. I scanned the savannah that gently sloped down to the Tsavo River. Not a single animal in sight. Paul had been studying the guidebook and showed me approximately where we were relative to the nearest civilization. The *Kitoni Lodge*, a small lodge north of the river, was about fifteen kilometers from our current location. Taking a deep breath, he said, "It is six a.m. now. If we leave soon while it's cool, we can be at the lodge by about 10 or 11 a.m., just in time for coffee and a nice breakfast." It sounded very tempting and might be a reasonable alternative.

However, I explained the risk: "The strict park regulation clearly states no one was to ever leave their car, let alone hike on foot for several kilometers in a wild game park." Paul added, "We have not seen any vehicle since we entered the park. It is obvious that the Southern Gate was seldom used. We have no cell phone coverage and are alone, except for all the wild animals that we cannot see, probably because they are sleeping late, taking advantage of the cool breeze." However, as the conservative one, I suggested, "We should not go for a five-hour hike in the wild game park, but should stay by the car, sheltered from the heat and wild animals, until we are rescued." Paul replied, "If we did that, we could use all our water sitting in the hot car and still be in the same place the next morning, dehydrated, without water, and no closer to civilization." He was right! How hard could it be to walk to the lodge? Maybe there were no animals in our area. Besides, we were both in good physical condition, went to the gym regularly, and hiked most weekends in Virginia. In addition, we were animal lovers and kindred spirits to the outdoors. Such bullshit! We were still stranded. This Kenyan bush environment was new to us. Before commencing our "*walk in the park*", we did a brief search around the tent and could not even find a stick or a medium-sized rock to defend ourselves against wild animals. Scrawny acacia bushes were less than waist high. There were no trees to climb to avoid an attack. We were dressed in t-shirts, shorts, and hiking boots. Each of us had a backpack that we could throw at an attacking animal. That would surely do it!

Our philosophy had always been, if you leave animals alone, they will leave you alone. That philosophy might be true for domestic dogs and cats, when you cross the road to avoid a large pit bull, but we were now in the home of hungry carnivores, such as lions, jaguars, leopards, hyenas, and cheetahs. They usually don't hunt during the day but wait until the late afternoon and early evening when it is cooler. I knew that coming upon any wild animal with a baby is extremely dangerous, because the mother will charge aggressively to protect her young. We also read that a buffalo will sometimes stalk you through the bush before attacking. Hippos look passive, swimming in the water, but are very aggressive when grazing on land and often attack humans. Enough of that. There was no way to compromise. We either stayed with the car or walked 15 kilometers through the wildlife park. Being up for an adventure and knowing that tourists never got to walk in a game park, I said I was "*fair game*", so to speak. We both were!

❧

We never discussed what to do if wild animals approached us aggressively. There was no place to hide, no tree to climb, and no rocks to throw. Our asses were literally swinging in the breeze, so I guess we figured, why talk about it? Our plan included ignoring all potential danger and taking a lovely walk in the park. Paul left a note on the car's windshield with directions for where we were headed on foot. We packed munchies and three eight-ounce plastic bottles of water, headed down the hill, leaving our locked car in the dust, and eagerly began our walking safari. We were both in excellent spirits, albeit naïve. A clear sky and a soft breeze cooled us. No sign of any animals gave us false confidence that we'd be just fine. The small dirt road wandered back and forth down the gentle slope to the Tsavo River valley. Confident and energized, I looked forward to this unique experience. I hoped we'd get to see some wild animals taking a drink in the river in the early morning. What an adventure! We had not gotten much sleep, but were invigorated and optimistic just to be experiencing this new, unexpected challenge. As we walked, back and forth, back and forth, slowly down the hill, I realized we were doubling our distance. We could both see clearly to the bottom of the hill and the river, I suggested, "Let's go 'off-road 'straight down the gentle hill." Paul agreed, and we took a shortcut off-road.

❧

What a different experience it was walking off-road. Now I knew we were in the wild. It was so cool! All kinds of scat, poop, from the little teardrop pellets of giraffes to cow patties of buffalo. Then, to a bunch of huge turds of half-eaten grass in a pile, the circumference of a large coffee mug—probably elephant. I also noticed the parched bones of some small animal scattered on the ground. The ultimate prize was finding many black-and-white porcupine quills of various sizes that told the story of survival of the fittest. I put a few in my backpack and trudged on. I was so glad we had brought heavy socks and our trusted hiking boots. Our heads were exposed, but at least our feet were comfortable and protected. The sun was slowly rising in the east and would soon be beating down on us. We brought sunblock, so there was no chance of sunburn, but heat exhaustion might deter us.

It was still early when we reached the Tsavo River. Not one animal in sight. I knew animals came to the river early in the morning to drink, but we saw nothing. Perhaps we were too late. A tall dirt berm ran along the entire edge of the bank, making it impossible for me to see down into the water. Paul stayed behind, but my curiosity got the best of me. I wanted to see if there were any animals by the river, and this was my chance. It was probably crazy, but I had no fear. When I reached the top of the berm, I looked down a sharp twenty-foot drop into the muddiest water I have ever seen. All at once, at least thirty huge hippos with cute pink ears turned their heads up and stared at me. Luckily, they were submerged up to their eyes. Even the baby hippos turned their little heads to say hi. They were having a cool time hanging out in the muddy, poopy river.

This river was about forty feet wide and deep enough for them to submerge. From my standpoint, I felt safe for now, but after a few seconds, better judgment prevailed, and I decided it was prudent not to upset the mama hippos protecting their babies, so I quickly retreated, walking slowly backward to the road where Paul was waiting impatiently. I described the encounter to Paul, adding," I should have taken my camera." He just shook his head and muttered impatiently, "Let's go."

❧

The map indicated a bridge across the river, so we continued parallel to the river until we encountered a sturdy rock-and-concrete road marker directing us to turn north onto the *Kitani Lodge* road. I climbed onto it, and Paul took my photo. We were having a cool adventure. Our spirits were high. We continued across a well-built concrete one-lane bridge over the river and noticed a few lazy alligators in the water below. On the north side of the river, we were now on flat ground. This flat bush was much the same as before, with small dry acacia bushes scattered about. If I ever had thoughts of refilling our water bottles from the river, I knew now that it would mean instant dysentery and total weakness. But, not to worry, we still had enough water to get to the lodge. It was essential for us to keep hydrated as the heat of the day approached.

About 9 a.m., the sun started beating down on us, without the slightest breeze. We trudged on. I spotted a solitary group of thin trees, no more than twenty feet tall, stripped of all their bark. "What animal had done that?" I wondered. It had to be an animal six to ten feet tall. Later, we learned that elephants used the trees to sharpen their tusks.

After another two hours, I was beginning to overheat. We should be close to the lodge, so I kept hydrated and pushed on until we finally saw the *Kitani Lodge* sign. What a welcome sight! We had made it! It was almost 11 a.m., and we were hot and tired. Following the signs, we soon found ourselves in a cool oasis with beautiful, huge, mature trees over thirty feet tall with lush green branches offering ample shade. Small cabins were located here and there under the trees. A huge water tank stood a short distance behind the cabins. Something was wrong. It was like the *Twilight Zone*, being at a lodge that had been abandoned, the locked structures in various kinds of disrepair. The water tank was completely empty! There was no front desk, no festive Kenyan workers to welcome us with coffee and breakfast, no hammocks, and, especially, no people. The most terrifying realization was that there was no water. The temperature was now in the high nineties. Thoughts of breakfast vanished, replaced by the reality of our dangerous situation. We were tired, sweaty, hungry, and thirsty humans stranded in the wild game park in the heat of the day, with no more water. What now?

24

After rationing our water during the morning walk, we reached our destination with nothing left. It was high noon, we were overheated, exhausted, with no water and no possibilities or ideas. "Shit! Now what?" I thought. Disappointed was not the right word for our scary situation. A frustrated Paul threw his empty water bottle as far as he could and cursed under his breath. I plodded over to pick it up. Devastated, I realized we were now in an extremely dangerous situation. After a few moments of rest, Paul soberly checked the tourist guide again. The nearest lodge to *Kitani* was the *Kiliguni Lodge*, an additional eighteen kilometers uphill. A closer destination on the map was *Mzima Springs*, maybe twelve kilometers directly to the East, over a significant ancient black lava flow, but that could be abandoned too. I no longer had any confidence in the seven-year-old *Travel Guide to Kenya*, but I knew *Kiliguni*, a thriving four-star safari lodge, was open because I had checked their website for their Christmas prices before departing.

We rested on a large log for a long time to cool down. The shade of the huge trees was welcoming. But, even in the shade, the heat was oppressive and would be getting hotter as the afternoon progressed. I didn't want to continue walking all afternoon in this heat. Still exhausted, I suggested we stay here in the shade of the trees and rest until late afternoon. Once it cooled off, we'd have the energy to walk the remaining eighteen kilometers uphill to *Kiliguni* without water. Paul laughed and exclaimed, "That is a great idea, except for the fact that the evening is when the carnivores go hunting." What if we sang as we went along the road in the dark?" I suggested. Paul didn't bother to answer. Once again, I realized my plan was dangerously flawed. Although we were extremely hot and tired, our best plan was to continue to the lodge during the day. I approached Paul, gave him a sweaty hug, and then handed him his empty bottle, suggesting, "You might need this to capture your urine to drink." The truth was, we never needed the empty bottles, because we never urinated again. We had sweated too much.

After a demoralizing respite, off we went, walking along a flat dirt road that seemed to lead nowhere. The unbearable heat of the sun scorched our bodies and souls. After another hour, I felt myself getting more overheated and recognized symptoms of a heat stroke—rapid heart rate, and lack of sweat. I had to rest. Seeking refuge under a scrawny three-foot acacia with absolutely no shade value, I lay down in the dry red dirt, with my feet resting on the trunk above my head.

Paul said he felt okay and did not want to rest, so he took off climbing over nearby hills of solid black lava rock in search of any civilization. It did not occur to us that separating would make each of us more vulnerable to an attack. What if Paul never returned? What would I do? What if he did return to find a bloody trail of me being dragged into the bush? It is better not to entertain that possibility.

There I was, lying under a small acacia in the middle of nowhere. I remember that time vividly. I was totally in the moment, concerned about retaining my strength and needing to cool down. Still, there was not even a glimpse of any wild animal, although I had an eerie feeling that I was not alone. I could imagine a few female lions lying lazily under a cluster of thick acacia bushes, dozing off as they watched. "Look at those stupid humans walking in the heat of the day," they mused, yawning, then they rolled over in peaceful slumber, waiting until late afternoon hunt.

Except for the obvious difference in landscape and weather, we could have been hiking in Shenandoah Park in Virginia. Since there were no dangerous carnivores, it was easier to ignore the overwhelming danger. Why waste energy being fearful? We were alone in the middle of the savannah, so quiet and majestic. And hot as hell.

I was still optimistic! We were strong and we were together, while, in the back of my mind, I was too aware of our vulnerability. After about thirty minutes lying down and dozing, I was refreshed.

Finally, I saw Paul from a distance, walking very slowly, obviously tired, with sweat staining his shirt. He had no news. We had been without water for over three hours. There was not much to say to each other at this point. We continued walking in the unrelenting sun and oppressive heat. The landscape was still flat, but the scrub acacia thorn bushes now became dense clumps about three to four feet tall. This made it hard to see any distance. What else could go wrong?

What would we do if lions emerged, coming directly towards us? Should we stand without making eye contact? Raise our arms above our heads and scream while slowly walking backward? We never discussed a strategy. I never thought it was strange until the ordeal was over.

After about another hour, I felt heat stroke emerging again, so I lay down under the nearest bush to rest. The air was cooling down a bit as the sun started its journey to the west. Relaxing and dozing off, I slept for a time in the stifling heat. Paul did another walkabout, searching in vain for human life or clean water.

A little after 3:30 p.m. The sun was farther off to the west, leaving a bit more shade. I was once more rejuvenated, ready to continue. Suddenly, Paul reappeared in the distance, limping toward me, exhausted. He admitted, "I've gone without water and rest, pushing myself for too long. "The dehydration and excessive sweating have caused my kidneys to be *"screaming in pain."* He dropped to the ground and admitted, "I can't continue."

❧

"Well, fuck, what do we do now?" I thought to myself. "What happened to my knight in shining armor?" He had pushed himself and was now out of commission. Now I was scared. I encouraged him to take it slow, and we walked a few more minutes and found a major intersection in the road. There was a sign posted that said *Kiliguni* was seventeen kilometers up a small hill before us. We sat down on the side of the road in silence. My confidence drained once I realized Paul was seriously compromised. He was my rock and protector. Why had he not said anything? Why are men so macho that they will not reveal their vulnerabilities? I know Paul felt responsible for our situation at some level, and I was sympathetic, but now we were tired, sweaty, and very vulnerable.

I was truly terrified! If he could not go on, we'd be sitting ducks after the sun went down. Was this how we were going to die? No one knew where we were. We would not be considered missing for another eight days. They might find the vehicle, but would they ever find our bodies? I recalled a book several years ago by Katie Payne, *Silent Thunder*, about her research concerning elephant rumbles that could carry for several kilometers but could not be heard by human ears. She told the story of a lion encounter she had while alone in the bush. She was resting under a tree when a large lion started to approach her from across the savannah. There was no place she could seek shelter. She remained silent, staying perfectly still, trying to avoid eye contact, and make herself look smaller. She waited, thinking that her book would never be finished. After what seemed like a lifetime, the lion stopped, yawned, changed direction, and went about his business. Could we be that lucky?

I knew female lions hunt in groups in the late afternoon. They look for the most vulnerable species, stalk their prey, and attack in unison. Once they capture their prey, the male lion enters the scene and is allowed the first serving, followed by the females, and finally the cubs. The disconcerting part is that they don't kill you before they start eating you. That was my new reality!

I had only one more option. We had done everything we could to survive, and now needed some serious help. Without saying anything to Paul, my silent prayer went something like this. "Well, God, you know that I don't pray very much because I feel you put us here to work out our own problems. But we have tried our best to get out of this situation, and we are out of options. Please, God, we really need your help, Amen." We sat in silence.

After about ten minutes, we heard a noise from the road to the north. It got louder as it approached, but I couldn't distinguish the sound. We both stood, not knowing what to do. What could it be? Could it be elephants or perhaps wild buffalo? A large, white safari van emerged from around the corner heading in our direction. The driver saw us and slowed to a stop, yelling at us at the top of his lungs, "Did you know that it is illegal to walk in the park? Last night, a lion killed a large zebra only half a kilometer from here. It is very dangerous! What are you doing here?" I approached the driver's window as his verbal rampage continued, interrupted him, and asked, "Do you have any water?" His demeanor changed instantly to compassion, and he handed me a large, cool water bottle. Paul explained what had happened to our car and how we ended up here. The driver could not believe we were still alive. Our life-threatening situation was finally over. We survived!

He explained that he was driving a young American couple to a safari camp further south along the Tsavo River. Drinking the water, we climbed into the van. We introduced ourselves to the young couple, and they seemed annoyed with our sensational intrusion on their holiday. He drove us toward the safari camp along the same Tsavo River we had crossed on foot, hours earlier. After five minutes, he stopped the van and pointed to the dead carcass of a half-eaten zebra that lay just off the road. Neither of us wanted to contemplate the "*what ifs*" of that alternate scenario, but we were grateful that the nearby lions had full tummies from the feast the night before.

I took a moment and thanked God for his intervention. We had been saved just in the nick of time. What a relief! How wonderful it was to drink the precious water. I never mentioned my prayers to Paul. But I knew God was with me. Upon arrival at the lodge, we checked in, showered, ate a small meal, and slept very soundly. Safely back in civilization, we realized how close we had come to a deadly end to our safari vacation.

Early the next morning, the driver and his assistant insisted on going to fix our rental car, returning late in the afternoon. What a blessing. Meanwhile, I had slept for ten hours and was resting outside the cabin, looking at the river, watching a variety of birds, including herons. Once more, I thanked God and told Him I owed Him. One day, I would pay Him back. Paul and the driver became buddies. The next day, he insisted that we follow his vehicle to Amboseli National Park because he felt our vehicle would probably not make the trip. He seemed to feel it was his responsibility to ensure the rest of our journey was safe. We gladly followed him, and soon the car had engine problems. We were forced to abandon it halfway to Amboseli, in the Maasai bush country. Mount Kilimanjaro, Africa's highest peak, majestically sits at the base of Amboseli, one of Kenya's most popular national game parks. Formerly the Maasai Amboseli Game Reserve, the park is a thirty-one square-mile ecosystem that spans the Kenya-Tanzania border.

After checking into the Amboseli lodge and having a wonderful meal, we called the Hertz in Nairobi, explained the car problem, and ordered a car to be brought to our Amboseli lodge. After spending a restful night and enjoying an amazing breakfast, we were refreshed and looking forward to our first game drive. Safe inside the safari vehicle, we saw herds of elephants grazing in a swampy area under the shade of Kili. The scene was breathtaking! As I gazed across the valley, I was overwhelmed by the natural beauty of wild elephants living free in their natural habitat. My emotions spilled over, and I started to cry tears of joy at the beautiful sight of mommas and their calves of all sizes following the old matriarch across the lush green grass on the plain. Paul understood and gave me a big hug.

We continued to watch them amble across the marshy savannah, then all the adults stopped and formed a circle of elephant bodies with each head facing outwards and their butts almost touching each other inside the circle. It looked strange until I realized that inside the circle were the calves. The females had made a day care center to protect the calves while they rested. How amazing! This was the Africa I had longed to see all my life. I was changed forever! The Kenya red clay had gotten under my skin, and I was hooked.

❧

The next morning, we arrived at the Hertz office in Nairobi and described our life-threatening ordeal, being stranded in Tsavo East for over twenty-four hours, walking for almost thirty kilometers to find help. Hertz was not a bit sympathetic. After we abandoned the vehicle, it had been dismantled by the Maasai and was now worthless. They showed us the fine print on the policy that stated we could not bring a sedan car into any game park. Paul had failed to read the fine print. The rental agent who delivered the car knew we were headed to a game park but said nothing. We were required to pay twelve hundred dollars in damages. But we walked away with our lives, not to mention the amazing story we tell our friends.

The last couple of days we spent in an air-conditioned hotel with clean sheets and hot water. What a luxury. On our final day, we journeyed from Nairobi to Mombasa, arriving at our resort in time for a tasteless dinner. After a restful night's sleep, we got up early and caught our ride to the airport for the return flight to Germany. No one had missed us! What would have happened if the safari bus had not come by to rescue us? Would we have ever been found? Hmmmm . . .

Part Five

25

After our Christmas adventure in Kenya, we returned to work in Virginia, but Paul soon became frustrated with his career as a contractor. He expressed a serious desire to leave the contracting rat race and return to Africa to support the humanitarian effort. He also knew I was only one year away from an early retirement option. We were both excited about the possibility of going back to Africa.

Paul began researching NGOs and reached out to the IRC, expressing his interest in joining their efforts. He quite frankly told that, although he had an impressive résumé in management, he was considered an unknown quantity in the vastly remote NGO world. They agreed to give him a chance to complete a ground-level assignment in an African mission before being considered for a position commensurate with his education and experience. He received a formal offer for a logistics officer entry-level position in the Democratic Republic of the Congo, DRC, in the small village of Lukalela, located along the bank of the Congo River.

I encouraged him to try it and see if he liked it. At the same time, I continued working in Virginia. He quickly submitted his application, was accepted, and immediately turned in his resignation to his company, preparing to leave for the Congo. We planned to use the same habit of recording conversations on mini-cassette tapes to stay in touch. My current assignment was at Andrews Air Force Base in Maryland, an hour away from home. The long drive was an excellent time to record how I was doing and how much I missed him. He lived in a small, mosquito-infested village on the shore of the Congo River, dealing with locals while delivering supplies up and down the river. He had delivered a baby, whom the mother named Paul, and needed to bury a dead infant brought to the office for help. He even adopted an abandoned baby spider monkey named Luke as a pet, which slept with him. It was a totally different world. Paul told me he never wanted another desk job. He had applied to the IRC for his next position. In August of 2001, Paul returned to Virginia with a new offer from the IRC to serve as the Deputy Director of the Uganda Mission. This offer would move us into a new world of adventure and freedom. We were ready for an African adventure.

I loved my work as a government contractor. It was diverse and challenging. I was proud of my career as a Senior Systems Engineer in middle management, working for the intelligence community on amazing, classified projects I cannot talk about.

I was fifty-four years old, not yet eligible for early retirement, so I arranged to take a year-long leave of absence without pay while we pursued our new dream. Paul just needed a medical examination to show that he was fit for service after his last mission, then we'd be on our way. I notified our landlord that we were leaving, and had started packing, this time only essentials.

On Tuesday morning, September 11, 2001, our day was packed with tasks to complete before our weekend flight to Uganda. Everything was on track. We even had our visas. There were just a few loose ends to tie up.

At 8:30 a.m., I was scheduled to meet with the TRW head of security for my security debriefing, required before I began my leave of absence. I walked outside our townhouse and stopped in my tracks before unlocking the door. I came out every morning to go to work and had never seen such a vibrant sky, weird, I thought. I got into my

Celica, drove to work, and went directly to the security office. Walter, the manager I had known for many years, welcomed me and began explaining the debrief process. After several moments, he got a phone call and appeared very upset. Hanging up, he resumed his briefing. After several more minutes, he got another short call. He hung up again and quickly turned on the television above his desk. CNN was broadcasting that two hijacked U.S. airlines had hit both World Trade Center Towers in New York City.

"We are under attack," he said.

For a moment, we watched both towers burning, belching black smoke. Each tower had a gaping hole where a plane had struck the building, many flights up. Walter excused himself and left, with more pressing matters to attend to. I was in shock at his remark. Were we at war? Who could have done this? No one knew what had happened. As I walked out of the building, everyone was glued to the nearest television, in total shock and disbelief. I proceeded in a daze to my next errand, my nearby bank, to deposit the payroll check I had just received.

At the neighborhood bank, I stood in an unusually long line. Everyone ahead of me was watching the live overhead television of the towers burning. Suddenly, the first tower imploded, and after a few seconds, the other tower followed. Then the massive Twin Towers disappeared in a colossal cloud of dust and debris, sinking in seconds to the ground. Everyone on the nearby streets started running for safety. I was feeling numb as I waited inside the bank in shock, watching events unfold. I quickly deposited my check and immediately went home.

That same morning, Paul was handling last-minute details of the job. He had completed his physical and the required lab tests and x-rays, but had gotten a call that morning from his urologist saying that, based on the bloodwork, he wanted to biopsy Paul's prostate. Paul did not seem alarmed by the request. Five years before, he had been diagnosed with an enlarged prostate and had taken medication to relieve the symptoms. He agreed to go that morning and get it done quickly. He left for his appointment shortly after I left. Paul returned around 11 a.m. He, too, was shocked by the news of the terrorist attack. He also had bad news from the doctor's visit. The biopsy had been very painful without an anesthetic, and the doctor took several little chunks of tissue around the prostate. I felt bad I hadn't been there, but our schedule was too tight. He said the doctor was optimistic but just wanted to be sure there was no cancer.

There was no history of prostate cancer in his family. Paul said, "The results of the biopsy will be back in a couple of days."

"What?" I said alarmingly. I was no longer focused on the terrorist attacks. "What?" I exclaimed a second time. "That is too late!" I explained that we'd only be getting the results the day before we got on the plane to Uganda. He would not have medical clearance in time for IRC to issue his official contract. When Paul asked, "Why couldn't we just wait and see?" I realized that he was either in shock or denial.

I explained, "Paul, today is Tuesday, the movers are coming on Thursday, we are cleaning and giving up our apartment on Friday, and flying on Saturday. If the test turns out positive for cancer on Friday, that would be horrible news in itself, but we'd then have no jobs and no place to live."

I suggested that he call the doctor back, describe the schedule we were up against, and ask him if we should postpone the trip. He called immediately, and the doctor agreed that Paul should put the trip on hold for just a few days. Paul then called IRC in New York, who emphasized that they must have medical clearance before they could accept him for the position and allow him to fly. I immediately called the apartment manager, explained the situation, and asked her to put things on hold for a couple of days. She agreed. Then I called the movers to put them on hold as well. The situation was nerve-racking for both of us, but I knew that Paul was very healthy and there was no way he could have prostate cancer.

❧

During that two-day wait, neither of us discussed the possibility of cancer. For the remainder of the day, we were distracted by the unfolding disaster on television as more tragic details emerged. All flights had been canceled nationwide. The Pentagon had been struck by a third plane, and a fourth was still missing. Journalists speculated whether the White House or the CIA Headquarters could be next. The world was going crazy. We had made the right choice, not only to move out of the Washington area, but out of the country. Given the current issues, when would that happen? We'd find out soon enough.

On Friday, the doctor called us both into his office for the results. That was not a good sign. The doctor said, "Paul does have cancer of the prostate. His prostate Gleason scale was zero to ten; his was six point seven, meaning the cancer would grow and spread rapidly. Due to his young age of fifty-three, the doctor recommended a radical prostatectomy—the total removal of the prostate. The doctor said the biopsies indicated that the cancer was contained within the prostate, so the prognosis was very good for total recovery. He immediately put Paul on female hormones to help shrink the tumor. In the meantime, he said we should consult one or two oncologists to discuss what other options were viable. The doctor also mentioned Paul would be on the female hormones for at least three months before any surgery was practical. It gave us a bit of time.

❧

Paul and I were both in shock. I went into my controlled analytical mode to avoid an emotional meltdown. Once home, we sat and discussed how we should proceed. First, I needed to cancel my leave of absence and get back to work. Second, we needed to contact the resident apartment manager and explain that we would not be leaving. Third, Paul needed to get oncology appointments as soon as possible, and most importantly,

Fourth, we both needed to quickly become very knowledgeable about prostate cancer, various treatment options, and the pros, cons, and prognosis for each. The internet was invaluable. The terrorist attack of September 11 fell into the background as we plodded through the medical options available. I tried to read Paul's emotional state, but it was well hidden. Mine was too. Our new focus was getting the facts and deciding on the best treatment.

❧

The next few days and weeks were a blur as we sought the advice of oncologists, both of whom strongly recommended surgery because he was so young. A popular new therapy, radioactive seed implants in the prostate, would save the prostate, but had not yet been proven to eliminate the cancer. Doctors were encouraging, but the treatment was less than ten years old, and long-term results were speculative at best.

My analytical skills were working overtime. I felt the bottom line was: What good was an enlarged prostate if, ten years later, you had more trouble peeing and still had cancer? Our lovemaking was always incredible and an integral part of our intimacy. It was closely intertwined with an essential part of our lives. If impotency were a result of the surgery, we'd still have the closeness of hugging, holding hands, kissing, and the special snuggling we always enjoyed. I felt we'd work it out. Paul's urologist and the two oncologists he saw recommended the radical prostatectomy, but Paul favored the less invasive radioactive seed implant. It was time to talk. I asked him to sit down. I spoke, and he listened. I told him how important this decision was to our future. I told him how much I loved him and wanted him to be my partner and soulmate, not just for now, but also how important it was for us to grow old together. If it meant trading the possibility of impotency for his life, I wanted him to live.

When all was said and done, he agreed to have the surgery, so we contacted the leading urologist at Johns Hopkins Hospital in Baltimore, who was world-renowned for his state-of-the-art, *nerve-sparing* prostatectomy technique. For the next three months, Paul waited. During that time, he felt fine but was unemployed and had nothing to do, which drove him crazy. He realized he could use this time to complete his flying lessons at a small airport in Maryland. He took lessons almost every day and received his pilot's license just before the end of the year. He was very proud. I continued to work. The surgery was performed on December 26, 2001. The doctor said it was completely successful. Great news! He was discharged three days later.

❧

Paul recuperated quickly, and we soon realized he had become impotent. Viagra did nothing. During the next few months, we tried to ignore the elephant in the room. Then we walked around it. Perhaps healing was required. He focused on his next position with IRC in Africa. Give it time, I decided. We were not having sex, and we were not talking about it. I still wanted to hug and snuggle, but Paul would not touch that elephant. When I snuggled next to his back, he'd lie there and not respond. Perhaps it's normal for married couples not to discuss sexual failures and possible alternatives. It was too raw a subject to even think about. Maybe in six months things would be back to normal. The good news was that the cancer was removed entirely. I hoped he was right.

Looking back:

Years later, I realized we should have gone back to the Johns Hopkins surgeon for a second post-op and asked about the impotency problem. Perhaps we would have received some guidance or a series of drugs to try, but we just both put our heads in the sand while Paul began planning for another opportunity with IRC in Africa.

I went back to work, engrossed in a new project. Paul had been through enough stress with surviving cancer and needed to get on with his life. It was unfair of me to pressure him to seek a solution from his surgeon. He should do that in his own time. This elephant in our life sat patiently in the corner. Good thing it never pooped! It soon became a regular pattern. Paul avoided kissing, hugging, or snuggling at night or early in the morning. We did not hold hands anymore. I recalled the Neil Diamond song, *"You Don't Bring Me Flowers Anymore."* Several times, I tried to initiate the closeness I craved, but the gesture was ignored as he'd casually roll over and go to sleep. That was not denial, it was intentional. The elephant soon grew to fill the room. Be patient, I told myself. It was a hard time for me. I had no one to confide in about the emotional void developing in our marriage. So, what did I do? I soldiered on.

26

Four months after his surgery, Paul had recovered from his prostate surgery and was offered a one-year position as Deputy Director of the IRC Mission in Nairobi, Kenya. He submitted his medical clearance information and was quickly approved. We hoped that he would become an asset to the NGO world, allowing us to remain in Africa as long as we wanted.

I prepared for the move by purchasing a digital Nikon camera, several Columbia cargo pants that I could quickly turn into shorts, and high-quality waterproof hiking boots with sturdy socks. After years of wearing contacts, then glasses, I splurged and had LASIK surgery on both eyes to eliminate my nearsightedness. Perfect vision would allow me to see African animals in the wild across the savannah.

I was finally eligible for early retirement. Yet, I still had a strong desire to make a difference and hoped to obtain a job with an NGO in Nairobi once settled. But for now, I was looking forward to the fantastic opportunity to live in Kenya, understand the culture, and explore the wild animals—especially the elephants.

❧

We had a solid, loving marriage for eight years. But now, the elephant in the room, I named SI, for sexual impotence, still sat silently in the back seat for now. I felt we still needed time to adjust.

❧

The thought of early retirement from my career was scary. The career I had established served as my touchstone and secure foundation for my life. I loved the challenging and rewarding work. The company was my security, stability, and almost family. But on the other hand, I knew there was more to life, and I wanted to experience it. Still a bit torn between security and adventure, I shared with Paul my feelings of vulnerability in relinquishing my career. I would be giving a huge part of my security in life to join him, as the sole breadwinner in a foreign country. Numerous friends felt I was crazy to give up a successful career in the intelligence community. I would also be giving up my top-secret clearance, my coveted security blanket. I asked him if he felt we were solid in our marriage and if I could rely on him without reservation. Without any hesitation, he replied, "We are solid. You have nothing to fear." Then he gave me a big hug. Okay, now I can relax, have fun, and explore.

❧

We arrived in Nairobi in May of 2002, with four suitcases each, backpacks, three parrots, and Eiger, our male German shepherd. I had contacted the U.S. Fish and Wildlife Service for the required paperwork to ship our animals. Paul's parrot, Quique, was a Blue Crown Conure with a vibrant green body and a light blue head. He was bonded to Paul and was very affectionate and talkative. Paul and Quique went everywhere together, even hiking along the Potomac River, truly joined at the shoulder. His friends often noticed a fresh streak of bird poop on his shirt, but it did not faze him. Quique's favorite phrase was, *"You're a brat! Give me a break!"* Since Quique had bonded with Paul, I purchased my own baby African Grey parrot. This baby bird had no feathers, so I needed to feed him with an eye dropper for weeks. We bonded quickly. I named him Cassidy and hiked with him too. African Greys have the intelligence of a two-year-old child. He would call, *"Paul,"* in my tone of voice, and Paul would answer. Cassidy was more subdued and very loving, but not chatty like Quique. Our third parrot was a rescued African Grey named Grumbles. He was frightened of anything big and scary that went by his cage, such as a large box, a suitcase, or anyone new. When he was scared, he would let out a loud, growling noise like a lion. The Kenya Wildlife Service, KWS officer reviewed our paperwork and said we had requested CITES authorization to export the birds from the U.S., but forgot to request authorization to import them into Kenya. After a brief discussion and many apologies, we agreed to home-quarantine the bird for thirty days and then provide the proper import permit to the KWS CITES office. The IRC staff picked us up at the airport and took us to our hotel. The next morning, we met the staff and attended a mandatory security briefing.

The Kenyan population was struggling to survive. There was a growing number of muggings, home invasions, and carjackings every night in the city. This news got our attention. This third-world country was not secure! We had left the relative security of the Virginia suburbs for a country of poverty, crime, and survival in the face of the HIV/AIDS epidemic. Paul's boss reassured us that the IRC takes extensive precautions to mitigate the security risks of its employees. We were required to rent a place that had a secure perimeter wall or fence around the entire property and a secure front gate. They would provide trained guards to protect our home twenty-four hours a day, seven days a week, but for some reason, the guards were not allowed to carry guns for self-defense. They had only nightsticks.

Working for an NGO felt like working in the U.S. military. We were now under their safety umbrella. The salary was only thirty thousand dollars a year, but the benefits enabled international staff to live in relative safety and comfort.

Paul's contract included a salary, plus the additional benefit of covering home rental costs and utilities. He also received a vehicle and driver, as well as a one-time allowance for home furnishings and appliances. We borrowed a few beds and a washer/dryer from the IRC surplus storeroom.

Nairobi's older communities were established during the British colonial era. These communities had lush green lawns, tropical gardens, and tall stately palm trees. Huge overhanging jacaranda branches with vibrant purple flowers provided shade along the roads. Tall bougainvillea living fences, in vibrant red, pink, white, and fuchsia, added vivid color to the tropical suburbs. The Nairobi City Center was modern, with numerous high-rise office buildings and a few five-star hotels. This impressive skyline had emerged from the arid bush. The Nairobi Game Park was located on the south boundary of the city. As soon as we arrived, we drove through the park, where elephants, zebras, antelopes, and giraffes lived with the modern Nairobi skyline serving as an unlikely backdrop to our photos.

KWS had an impressive army of fully trained soldiers who were very serious about protecting the country's parks and wildlife. There was a constant fight against poachers killing elephants for tusks, rhinos for horns, and antelopes for bushmeat.

Swahili is the native language of Kenya, but many Kenyans learned English during British colonial rule. As a result, the United Kingdom English was commonly used. Entrepreneurs from India also settled in Kenya during the colonial times, becoming successful merchants and owning many retail stores. It was surprising to see Indian merchants among the sea of Kenyans.

❧

I quickly adjusted to living among the Kenyans and did not feel insecure or vulnerable, except when a Kenyan walked down the road toward me carrying a large machete. It reminded me of the Rwanda genocide years before. I learned it was a standard tool used in farming, and before long, I had my own machete for gardening.

Paul's driver took us to various rental listings and explained the pluses and minuses of each. He was very cordial, spoke good English, and could speak Swahili with the landlords when we had questions. Gradually, we became familiar with the middle-class communities surrounding Nairobi. Some areas were mainly Caucasian, and others were primarily Kenyan. Everyone was very polite, and it was customary to offer us a tiny amount of very sweet tea. We focused on houses in the suburbs that would be an easy drive to Westlands, an upscale, safe, middle-class suburb, thirty minutes north of the city. We viewed many homes and a couple of apartments, each with beautiful, large trees, luxurious lawns, and perfectly manicured gardens. Still, we always had to be mindful of the IRC security. A few quaint, one-story homes built in colonial times were constructed of limestone, with massive fireplaces and lovely parquet floors, but lacked the required security fencing. Others were more modern, multi-storied dwellings in gated communities. There were also condominiums in more congested areas closer to the city. The homes usually had fans in every room but no air conditioning. Due to the climate at six thousand feet, midday is generally very hot in the sun, and in the late afternoon, the weather becomes cooler. Each dawn would be chilly. After almost three weeks of searching and having two homes rejected by IRC security, we decided on a lovely, huge, stone, two-story house in the prosperous gated community where many expatriates lived. The downside was that it was an enormous house with five bedrooms, three and a half baths, a three-car garage, and separate servant quarters. A wealthy Kikuyu gentleman built this huge two-story home. It seemed like a castle with heavy gray limestone blocks, a common form of construction in the area. A spacious stone veranda, adjoining the ground floor, overlooked the gardens below. The sturdy six-foot stone wall encompassed the entire property. This home was much too large for the two of us, but the IRC insisted that it was secure and did not balk at the rent. I felt self-conscious in such a huge home we did not need, but Paul took it in stride. I was surprised to see the live-in servants' quarters, but they were standard from colonial times and continued to house workers after independence. A typical middle-class family, regardless of race, had a housekeeper, a gardener, and a security guard. Many also had a cook and a nanny. I was going to be spoiled! We hired a housekeeper once a week and needed a full-time gardener, who lived in our servant quarters. Here we were now living like royalty.

To furnish the house, we purchased handmade, wrought iron, and bamboo furniture from vendors on the side of the road. It was fun to select everything new while staying on a strict budget. A nearby Walmart-like store, Nakumatt, stocked groceries, linens, kitchen items, and appliances, including fresh produce.

During our previous vacation in the country, we realized a rugged, 4x4 vehicle for safaris was essential. At a Saturday afternoon used-car fair, we purchased a used, dark blue Mitsubishi 4x4 from a white Kenyan man over eighty years old who had lived in Kenya his entire life. He had a beautiful, tall, young Somali woman as his partner. We became friends. After a couple of beers, he would share exciting stories of the old days.

I now had a car and could start to explore. My confident nature and positive attitude served me well. I did not feel shy or intimidated in this new culture. If I got lost, I'd pull over and ask the nearest Kenyan where to find City Center, Westlands, or the Nairobi Museum. Sometimes they gave me accurate directions, and sometimes they didn't have a clue, but gave me directions anyway. Eventually, I learned that Kenyans don't want to disappoint you, so they may provide inaccurate directions and send you to get lost. Kenyans walk along the road or take a matatu, a colorful local bus, to and from work. Many only knew the familiar footprint between work and home. As a result, it was difficult for us to find a good Italian restaurant because the locals had no idea where one might be. It was outside their footprint. Neither WAZE nor Google Maps nor smartphones had yet been invented.

❧

Paul contacted his business associate and friend, Howard Crooks. He and Nancy were an American couple married for over fifty years, twenty-five of those years were in Kenya. Howard was a successful African businessman, well-known in the security business. We were immediately invited to their house for a drink. Their home was built with the same gray limestone block as our house. It was a stately two-story house with a large living room, adjoining library, and a huge fireplace. African art collected over the years accented the walls and floors. It was like a museum. The entrance had a private gate with a security guard. There was also a small guest house. Servants included a young Kenyan housekeeper, a male cook, and a gardener for the vast lawn, gardens, pool, and, of course, the 24/7-hour security guards.

They welcomed us like old friends. Both were warm and eager to have new Americans in their midst. We soon became trusted friends and learned much about Kenya that is not in any travel guides. Howard was a tall, stately man with a warm smile and a thick white moustache. His thick, gray hair was buzz-cut by Nancy.

Nancy, a tall, thin, handsome woman with short gray hair, had a very warm heart. She gave me endless advice on where to find what. Nanc, as Howard called her, had recently retired as a high school English teacher at a nearby private international school and was now starting a small NGO to bring solar cooking to tribes in Northern Kenya. Nancy was the first American friend I had in Kenya. I had a great deal of respect for the adventurous life she was living with Howard. She was confident, self-assured, and an excellent international role model. Both were fluent in Swahili and were very well-connected in the Kenyan business community. We were no longer alone in this strange new country. They loved Africa and had many exciting stories to share, like when Nancy was arrested and sent to jail for several days. Howard was in his seventies but still traveled internationally frequently for business. They insisted that we stay in their guest house until our rental house was ready. We accepted, thankful to have more room for our pets. Before long, we met several of their friends and colleagues at their festive dinner parties, Fourth of

July celebrations, Thanksgiving, and Christmas as part of the family. We also made friends through Paul's work and began to lead active social lives. Paul stepped into his job with ease and was soon taking trips into war-torn South Sudan to support the mission.

❧

I was now a stay-at-home housewife, a strange new paradigm for me, which morphed into exciting experiences.

I had to quickly learn how to drive on the left side of the road. The steering wheel was on the right side. If I entered a roadway with no traffic, sometimes, out of habit, I automatically reverted to driving on the right, only to realize my mistake when irate motorists began gesturing and honking. Luckily, I had no accidents.

Occasionally, I would browse the Friday Maasai markets in the City Center and negotiate a good price for old masks among the sea of art and crafts. The art of saying no and walking away always brought the price down from a *mzungu* price to a fair price. It was fun, and I always felt safe. I was fascinated by the colorful clothing worn by many of the Kenyan women. Nancy gave me directions to a textile area in town that carried bolts and bolts of all the bold, colorful batik patterns. I was in heaven, and even though I no longer sewed, the brightly colored kanga made stunning tablecloths and gifts.

❧

In the past, I read all I could about elephants, but I had only seen elephants in the circus or a zoo. These savvy giants have a gentle, caring family nature. I learned that the matriarch, the oldest and wisest female in the group, was responsible for leading the group to good pastures, adequate water, and safety, based on her vast memory. A group usually includes between six and twenty members, normally relatives of the matriarch. Young males remain in the group of females until they mature between the ages of ten and twelve, when they are ousted to prevent mating with family members. Males, however, remain loners, wandering alone or in pairs searching for mates, perhaps like humans today. Periodically, fully grown bull elephants enter musth, a condition characterized by highly aggressive, unpredictable behavior, triggered by a significant rise in reproductive hormones. Testosterone levels in a bull in musth can be, on average, sixty times greater than during regular times. He could become frantic, unpredictable, and very dangerous during that period.

Nancy told us about a lecture at the Nairobi Museum given by Ian Douglas-Hamilton, a famous elephant researcher and founder of Save the Elephants, STE, an NGO established many years ago in Nairobi. I was familiar with his research after reading one of his early books, *Among the Elephants,* and was excited to hear him speak. Paul and I attended with Nancy and Howard. After the lecture, I went down to the stage, introduced myself, and explained that I was new in Kenya and had a background in computer database technologies. I added, "I love elephants and want to volunteer with your NGO."

"Really??," he said, with an inquisitive grin.

"Yes," I replied enthusiastically, smiling in return. We set up an interview at Ian's office in Langata, on the edge of the Rift Valley, almost an hour's drive from the house. We met in his office, and after a brief discussion, he admitted he had many challenges with the ever-changing IT environment and agreed to let me help. I was back in a working environment—this time, learning so much about elephants.

Over the next several months, I worked at the STE Langata office four or five days each week and had to learn the Apple Mac system they used, which was new to me. Once I realized their entire library of videos and photos was on one computer, which had never been backed up. I recommended, procured, and set up a backup system to capture and save their entire media history. Ian had established a STE research camp in the Samburu National Park, six hours north of Nairobi. Selected researchers from all over the world performed research for their Ph. D about a specific aspect of elephant life.

Occasionally, I was allowed to stay at the STE research center to understand the researchers' data requirements. I'd usually spend about two weeks living in a small tent, working in the small facility, and riding along with researchers to see the data they were collecting. It was a once-in-a-lifetime opportunity for me to see elephants up close. Slowly, I became more familiar with their behaviors and mannerisms. I did not make any money, but I was learning treasured volumes about these African elephants.

One exciting project was to monitor the migration of the various elephant groups through the park, especially when they ventured outside the park boundaries into rural villages., often causing havoc with the locals Once a Global Positioning System, GPS collar was installed around a matriarch's neck, a special software program could plot the movements of different elephant groups to monitor their migration patterns. To do this, a selected matriarch of a group was fitted with a durable GPS collar supplied by a company in South Africa. This project had been ongoing for two to three years, and the batteries were going dead and needed to be replaced. This web-based program successfully tracked elephant groups throughout the Samburu region over a specified period. This program told a very interesting story. Usually, elephant groups stay within the protected national park, because it is safe. However, a few groups would take different instructions from the matriarch, we'll call her mom. She wisely waited until after dark, then quickly and quietly led her group out of the park, racing the entire way until she found a new grazing area or a valuable water source. Then the entire group would relax and graze. When Mom decided it was time to return to the park's safety, she waited until the dead of night and, once more, raced the entire group back into the park. Their instincts and intelligence fascinated me.

❧

I was very fortunate to observe the battery replacement procedure, in which the matriarch would be darted, then the battery in the collar would be replaced. The first time, the matriarch and her group had no idea what was happening. But the next time, the wise old matriarch thought, "Fool me once, shame on you. Fool me twice, shame on me." This group remembered their frightening ordeal several years ago involving a vehicle that had attacked their matriarch. As soon as the vehicles approached the target group, all the elephants took off in different directions. Several members of the group ran interference to allow the matriarch to hide. They were truly clever, and it took the veterinarian some time to get a good shot of the matriarch's rear end to sedate her. Once she was darted, the huge elephant staggered around like she was drunk for a few minutes and then fell unconscious. The elephant's health and well-being are always paramount. The battery replacement had to be performed quickly to prevent the animal from going into distress. As the team worked quickly, other researchers gathered blood, hair, and perhaps even spores for analysis.

It was vitally important for the rest of the group to remain at a reasonable distance from the researchers. Concerned aunties and young calves became upset, so a vehicle was used to deter the group members from swarming around their unconscious Mom. Confused and concerned about their unconscious leader, they may have charged. This vehicle circled the downed matriarch until the procedure was completed. While the matriarch was unconscious, the vet monitored the heartbeat, breathing, and other vitals constantly. If she ever became distressed, he would terminate the procedure by administering an antidote to wake her up. As an observer, I stood by the researchers and sometimes helped by moving an ear out of the way, but otherwise just stood in awe. I was able to touch her coarse hide, which had tough black hairs protruding here and there. The deep hollow of her breathing through her trunk sounded like she was breathing through a pipe. She was, indeed. Her breath was warm and moist. The team always wet down the elephant's hide to avoid her overheating in the sun. I slowly walked around this huge sleeping giant, touched the cushioned soles of her feet, and examined the cute toenails. Elephants have amazingly soft feet—no wonder they move so silently.

Once the battery was replaced and the battery was functioning, the veterinarian gave her an injection of a potent antidote, allowing her to wake up immediately. As soon as he got the injection ready, everyone ran to the safety of the nearby vehicles. We stayed in the vehicle and watched from a safe distance to be sure the matriarch woke up and began walking normally. The whole process took less than an hour. I felt very privileged to be part of such a significant effort.

27

I finally acknowledged a small crack in our relationship. We had settled into our castle and become comfortable, but I began to realize that the impotence had affected Paul in ways I had not expected. Our passion for each other was still alive, but the shroud of impotence had settled over us. He tried everything—Viagra and Cialis—but when nothing happened, Paul was frustrated and helpless. Something had been taken away. After several attempts, the elephant in the room said, "Don't bother, it's too embarrassing and too stressful to try again." I tried to understand and be supportive, but at the same time, I craved our closeness in the form of hugging, kissing, and holding hands as we had always done in the past, and I told him so. We discussed our dilemma, and he decided to see a urologist at Aga Khan Hospital, a well-known and trusted hospital. We arrived at the hospital, and a very experienced Indian doctor took Paul's history and examined him. Paul told him of his frustration because neither Viagra nor Cialis worked at all. The doctor discussed alternatives, such as injections or, ultimately, a surgical implant with a pump. These were bizarre, unwelcoming alternatives.

But Paul was willing to try injections, so after a quick trip to the pharmacy, we were excited to give this alternative a try. To me, having to inject medicine into one's penis sounded like planning a missile strike: get ready, inject, wait, boom! But Paul was willing to try. The downside was that it took all spontaneity out of lovemaking. I waited as Paul injected his projectile. Within a few minutes, he got a full erection. Wow, this was amazing. Hallelujah! It was great! Problem solved! Maybe not the best alternative, but a viable one. A few nights later, we tried it. It worked well, but this time, his erection did not subside. I was overwhelmed with pleasure, and Paul was in pain and did not subside. Be careful what you wish for, I thought. The doctor told us about this potential side effect. If the blood in the engorged penis does not recede, it can become dangerous if not treated. After a few minutes of waiting, with no decline, we dressed and took off to the Aga Khan Hospital. After driving about ten minutes, Paul announced that the erection was subsiding on its own. What a relief! I turned the car around, and we both agreed that the injection was not a good idea.

Sex without spontaneity is a physical release but not an emotional one. Our extraordinary lovemaking had spoiled us. We finally accepted sex was no longer in our lives, but other forms of affection came to a screeching halt as well. No holding hands, no hugs, no snuggling, and especially no kissing while hugging. It was as if affection was sexual foreplay, and he had rejected it all, but he never explained to me why. We used to talk about everything, but this trauma caused him to become silent. He accepted my hug but did not reciprocate. It was like hugging a streetlamp in the dark. I told him I wanted his hugs, but for some reason, he would not discuss it. All the loving gestures were a thing of the past. I knew he still loved me, but I still felt unloved. After months of no affection, I decided to let it go. We had this amazing adventure, and I tried to focus on all the other stimulating things we were doing, like learning about animal dung!

❧

Paul heard about a new, one-week safari guide certification course in the Masai Mara National Reserve. The teacher was a South African wild game hunter turned conservationist. Paul signed me up as a surprise. What an excellent way to get an overview of the natural flora and fauna. There were about fifteen students. Most of the Kenyans were already experienced safari guides, now seeking official safari guide certification. Then there were a few curious gringos, three Brit birders, and me.

Our campsite was a quiet, secluded, tented camp in one of the coveted shady areas in the middle of the Mara. I shared a tent with a young local woman who was learning to be a safari guide. The course was terrific for a novice to Africa. It was truly amazing to be living in the bush with the animals. Every morning after breakfast, we'd have a lecture followed by a show-and-tell as we walked through the bush. In the afternoon, we'd take an open safari vehicle to see giraffes, zebras, antelope, lions, elephants, wildebeests, cheetahs, and leopards, then back to shower, relax, and have an incredible safari dinner. Did you know that there is a difference between healthy and unhealthy pasture, called Velt? I didn't. Next, we learned how to track animals by looking for actual tracks, broken branches, and spoor.

Tracking was followed by an intense course on spoor, or shit, as I call it. We could easily identify elephant poop, a compact pile containing many droppings of round, compact dung, which looked the size of a package of Gouda cheese, without the red packaging. Next was giraffe dung, which looked like chocolate kisses, then there was antelope dung, similar to rabbit poop. I can honestly say I became an expert in identifying shit. The years working for the government had given me more than an introductory course.

❧

One morning, the instructor told us we would be tracking a group of elephants on foot. I was excited about doing it, but one of the experienced Kenyan guides, a tall, black, gentle man named George, said, "That is crazy. You do not track Kenyan elephants on foot without putting your life at risk." Three Kenyan guides refused to participate. They stayed back at camp. The Mara terrain is flat for miles, with a Velt, or grass, about a foot tall, and thorny acacia trees dotting the landscape. No large trees were in sight if we needed to get out of the way of a charging elephant. It was a clear, lovely morning with a hint of cool breeze before the onslaught of oppressive heat. We novice students began our walking safari in a line behind the instructor, staying directly behind him and being very quiet. After about a kilometer, our instructor spotted a small group of about six adult female elephants, with a couple of young calves nearby.

❧

The bad news was that we were upwind of the group, and they caught our scent immediately. I looked around for some nearby shelter, a large rock or kopi, but there was no place for any of us to hide from charging elephants. The instructor urgently whispered for us to stay perfectly still and quiet. The matriarch shook her head and advanced a few steps toward us in a mock charge. A few of the other females joined in, then stopped short. That was enough for our brave instructor, who began walking backward slowly and quietly, telling us to do the same. We continued to face forward, walking backward, peeing in our pants. She watched our retreat, with ears flapping, kicking up the dirt. She probably didn't want to charge unless forced into a confrontation. Neither did we. Finally, there was enough distance between us that she turned slowly and moved the group in the opposite direction. What did we learn? Don't try to track elephants on foot in Kenya, and don't let anyone convince you it is not dangerous. Later, at lunch, the instructor apologized to the Kenyan guides who had refused to go, telling them they had been right. South African elephants have a different temperament from Kenyan elephants. Well, good to know.

❧

On the last evening of the course, we were served a delicious barbecue chicken meal prepared by our camp chef. Everyone was relaxed, drinking beer or wine and sharing safari stories. After a lull in the conversation, I shared with the group how my husband and I got stranded in Tsavo East National Park. All at once, I had a captive audience as I described renting a saloon car, traveling from Mombasa to the southern Voi Gate of Tsavo East Park, and entering the park in mid-afternoon. When our vehicle became disabled, we pitched a tent for the night. The next morning, when no cars had passed, we hiked eighteen kilometers to the nearest safari camp, which we found abandoned.

George, the wise safari guide, asked, "Exactly where were you?" When I told him we were on a small hill that led down to the Tsavo River, he exclaimed, "I know exactly where you were," and shook his head several times and finally said, in a serious tone, "I cannot believe you are here to tell us about it." He was visibly shaken and mentioned the man-eating lions of Tsavo. He added, "The fact that you and your husband are alive is a miracle." That gave me goosebumps." We did not see any large animals during the ten hours of hiking," I replied. With a slight smile on his face, he soberly added, "They were watching you! Their stomachs must have been full." I became quiet and said a short prayer of thanks.

❧

One of Paul's top priorities was to have his private pilot license recognized in Kenya, so he went to Wilson Airport in Nairobi, showed his license, and had a successful check-ride. For one hundred and fifty dollars per hour, he could rent a single-engine plane. At first, he flew with an experienced Kenyan pilot who showed him the ropes. Nairobi's altitude is six thousand feet, so a plane is already high above sea level when it takes off. When he asked me to join him, I did, but it was a bit scary getting into such a small, single-prop plane with such a fragile aluminum fuselage. He contacted the tower, and soon we were allowed to take off. I looked over at him with pride. He was a confident, capable pilot. It was like a scene from the film *Out of Africa*, with Denys Finch Hatton at the stick and Meryl Streep as the passenger.

We soared out of Wilson Airport, banked right over the edge of the Nairobi National Park, and headed south toward the Ngong

Hills. Paul dropped down into the Rift Valley, a dry savannah with only a few small acacia trees. The view was amazing, so vast and flat, with a few Maasai mud huts here and there, and a small herd of scrawny cattle nearby. Paul explained that he had to continually scan the ground for a potential emergency landing spot if he lost engine power. He was totally focused, composed, and confident. I was so proud of him. It was his dream come true.

We had a fantastic adventure on one long weekend. Paul flew us across Kenya to Zanzibar, the Tanzanian Spice Island just off the coast of Tanzania. The Old Town was once a Swahili coastal trading post dating back to the eighteenth century. This town had an unusual look. Block after block of what looked like large apartment buildings were joined together, four to five stories high, in a labyrinth of narrow pedestrian alleyways, only wide enough for a donkey, two large women to pass. These tall alleyways were built to be cool, allowing no sunlight, but welcoming ocean breezes. It was ingenious. However, the sweltering heat hit us as we exited the labyrinth. These buildings contained homes, restaurants, shops, a mechanic shop, and a pharmacy. It was like going back in time. Our hotel was a narrow, multi-floor building with rooms on each floor and a lovely restaurant on the roof. Each entrance featured a thick, ornately carved door. It was a sign from the past. Beyond the entryway, we encountered a large open courtyard with bright bougainvillea along the walls and a cobblestone floor. Numerous tables and shady sitting areas invited us to relax.

❧

We were flourishing in this amazing environment. There was so much to explore. Everything was new, and we tried to absorb it all. Paul was enjoying his job, and I was enjoying being part of the STE team. Our experiences were unique. SI, the elephant in the room, was relegated to a bookshelf. Paul was alive and well, cancer-free.

Part Six

28

The IRC office received a USAID contract to perform an HIV/AIDS study in war-torn southern Sudan. The team leader, Judith, needed a consultant with management experience to assist in the two-week, boots-on-the-ground project. I was interviewed and got the job. Before I knew it, Judith and I flew to Rumbek, a small town in South Sudan. A small UN camp nearby provided us with room, board, and much-needed security. The rooms were tiny, single-person tents with screens all around. A shower and bathroom were at the far end of the compound. Flashlights, sunblock, and bug spray were mandatory. Air-conditioning was nonexistent. My tent had a dirt floor with a single bed against one wall, and a table with a small fan that helped circulate the hot air. I slept in a tank top and panties under a damp sheet.

An open dining hall, called a canteen, served breakfast and dinner. A picnic lunch was prepared for us each day. We had ample bottled water and were encouraged to stay hydrated. The canteen food was UN-standard, so I never got sick. For the most part, I kept my own counsel, working all day with one of the teams in extremely hot sun. Exhausted, after dinner, I returned to my tent to avoid malaria-carrying mosquitoes. I brought my laptop, and there was Wi-Fi in the compound, so Paul and I kept in touch.

The war in Sudan was ongoing, but the Rumbek area was not in active conflict, and it was supposedly safe. For the moment, anyway. However, evidence of the war was everywhere. I was warned to always stay on dirt roadways and well-beaten paths and never walk off the path. Land mines were still buried. I saw numerous round depressions in the ground, some ten feet across, made by an exploded rocket.

The Rumbek area was a very flat, dry, dusty savannah, with no green vegetation in sight except for the occasional mango tree, which offered a little shade. The local, tall, stately Dinka were nomadic pastoralists. Men and boys moved across the scorched savannah with their small, skinny herd of longhorn white cattle to find meager pastures and the occasional water hole. Women and girls stayed behind in small villages, caring for the home and younger children. Each family lived in a small, perfectly round straw hut with a dirt floor. The women cooked outside over a small fire, using scraps of wood, leaves, or sticks that were almost impossible to find.

❧

The purpose of the HIV/AIDS study was to determine if the epidemic proportions across Africa were also as high in this war-torn country. Due to the war, the UN had no data on the extent of infections throughout that country. The study was very well planned, with detailed questionnaires about confidential sexual practices. Tribal elders in the area had been briefed in advance and had given consent for their village to participate.

There were four teams, each with two local, bilingual Sudanese and one group leader. We all attended a two-day training course in English and Sudanese in an old concrete school building. Only the women were to be interviewed.

In the initial part of the interview, the Sudanese interviewer described the study to the women of the household. He obtained written consent from each adult woman in the household before proceeding with the survey. The questionnaire inquired about sexual practices, multiple partners, etc. The woman was then instructed about the risk of sexually transmitted diseases, STDs. She was taught about the importance of using condoms to avoid HIV and STDs. Each team had a male Dinka interviewer, and I wondered if the Dinka women would provide candid answers about their private sexual activities to a male. A few declined to participate, but most women were curious and cooperative. After all, their spouses were away somewhere in the desert herding cattle. During the second part of the survey, a blood sample was taken to check for STDs. If a woman tested positive, the team would return to provide her with proper counseling and the proper medication.

Early each morning, a driver would pick up our team, and we would drive out to a new village. The male interpreter of our team approached each village woman, who was usually cooking on a small fire or nursing her baby. During the interviews, half-naked children of all sizes gathered around us, very curious about our white skin and different language. Babies remained naked and were cared for by their siblings. We interviewed at least six or seven women per day from the same village, and each interview usually lasted about two hours. This was an opportunity for these women to discuss sex confidentially. I was impressed that these women were so candid about their sexual lives. I felt privileged and humbled to be allowed into their personal spaces, next to their huts or sleeping quarters. I gained a great deal of respect for these families, especially the women. They survived on so little. At the end of each day, the team would compile the completed questionnaires and blood vials and deliver them to Judith, who had an office in the UN compound. She and I later organized the surveys and turned over the labeled blood samples to technicians and doctors working with us. A laboratory was set up behind the canteen to process blood results quickly and safely. Positive STD results were returned to the affected participant with the necessary medical treatment.

At the end of two weeks, Judith and I boxed the results and flew back to Nairobi. It had seemed like a month, doing the same thing every day in such oppressive heat. My total remuneration was thirty-five dollars, but the unique experience of living briefly in war-torn Sudan with this tenacious tribe was priceless. Time flew by in those days. Paul's rat race was navigating IRC management politics. I began exploring another epidemic that disturbed me—homeless street kids.

29

Homeless street boys gathered in large towns and cities across Kenya, living on the street and begging daily for food. They were considered a *"blight on Kenyan society"*. Teenagers and boys congregated as small groups in roundabouts near bustling business areas frequented by locals. Some approached cars and begged for money, while others were sleeping, high after sniffing glue to eliminate the constant hunger pains. Girls were ever visible. If they were lucky, they would be taken off the street by a caring church. Otherwise, they turned into prostitutes.

Westlands, an upscale town near our home, had a variety of shopping, restaurants, a craft market, and the Sarit Center, a three-story mall. Paul and I had to drive past Westlands' two roundabouts to get anywhere. Seeing these thin boys in tattered clothes was gut-wrenching to me.

Our friends, Howard and Nancy, warned us, "Always roll up our car windows when you slow down at a roundabout because the street kids will try to grab your necklace or watch. If you don't give them a few coins, they will even throw their shit in your window. Just ignore them, don't talk to them, and never give them money. They will just spend it on shoe glue and get high, spending the day in a stupor. If you are on foot, they could mug you for your purse or wallet."

To me, they looked vulnerable and helpless. Each time I saw the street boys, my heart went out to them. They were ignored by everyone who went by in this sea of disregard. Unwanted, hungry, dirty, ragged kids came from various tribes in rural areas to prosperous towns, especially Nairobi, seeking refuge and hope. They congregated in Nairobi, targeting middle-class patrons near hotels, restaurants, and shopping centers. They hung out in the roundabouts waiting for traffic to back up. It was not surprising to see several boys of different ages sprawled out on the roundabout grass, high on glue.

No one knew how many were HIV positive. Some kids had lost parents to AIDS. In other cases, one parent dies, and the other marries again. Children who find themselves with a new stepparent are often considered unwelcome and are neglected and abused. These kids become desperate and eventually run away, ending up alone on the street, surviving as best they can with no protection, shelter, or food. Usually, each child finds a small group of other street kids and forms a group, a sense of brotherhood, companionship, and most importantly, protection.

I had never seen such helpless, innocent kids. Their ages ranged from five or six to their twenties. Occasionally, I'd see a solitary homeless man who acted as a guardian to the boys to minimize harassment and beatings by the police. This blight existed nationwide, and everyone seemed to ignore it. There were no homeless shelters, only juvenile detention centers. Police were quick to arrest these kids if they were suspected of stealing or harassing tourists, the country's lifeblood. If an international dignitary, like the Prime Minister of the United Kingdom, was visiting Nairobi, the police would round up kids living on the street and take them to remand centers, i.e., juvenile detention facilities. I had heard remand was worse than being homeless. However, there were never enough remand centers to get this growing population off the streets.

❧

America has homeless shelters for adults in almost every major city to provide a place for the homeless to sleep. Destitute souls lived in doorways, sleeping in parks, under bridges, and walking along the city streets with a shopping cart full of their belongings. In the winter, they huddled over heating grates in the cities or made shelters from used cardboard boxes. Newly homeless families might still be living in their car, hoping for work. In the U.S., cities have homeless shelters and soup kitchens that provide meals, but you rarely see solitary children on the streets. The kids are picked up by police and placed in foster homes or returned to their own homes.

There were several very nice restaurants in the Westlands area, not far from our home. I was never fond of cooking, so Paul and I often went out to dinner. In a flash, a street boy would appear out of the darkness, not begging for money but to tell you he would watch your vehicle to ensure it was safe, thereby making a verbal contract with you. These boys had their pride. Many spoke English, German, French, and Swahili to interact with the tourists. We always said *masuri sana*, thank you, for the car to be watched. When we returned to our car after a meal of Italian, Chinese, or Indian cuisine, the boy would appear out of the darkness once again. We would pay him a few shillings and perhaps offer him a doggie bag as well. His eyes would light up with a big smile if you offered him leftovers.

❧

I always passed the Westland roundabout to get to the STE volunteer office. Without fail, I saw several hungry street kids, asleep on the grass of a roundabout, but I knew not to stop. This routine continued for a few months, and finally, I decided to investigate on my own. I learned the government was not in favor of adoptions, but they wanted their people to stay within their culture, not be flown to Canada or America to grow up as Westerners. This attitude was very different from Kenya's northern neighbor, Ethiopia, which had a thriving international adoption program that welcomed Westerners. Agencies and procedures were in place to facilitate placement. It was called adoption tourism. When we visited Ethiopia, we met several excited young American couples who had come to pick up their new adopted child. Kenya, on the other hand, had children's homes throughout the country, with children from one day old to eighteen years old who would live in the houses and attend church and school. Due to the rampant HIV/AIDS epidemic, a few of these homes became specialized for HIV/AIDS children only. Parents living in the slums who died of AIDS often abandoned their HIV positive babies and small children.

❧

During a luncheon at Howard and Nancy's, I met a gentleman named Sam who was involved in the local children's home. After a discussion, he invited me to visit the Nyumbani Children's Home, a Catholic children's home in the nearby town of Karen. Karen is a well-known small colonial town south of Nairobi, named for Karen Blixen, author of *Out of Africa*. Nyumbani was founded by Father Angelo D'Agostino in 1992 to serve abandoned HIV positive and sick children with AIDS.

I took him up on his offer, and Sam welcomed me to Nyumbani and then introduced me to Father D'Agostino, the founder. Next, we toured the home and its lush vegetable gardens. In the back was a small cemetery for the children who had died of AIDS. Tiny headstones dotted the lawn for more than fifteen souls. It was a sobering reality. The occupants of the home were adorable kids of all ages, with bright eyes, clean clothes, and smiling faces. The kids seemed calm and happy, but they were all infected with HIV or AIDS. I toured the spotless, large kitchen where the food was prepared. A clinic was run by a nurse and other trained staff who examined kids regularly and administered the precious HIV/AIDS drugs.

After the tour, Sam and I sat down in his office. I asked him about the street kids and what social programs were in place to help them. He sighed and said, "Really, nothing has been done to improve the situation. It's a big problem." He got up, went to the bookshelf, and returned with a VHS tape. It was labeled *Left Behind*. He explained that a young journalist from the United Kingdom visited Nairobi a few years ago and made a documentary about this very problem. "Take a look at this," Sam said. "This is the harsh reality, and it will change how you feel about the homeless." He told me to keep it. I thanked him, and he wished me the best. That night, I watched Sam's video. It was hard to watch the horrible problem that existed in the Kibera slums, tin shelters for over two-hundred and fifty-thousand people on less than three acres. I will never forget this haunting interview with a homeless man, who said, "We exist! We are human, yet you drive by with your fancy cars with your windows rolled up, the air conditioning on, looking straight ahead, pretending we don't exist. We do exist, and we need your help." I was in tears and can still see his face. What could just one person do to make a difference? I had no clue. Sam had succeeded in changing the way I looked at the homeless. I now saw these helpless adults, children, and teenagers, without a home, victims of a society that had turned its back on them. My heart ached. This problem had mushroomed in recent years due to the AIDS epidemic sweeping across Africa. The uncontrolled virus had wiped out entire families, especially those living in the close quarters of the slums. Billboards talking about condoms were now prominently placed, but it was too little, too late. If that were not enough, in many Kenyan tribes, a man may have many wives over his lifetime. If he gets infected, the virus quickly spreads to the other wives, who become mothers with HIV-positive newborns. When the parents die, the children are left with relatives who may be too poor to care for them. Hence, the explosion of homeless street kids.

☙

A month or two later, I had just finished my shopping at Westlands and was walking back to my car parked along the side of the road, when a young street-boy of about eight years old came up to me, smiled, and asked in English,

"Mum, could you please give my friends and me some money for food?" A couple of his friends were trailing behind him, but he was the charismatic spokesman. His name was Albert. He looked Somali and was as cute as a button, with a wide, innocent smile that warmed my heart. I continued walking and told him I would not give them money but would buy them milk and bread at the petrol station ahead. They followed me into a small snack shop.

The security guard asked if they were harassing me, and I replied, "No, they are with me." I purchased enough for the three boys, returned to my car, and said goodbye.

Peter, the oldest, asked, "Mum, can I have your cell number, please?"

I laughed and said, "You don't have a phone. Why would you need my number?"

He said, "We may need it in case we get sick or into trouble with the police."

I had been set up and had fallen for it. I gave him my number and waved goodbye, chuckling to myself. They were an odd threesome. Three boys of different ages, each from a different tribe. It felt good to have helped them.

❧

After dinner, Paul and I were upstairs reading in bed around 9 p.m. when my cell phone rang. Paul shot me a curious look as I answered it. No one called me at this hour.

It was Peter asking, "Can you come to see us tomorrow morning at the same place, same time?

"Without thinking, I said, "Sure, I'll see you at 10 a.m. at the same place." Then I told Paul the story about meeting the boys.

He expressed his concern, saying, "Be very careful." I understood his concern and promised I would. The next day at 10 a.m., they were waiting, and I bought them more food. Through the days ahead, it became a daily habit, and I got to know them better. Each boy told me his story of becoming homeless. Peter, Steven, and Albert became friends when they became homeless, forming a sort of street family that looked out for and protected each other.

Our breakfast meetings continued for a couple of weeks. I asked where they slept and how they hid the money they earned from begging. They told me they took a bath at the city mortuary in the wastewater that came out of the building. Yuk! They didn't smell like formaldehyde, so I hoped it was just gray water.

One day, I asked a nearby security guard if these boys were honest. He told me, "I see these boys every day. They are well-behaved and do not steal or sniff glue. They were good boys."

Albert Raju was the youngest, with an adorable smile. He was only eight years old, the youngest child of a Somali family living in the Nairobi suburb of Eastleigh. He was born in 1995. After his father died, his mother remarried, and the stepfather started abusing him. Albert resisted the abuse and often ran away, but was always caught, returned to the house, beaten, and then chained to his bed without food. Finally, he successfully escaped and went to the street in July of 2001. I could tell he craved a mother's love and guidance.

Stephen Wachira, the middle boy, was ten years old, a Kikuyu from the Eldoret area. He was a very shy, quiet boy with an accent that was difficult for me to understand. Born in 1990, he lost both his parents in the 1992 Mau-Mau uprising. As a two-year-old orphan, he was sent to live in an orphanage near the Ngong Hills with his older brother. After a time, his older brother ran away to the street, and Steven started being abused. He also ran to the street life in 1998.

Peter Bosire, the oldest, was a tall, thin twelve-year-old child from the Kisii tribe, near Lake Victoria. Peter told me that his mother was promoted to a supervisory position at her company, where a jealous co-worker poisoned her with chameleon ash poison. After his mother died in November 2000, he and his siblings stayed with an uncle. His older brother left, leaving Peter alone. He ran to the Nairobi streets in September 2001.

❧

I explained to Paul about meeting the street boys and how much I liked them. They were very polite, kind, and spoke English very well. After another three weeks, I took Paul on one of my milk runs, and he met the boys. He was impressed by how neat, clean, and polite they were. Peter told me that they would like to enroll in the new *"free school"* in Kenya, a law that had been enacted. Maybe I had too much time on my hands, or maybe it was karma, but I said I'd try to help. First, I made an appointment with the principal of Westlands Elementary School. I told her the story of meeting the boys, getting to know them, and asked how they could get into school.

She sympathetically replied, "It is not possible. These Westlands street boys would be recognized by the other children who live in Westlands, and they would be afraid of them. Where would they store their books? Where would they get their uniforms and how would they keep them clean? Where would they eat regularly? Living on the street makes it impossible."

I finally realized, more than ever, that the street was a dead-end for these kids. She continued, "If you are serious, the best solution is to find a rural private school that is willing to accept them." Wow, that would be a huge commitment and investment!

I met with other principals from nearby public schools, and the answer was always no. The boys needed a secure home before school would be an option. Maslow's Hierarchy of Needs. I really wanted to help them, but saw no clear way forward.

30

Kenya's rainy season starts in mid-December. It was an early evening in January of 2003, when ominous clouds swept over our area just as dusk settled. At 6 p.m., a thunderstorm struck without mercy. Sheets of icy rain hammered the tin roof of our stone house while thunder, like a furious lion, roared above us. Lightning lit up the sky before vanishing into the consuming darkness.

Paul and I had just finished dinner, I had done the dishes, and we retired to our living room. The wind was wild, with rain blowing in through the open windows. I grabbed the brass levers and quickly closed them.

Our furniture consisted of a bamboo sofa with two matching bamboo chairs, custom-made by roadside vendors. Brightly colored jungle prints of green, tan, and yellow covered the Styrofoam cushions.

Our large, beautiful living room, about twenty-by-twenty square feet, had large windows on two walls. The best part of the room was a stone wall that divided the kitchen from the living room. A massive stone fireplace covered that entire wall with a separate pit for storing logs.

The temperature had dropped from a comfortable level to about fifty-five degrees Fahrenheit in ten minutes. Paul quickly got to work building a fire, and soon we had a large, crackling fire to warm us. Our new bamboo sofa was pretty enough but not very comfortable, so we gathered a few large pillows we brought from the U.S. and lounged in front of the roaring flames. We were talking about our day as a powerful storm slowly intensified. Suddenly, hail the size of golf balls began to pummel the tin roof, making such a loud clatter that it sounded like a band of rain fairies playing giant pots and pans. It was deafening. Then the lights went out in the entire house. Our only light was from crackling flames. But I could not relax. My thoughts drifted to this foreign country where we were living. Lying on a pillow, relaxing, I recalled the song, *"I Miss the Rains Down in Africa,"* by Toto. "Would I miss them someday, I wondered?"

Looking back:

I do miss the rains in Africa. Kenya has a way of pulling you into its heart and holding on fast. I still feel the strong pull back to the bush, the arid plains, in all its vast beauty.

The storm continued to build, with increasing gusts. It would probably last all night. At 9 p.m., we agreed to go to bed. I will never forget that night! Our bedroom was almost as large as the living room below, but it was much colder because the warmth from the fire had not drifted upstairs. We brushed our teeth by candlelight. The warm, king-sized featherbed duvet on top of our bed beckoned to us. The sheets were freezing. I was still wearing yoga pants and a long-sleeved top, as I snuggled under the down duvet, but my feet were still freezing. Perhaps I should get up and put on socks. But I could not budge. Paul settled his body beside me, and I snuggled against his warmth. As I tried to doze off, I listened to the powerful energy of Mother Nature in this utter blackness, the gusts of wind shaking the windows as lightning lit up the sky. Man had landed on the Moon but was still unable to harness the power and force of the weather. Sleep refused to come as my thoughts drifted to Peter, Steven, and Albert, lying under a large tree or maybe huddled in the doorway of a closed shop, trying to get warm. The boys had to be freezing with only the rain-drenched clothes on their backs. My heart ached for them! Images of them huddled together, suffering in the cold, came to me like a bad dream! The wind continued to howl as rain and hail pelted the tin roof.

Carefully considering their dilemma, my heart and mind always came to the same conclusion. These were innocent boys trying to survive as best they could. I knew they were honest, clean, and polite. They had wooed me and were already calling me "Mum." I could not step aside and do nothing, as everyone in the video had done. My mind was made up, and I hoped Paul would agree to bring them home.

I nudged him awake and said, "I cannot just stand by and do nothing! Tomorrow morning, I'm going to bring the boys home to live."

He remained silent for several moments, then chose his words carefully, considering how best to answer me. After what seemed like minutes, he finally said, "Be very careful."

I told him, I understand, and I will be careful." Soon, I drifted off to sleep.

Rescuing these street boys went against all the security advice we had been given from everyone, especially Howard and Nancy. I knew I was not being foolish but compassionate; not reckless but determined; not naïve, but caring! How did I know these things? I had learned many years ago to trust my gut. This decision would change my life and theirs forever!

The next morning, I met the boys at our usual meeting place and explained that I could not stand the fact that they had been out in the storm last night, and that "Paul and I decided to bring you to stay with us." I asked them to gather all their belongings and meet me at the car.

At first, they were speechless, but then they said that their only possessions were on their backs. They were ready. They said goodbye to a couple of women shopkeepers who had befriended them and piled into the car to come home.

We didn't tell our friends Nancy and Howard about my decision. They had warned us: "If you let a street kid into your house, they will slash your throat and rob you blind." I didn't think so, but Paul told me to be careful, so I decided to take it slow.

At first, they would live in the three-car garage that we never used. I turned it into their dormitory, moving some used single beds from the upper bedrooms to the garage. Then I arranged a table and chairs for studying and eating meals. They could use the outside shower and toilet that were on the side of the house. This was going to be a trial period. I wanted to see how things went, and I still wanted privacy for Paul and me.

I explained to the boys that I could not bear that they had stayed on the street after the chilling cold storm the night before. I would help them try to get into school, but in the meantime, I'd get them school supplies that they could use to study at home.

The next morning, we hit the road to get them more clothes and other supplies. Outdoor markets sell used clothing from all over the world in huge sacks for almost nothing. Clothes for children and adults were spread out on tarps in a parking lot area. I suggested they find three shirts each and three pairs of pants. It was so much fun for them to pick out what they wanted and negotiate a good price.

They needed shoes too. Nakumatt would have underwear and socks. They also needed toothbrushes, toothpaste, soap, shampoo, and, of course, Vaseline to moisturize their skin. It was like Christmas for them and a new adventure for me. I was a mother again, and I felt I was doing something worthwhile. There were plenty of linens and blankets at home. We arranged for our housekeeper, Grace, to come daily to cook the customary Kenyan food. As I would learn, breakfast consisted of hot tea with bread and butter, or porridge. For lunch, she fixed *skuma wiki*, chopped kale cooked with onions and garlic. Then she would prepare *ugali*, maize, water, and spices, which she cooked into a pliable paste. Instead of forks, the boys used their thumbs and first two fingers to dab a little ugali, then scooped up the *scuma wiki*. Dinner was rice and beans with chicken. I was surprised when the boys cracked open their chicken bones and sucked out the marrow. Their appetites were good. They seemed happy with their new surroundings. Time would tell.

I'm sure they were a bit scared and unsure of what was going to happen, but they didn't have many questions. I established some rules of the house and explained them all. There were basic rules my sons had when they were young. They all spoke English with strong accents. At first, I had difficulty understanding them, so I asked them to speak slowly. When they were together, they spoke their native Swahili. All I knew was *jambo*, hello, *habari*, how are you, and *sante sana*, thank you.

❧

I decided to call them my Kenya boys. They were *'blank slates'* in terms of how to live a normal life in a nice home, how to take care of themselves, their clothes, personal items, and clean their room. They always looked clean and neat on the street and had a street-adapted concept of personal hygiene. I didn't ask them what it was; I just showed them how I expected things to be done in our home. I told them they should take care of their area, keep it neat and clean, wash their dishes, and put the clean clothes in their own drawers. I showed them how the shower worked with hot and cold water mixed, and asked them to hang their wet towels on a hook to dry. They always washed their hands before meals and then said a prayer of thanks to God. I showed them how to make a bed with sheets, blankets, and a pillow, and asked them to make their beds every day before breakfast. I washed and dried their clothes and showed them how to fold items and put them in their assigned drawer.

Keeping the papers, pencils, and crayons in order and cleaning up after themselves was a challenge. On the street, they had had nothing but the clothes on their backs, and perhaps a few shillings for their next meal. In the garage, I prepared an area for school supplies, including several coloring and exercise books. I asked them to clean up the area at the end of the day and to keep their work area neat, not spread out all over the floor.

❧

The boys had a strong Christian faith in God, who, they trusted, would take care of them. Whenever I went shopping, the boys always wanted to go. One day, they showed me a tiny newsstand with a tin roof where they had slept during that bad storm. I took a photo of it with them inside. We took things slow. I didn't allow them in the main house. It was a probationary period. Paul was pleasant and cool with the boys, leaving the rearing and discipline to me. This was my project. In the future, we'd have to find a private school for them and pay for it ourselves, but Paul never objected.

After a few days, we broke the news to Howard and Nancy, and they were horrified. "What do you think you are doing, bringing street kids into your home? It is dangerous. They will steal from you and take advantage."

We asked that they meet the boys, so they drove over to our place and met each of them. They realized these boys were just kids with unfortunate lives. Nancy stood there in the driveway, with a big smile, and said, "Nice to meet you, boys. Do you know how lucky you are?"

They replied, "Yes, Mum, we thank God every day."

She turned to me, shaking her head in disbelief, and said, "I hope you are right, for your sake. I am amazed they are so polite, well-spoken, and well-mannered."

Nancy soon grew to accept them, even inviting us over to use the pool and teach them how to swim. Howard just shook his head.

❧

After a lengthy investigation and talking to private schools in our area, I realized it was impossible to place them nearby. These schools refused to take street kids, even if they had a home. One of the principals mentioned a new school starting up in Naivasha, about an hour north. I made an appointment, and we drove up to meet the director, Winnie, at the brand-new Valleys Lily School, grades one through twelve, located on a small hill overlooking Lake Naivasha. I introduced Paul and myself, and explained that Paul worked for an NGO. I then explained how upset I was to see these helpless children. Finally, I told her how I met the boys and slowly got to know them. I let her know that I had interviewed nearby security guards, who said they were good boys who did not steal or sniff glue. Finally, I told her about the terrible storm and our decision to bring them home. When I was finished, she was in tears. "Bless you, child," she said.

After a few moments to collect herself, she stood and said, "I would like to interview each of the boys." After their interviews, they toured the school compound, chapel, dormitories, classrooms, and dining area. Winnie met with Paul and me later and agreed to accept them on a provisional basis. "They will have a big challenge, adjusting to the new environment here as well as beginning to learn and study. But I'm willing to give them the chance."

We thanked her and collected the requirements for uniforms, books, and items to bring to the dormitory. I smiled, shook her hand, and heaved a sigh of relief, so happy that they could finally attend school, make friends, and play sports like normal kids. She had heard my plea, and she understood my motive as a mother. We were going to give them a chance for a good life.

I quickly got the boys a set of uniforms, shoes, and the required books. The school was brand-new, and the semester had already begun, so the environment was new to all the kids. We got duffel bags for their belongings and took them up to drop them off on opening day. Paul and I were the only white parents in the sea of Kenyan parents and their kids, but everyone welcomed us. The boys stood in their new uniforms, putting on brave faces for everyone. They hugged us and waved goodbye when we departed.

❧

Things got back to normal at home for Paul and me. We made trips to Naivasha on Sunday for Parents' Day and whenever they had ceremonies. The boys returned at the end of each semester and came home to stay with us on their break.

They had wanted to go to school but had no idea how hard it would be. Each boy was behind the others in their age group, and I was sure they were self-conscious. They struggled to learn how to read, study, and complete their homework assignments.

Suddenly, they had all this structure, schedules, and discipline. Life on the streets was harsh, but they lived free. Would they regret wanting to go to school? I wasn't sure.

Peter, the oldest boy, sometimes rebelled against the rules and bullied Albert. Steven and Chap 30Peter were close friends and got along well. At home, Peter started challenging authority, becoming belligerent, and sometimes lying about his behavior. He began fighting and bullying Albert. I disciplined him several times, and nothing worked. Finally, I told Peter to go back to the street if he could not respect and obey the house rules. Steve always went with him, but without fail, they always called me after two or three days and repented, "We are so sorry, Mum. Please, can we come home?" I took them back again and expanded the punishment. It was a work in progress for all of us.

I asked the boys what street life was like. They eagerly shared their stories of life on the street, describing a very hostile environment in which each boy could not trust the others. If they received some coins from begging, they had to hide their money at the end of the day. They would dig a small hole and deposit the coins there. Otherwise, it would be stolen when they slept. They had only the clothes on their back. They became a street family for safety reasons. When they slept at night on the grassy roundabouts, they would take off their shoes, tie them together, and sleep on top of them so they would not be stolen. They once introduced me to a tall, young homeless man who they said protected them from being beaten by the police. In bad weather, they would try to find shelter in storefront alcoves. A few kind shopkeepers in the area would look after them. They were true survivors!

I felt I was doing something important. The boarding school gave me time to do volunteer work. Paul and I continued to travel as often as we could. Paul was very supportive and kind to the boys, leaving me as the "serious parent." I used the same guidelines I used in raising my own sons. It seemed to be working.

Part Seven

31

RECAP

This book's prologue describes the day when Paul was critically injured in a UN terrorist bombing in Baghdad—August 3, 2003. He suffered a fractured skull with hematomas in both frontal lobes. He was stable enough for the U.S. military to evacuate him to Landstuhl Hospital in Germany for further treatment. I had boarded a plane from Nairobi to Germany to be with him. . . .

The jet had finally taken off from Nairobi on August 3, 2003. At last, I was on my way to be with Paul at Landstuhl Military Hospital in Germany. I ordered a gin and tonic, reclined my seat, and closed my eyes, trying to make sense of everything that had happened. In a split second, our comfortable lives had been shattered by terrorism.

My flight departed Nairobi International Airport and leveled off at thirty-eight thousand feet on its journey to Frankfurt, Germany. I wondered how the future would be written and whether Paul would ever be his old self. Our marriage had been a sweet love story of mostly highs with a few lows we weathered together, resulting in an enduring love and complete trust in one another. I felt optimistic that Paul would survive his extensive injuries. I was still in my controlled crisis mode, numb yet hyper-alert, my mind focused on the facts, suppressing any worry or doubt. I refused to think he might die.

The cabin lights dimmed for the long overnight flight, and I dozed off. After a while, I got up, went to the bathroom, and then returned to my seat. Most of the passengers were sleeping. However, my mind was in overdrive about the unknown; there would be time to fall apart and grieve.

❧

I remembered that Paul and I had been through a lot in the past few years. While living in Northern Virginia, Paul had been diagnosed with prostate cancer on September 11, 2001, the day of the 9/11 terrorist attack, a double tragedy for us.

During the two-month pre-surgery treatment to shrink the tumor, Paul decided he would complete his final flight school lessons. By December, he received his single-engine, private pilot license. Over the Christmas holiday, Paul had surgery at Johns Hopkins Hospital in Baltimore, successfully removing all the cancer. After a few months of recuperation, we resumed our plans to sever our lifelong careers in the hi-tech world, completely changing our lives by moving to Africa for Paul to work for a UN humanitarian organization. His cancer was part of the past.

32

My flight was scheduled to arrive in Frankfurt at six a.m. Paul, and I met in Germany in 1989, when I accepted a one-year overseas assignment with the Army in Heidelberg. I was familiar with the area and comfortable with my limited German. I had rented a car and knew the route toward the French border to the Landstuhl Military Hospital, near Ramstein Air Force Base. As Paul's wife, with a military-dependent identification card, I should be able to get on the base without a problem, but I realized that, since the 9/11 attacks, U.S. security would be tight.

❧

In the past, I had always had my two boys with me. Now, Momma's chicks had grown up and left the nest, becoming independent, confident, handsome young men with lives and families of their own. I loved them more than anything. But at this moment, I felt very much alone.

The last time I spoke to Neil, he was trying to get a flight to Germany. I had only my laptop and email, but no cell phone for communication, because my Kenyan cell phone would not work in Germany. Today was 2003, before *smartphones*, *WhatsApp*, or *Zoom*, which would make international communication easier.

❧

Time dragged on. I tossed and turned, but I could not sleep. I noticed a large manila package in my backpack. Wayne had handed it to me just before I left for the flight, saying that it was mail that Paul was still getting at the IRC office, his last job. Someone thought there might be something time-sensitive that needed my attention. Our mail for the past year had all been forwarded to the IRC office, and Paul always brought it home. Since he no longer worked for them, the mail had been piling up. I opened the package and browsed the contents. Many items were ads that I separated for disposal. I received information on my new retirement package, which I put aside to review later. There were no personal letters because we used the internet to communicate with friends and family.

Next, I went through Paul's mail, mostly credit card bills, to see what might need to be paid. The first credit card bill was for twelve thousand dollars, with the explanation *"previous balance forwarded."* There was no indication of what had been purchased months before. The bills made no sense to me. We always paid off our credit card balances each month and had no other debts. The next credit card was for over nine thousand dollars, *with "previous balance forwarded."* "Oh my God, what is going on?" I thought, my mind now racing. The last bill was the largest, fourteen thousand dollars: *"previous balance forwarded."*

I was in total shock and could not fathom how Paul had accumulated over thirty-five thousand dollars in debt. It was more debt than his entire year's salary with the IRC! The *"previous balance forwarded"* meant he had these bills accumulating for some time. He had deliberately hidden this debt from me. After he retired from the army, Paul had numerous business credit cards because he often traveled internationally. He always handled his own accounts. I had no access or interest in his business finances. Slowly, I began to realize the depth of his deliberate deception. The bile in my stomach rose into my throat as I continued to deny the huge debt in front of me.

My mind continued to spin in confusion and disbelief. I was seeing a deliberate, deceptive, toxic cocktail that I was forced to drink. This betrayal of honesty in our marriage choked me and left me helpless. It was not the debt that angered me; it was his blatant betrayal of trust. He knew I would never see his credit card bills because he kept them at the office. How convenient! The overwhelming pain quickly turned to anger, becoming a large, dark cloud that hovered over me. Was there any love left outside that cloud? I could not feel any at that moment. My marriage was just a sham, and my love for him was a hollow vessel filled with unspoken lies. Was it possible for my world to be shattered twice in one week? The answer was yes! That is precisely what had just happened. *"You made your bed, now you have to lie in it,"* was the famous mantra Mother shared with me decades before. I had cherished the honesty and trust we had built. What did that even mean anymore? My marriage was now a joke, but I was not laughing! I thought we shared everything and had nothing to hide from each other. That was a big mistake!

❧

My mind swirled with questions I could not answer: How old was his debt? Was there even more? Did he have a mistress or a child with someone else? Was he now paying child support? Did he have a gambling problem? I never saw him gamble. Was he hiring prostitutes for blow jobs? I doubted it, but since his cancer surgery and subsequent impotence, I could not dismiss it. What was this secret side of his life? He had always seemed so open and transparent.

The critical question was, "Why had Paul deliberately chosen to lie by omission about this part of his life? Why had he done this to me?" The reality was that none of it made any difference. The issue was not the debt, his explanation, or how the money was spent. It was his casual betrayal. It was also the complete disregard for the trust and transparency I thought we had cemented in our marriage. That realization tore my heart apart, exposing my naked, vulnerable soul. The foundation of our marriage had been destroyed just like the

Canal Hotel had been destroyed. It was only because he had become a victim of the terrorist bombing that I now had hard evidence in my hand that our marriage was a sham, riddled with deception and lies, with secrets, a bold forgery of trust.

I felt totally alone in this new reality. Paul's Pandora's Box had been opened, exposing his deceit. I was untethered, blowing wildly in the wind, totally out of control. I just wanted to scream, but instead, I sat there, with my seatbelt fastened, silently choking on the bile of his deceit as the other passengers slept soundly. At the same time, Paul lay in a peaceful coma on his medevac flight to Ramstein. I never would have left my fulfilling career and moved to another continent if I had felt we were not in a solid marriage. I remember we talked about me giving up my career at its prime. He told me, "We are solid." Ya, sure!

I didn't even want to see him. I hated what he had done to me. How could I act like a loving wife when I knew our marriage was a fraud? The icing on the cake was that there would be no answers anytime soon, because he was still peacefully sleeping in his medicated coma. All previous concern for him turned to an all-consuming, pain-fueled rage sprinkled with shards of hate. Should I turn around and leave him? No, at the very least, I needed an explanation.

❧

Around 6 a.m., the United flight began its descent into Frankfurt International Airport. I was eating the popular German continental breakfast of small hard rolls with lots of butter, cheese, and assorted cured meats. The meal brought back memories from my time living in Germany. The strong coffee and thick cream gave me the renewed energy I would need for the day ahead.

Looking Back

Reflecting on my childhood, I recalled a picture of me, a four-year-old, in my kindergarten band uniform, playing the tambourine. That little girl was now a fifty-eight-year-old successful woman who had loved and trusted her husband completely. Was I that gullible and stupid? No, I had just trusted my husband. I wanted to take that tambourine back so I could pound on it until this horrible new reality disappeared and I could have my life back to normal.

33

After a smooth landing, I collected my luggage and my rental car and took off south on the autobahn, once more back in Germany, where I had lived for many years.

I knew I must put the betrayal issue aside for the moment because I could solve nothing. I was his wife and should be with him. How could I see him and not show disgust? Well, he wouldn't notice until he woke from his coma. I had time before I confronted him. I wondered to myself, how long would that take?

I drove through the gates of the Landstuhl Military Base with my military identification card and quickly found the Landstuhl Hospital and the Neurology Intensive Care Unit, ICU. A nurse informed me that the military C295 medevac plane from Kuwait would be landing soon. The injured would be transported to the hospital by a special bus. Many injured civilians were from the Canal Hotel Bombing in Baghdad. She said I needed to stay out of the way as they brought the injured inside. She showed me where I could stand, opposite the elevators on the second floor, to see each gurney arrive. Waiting, waiting, and more waiting again.

Two bright yellow school buses pulled up in front of the hospital. Each patient was offloaded onto a gurney, brought up in the elevator, and then wheeled through the ICU doors. All the patients were sedated, intubated, and covered in clean sheets, with bandages covering the numerous injuries. I knew I'd recognize Paul; however, the last gurney arrived on the floor just as the elevator doors shut. I stood there wondering if another bus would come.

❧

A young nurse in her twenties came out and sat down next to me. She was visibly shaken, fighting back tears. "Are you okay?" I asked.

She replied, "This group of patients is in very bad condition. Most of the injured are from the Canal Hotel bombing."

I introduced myself, "My name is Barbara Wolfe-Johnson. My husband was a victim of the bombing. His name is Paul Johnson. Has he arrived?"

She self-consciously said, Please forgive me for this emotional reaction."

"I admire your compassion and caring. It must be hard, day after day, seeing nothing but the badly injured," I replied.

She stood up and offered to check the list for Paul Johnson and returned to tell me, "Major Paul Johnson has arrived and needs to be cleaned up. Then you can see him."

It troubled me that I did not recognize Paul, but several men had head bandages, and all of them were intubated and very swollen. It wasn't easy to recognize him in a few brief seconds.

After ten minutes, she brought me to his private room in the ICU. There were machines everywhere—IVs, oxygen, intubation, and other monitors for heart rate and blood pressure. He was lying there in front of me, but it was not him. I felt sorrow for his condition, but only contempt for him as my husband. Deep down, I knew I probably still loved him, but my wound was so deep that I could not control my contempt. He was the man I had married, but I could not identify him.

❧

There was no one I could talk to. My best friend, Gloria, was in the U.S. I didn't want to share this with my sons, and I had no one in Kenya who would understand. His entire body was swollen. His head had been shaved and showed a neat craniotomy incision that went from ear to ear, now closed with staples. Numerous minor scrapes and cuts were visible on his face and seemed to be healing. His nose had a nasty cut on it as well. I could tell from the indented scar on his left cheek that this was where the shrapnel had penetrated.

The white sheet came to his waist, and various sensors were placed around his chest. The ventilator was doing the breathing for him. I should not have been distracted by his broad, hairy chest, still tanned and looking sexy, but I could not resist. The nurse told me that he had been fitted with a feeding tube on the left side of his chest, which went directly into the stomach. I took his hand and told him he had been in a bombing, but that he'd be okay. I still believed that. I maintained an emotionless demeanor when the nurse explained that the intubation tube would need to be cleaned at least once a day to avoid mucus buildup. She then left the room. I continued to stare at him.

After a few minutes, Paul started coughing and seemed to be choking on the tube down his throat. A loud beeper went off. The nurse ran into the room, turned off the beeper, and explained that the air tube was filling with mucus, and she needed to clean it. I watched as she disconnected the air tube and quickly cleared the blockage. She turned to me and asked, "Are you a nurse?" I said,"

No, why do you ask?"

She said, "Because you kept so calm, most family members freak out, thinking the patient is dying."

I said something like, "I knew it wasn't too serious. "Should I tell her I hated him and wanted to pull the plug?

❧

Later that day, an ICU doctor came in to say he had reviewed Paul's records and was going to do another CT scan of the head and neck. Facial bones had been fractured, and some bones were floating, causing a fragment to lodge near the left optic nerve, which resulted in a lack of dilation response. He was concerned that the eye might be lost, but wanted it confirmed.

❧

Relatives of the other injured personnel in the bombing had also arrived. Representatives from the U.S. Embassy Consulate in Germany arrived at the hospital that morning to assist the families of the injured. A very caring embassy-consulate staffer told me that all of Paul's belongings had been retrieved from his hotel room in Baghdad and that the package was transported with him on his gurney, including his medical records. She also mentioned that all rings, including his wedding ring, had been removed upon arrival for his first triage in Iraq, but his wedding ring had not been found. I described the ring to her and requested that she try to find it. We had matching wide 18-carat gold bands specially made for our wedding. They were very special. The ring was never recovered. Was that a sign?

The Embassy staff were very professional and compassionate. I could tell they had done this, many times. They briefed us on Fisher House, a small house next to the hospital that provides rooms for families of injured patients. I'd be staying there. They issued each of us a mobile phone for use while in Germany. What a blessing. I also received a base entrance card for my rental car. The staffer added that the Embassy was processing new U.S. passports for all the injured. She provided her card and asked me to call if I needed anything or had any questions. I was so reassured and comforted that we were finally under the protective umbrella of the U.S.

The military in Baghdad must have checked his wallet and learned Paul was a retired army major. Even though he was now a civilian, he was being treated as Major Paul Johnson, U.S. Army (retired). It was not long before a representative from the IMF in Washington, DC, who knew Paul, called to comfort me and offer any support possible. He had agreed to fly Paul's oldest daughter, Ruby, to Germany. Both Neil and Ruby were on their way.

I stopped by the post exchange on base and bought a compact disc player for Paul to have in his room. He loved classical music, and it might soothe him. The compact discs include his favorites, Enya, Beauty and the Beast, Kenny G, and The Four Seasons. Finally, I went to Fisher House and settled in. It had been a long day.

❧

Finally, Neil emailed me to say he was already at Landstuhl, so we met up. He had already seen Paul and said he looked very critical. I could tell in his eyes that he thought Paul might not make it. I understood. It was so good to have Neil there, and Ruby arrived later that day. We all took up residence in my room at Fisher House, with Ruby and me in the double bed and Neil sleeping on the floor. Finally, family was by my side.

Early the next morning, I entered Paul's room, and they were preparing him to be transported to another hospital. The doctor told me that Paul had severe head trauma but that the latest CT scan looked good. They had also done a CT scan of his neck, and it was not broken.

They wanted a German specialist to determine if the optic nerve of the left eye could somehow be repaired. They put him in an ambulance, and we followed it west on the autobahn to Homberg Hospital. He was now under German care, which meant dealing with the language barrier and strict German hospital rules. Visiting hours were restricted to two hours, from 11 a.m. to 1 p.m., in their Neuro ICU. At Landstuhl, I could come and go whenever I wanted.

❧

The attending neurologist said they would check his optic nerve. Because it had been more than three days since the accident, he doubted that anything could be done because of the loss of blood supply to the nerve itself, but he would examine him to be sure.

Neil, Ruby, and I had nothing to do after 1 p.m. on that Sunday, so we went to the old town of Landstuhl, walked around the castle ruins, and had lunch in the small village where we recognized other families who were also living in Fisher House. We soon formed a loose support network with each other. We were comrades in this tragedy.

The next morning, Neil, Ruby, and I drove to Homburg to see Paul again. He was still heavily sedated. After visiting hours, I drove them to Heidelberg to show Ruby the Heidelberg Castle Ruins, and we had dinner. It was a diversion for all of us, amid the crisis that we had no control over. Their caring was a balm to my pain.

I returned to the ICU in Homberg the next day, and the attending physician explained that the optic nerve was severed and the sight in the left eye was permanent. A male nurse said they were reducing the coma medication to try to wake him up. That made me very upset. Why would they attempt to wake him now? There was no point. If the eye was gone, he should be returned to Landstuhl. I asked why and got an answer in German.

Ruby and I approached Paul, and he moved a bit. I took his hand and told him again that I was here, that he'd been in a bombing, and that he was going to be okay. I asked him if he understood, and he nodded. Then, he gave me a firm shake of his hand, a signal I recognized so well. I broke down in tears. The heavily guarded floodgates had opened. He was still in there and knew me. At that moment, nothing mattered except that he was still alive. My heart surged with the same intense love I always had for him.

❧

There was no longer any reason for him to be in the Homburg hospital. I called the Landstuhl ICU doctor and told the doctor that the eye was gone. The doctor said Paul should not be woken up but should be returned to Landstuhl. He issued the order. Then I went back into the Homburg ICU and told them to contact Landstuhl. They should not wake him up, but rather sedate him again and return him to Landstuhl. I had been told that his pain would be excruciating if they woke him up. I did not make friends with those German doctors, but I asked questions, gathered information, and acted.

❧

Once he returned to Landstuhl, they checked him over. They determined he was stable enough to be scheduled on the next available medevac plane, along with me, his wife, to Andrews AFB in Washington, DC, and from there, taken to Walter Reed Army Hospital for continued treatment. This came as a huge relief to me. Walter Reed was the very best!

Neil and Ruby had to return to the U.S., but both were encouraged by the progress made at Landstuhl.

34

At 6 a.m., I was standing in Paul's room at Landstuhl Hospital, ready to accompany him on a military medical evacuation flight to Washington, DC, then transport to Walter Reed Army Hospital in Bethesda, Maryland.

The doctor explained they had put Paul in a deep coma for the flight. He was so swollen he looked like a mannikin on the gurney, covered with white sheets, with at least four machines lined up between his legs. They wheeled him down to the hospital's main entrance, where he was loaded, along with many others, into medical transport buses for transport to Ramstein Air Force Base. The Air Force C-295 jet on the tarmac looked like a huge guppy with its mouth open, but in fact, the plane's tail was wide open. Walking up the metal ramp in the back, I saw no first-, business-, or economy-class seats; just rows and rows of gurneys as far as the eye could see. The gurneys were stacked three high, like bunk beds extending the entire length of the plane. Each doctor sat in front of their assigned patient. I sat next to Paul's doctor in a jump seat attached to the plane's fuselage. Paul was in front of us at eye level.

I took it all in and was stunned. This huge jet had been modified solely for medical evacuations. It was shocking and eerie at the same time. However, it was today's reality! You'll never see the inside of this plane on the news. How practical, yet how sad, that the U.S. needed these sophisticated, medically configured jets for the medical evacuation of its service members.

Huge engines were so loud that it was impossible to talk to Paul's doctor, who was sitting next to me. They passed out earplugs to dull the roar, and I tried to sleep but could not. I was in a trance, moving forward in time but not knowing what would hit me next in this cruel joke of reality. It was a very long flight with no meals, coffee, or movies. I brought a book to read, but the lighting was poor, so I just stared at Paul in front of me.

We landed at Andrews Air Force Base in Washington, DC, at 3 a.m. It was still dark. Military buses were waiting on the tarmac. I watched as each patient was removed from the plane and placed on a medical transport bus. As a military dependent, I was told I would go in a van. I realized that I was the only next of kin accompanying an injured person. Most families of the wounded were already waiting in the U.S.

The van departed with other medical personnel and me to Walter Reed Army Hospital in Bethesda, Maryland. We drove through the security gate, and they dropped me off at the front of the hospital, alone in the darkness.

❧

As I made my way up the front stairs, I noticed a female nurse walking out of the building at the end of her shift. I guess I looked strange standing there at 4 a.m. because she asked, "Why are you here?"

I replied, "My husband was in the Canal Hotel bombing in Baghdad and had been medically evacuated here with a TBI." She replied, "Well, he won't be out of here in a week." Her candid answer hit me hard, but was probably very accurate. I wished her a good night, then, totally exhausted, went to the front desk, explained why

I was there, and was escorted to another Fisher House in the back of the compound. After a few restless hours, I walked to the rear of the hospital, trying to get my bearings in this huge facility. Signs directed me to the front lobby.

The ceiling of the main lobby extended through the second story and was bathed with light from large windows above. There were several seating areas, plus an excellent coffee bar. A woman at the information desk gave me directions to Paul's ward in the neurology ICU. Next, I was introduced to Paul's case manager, who described the procedures to expect within the hospital. I handed her a thick paper file containing all his medical records from Iraq. The case manager was my single point of contact, and I got her card. I requested the name of the doctor in charge of Paul, whom I would meet to learn the plan for his recovery.

I realized I was starving, so I had a quick breakfast in the expansive cafeteria in the rear of the building. After a satisfying American breakfast of hot scrambled eggs, crisp bacon, hash browns, coffee, and fresh orange juice, I was ready to face the day. I had only packed a few casual outfits when I flew to Germany. My garments were limited, but it didn't bother me at all. I was not here to make a fashion statement. I was dressed in jeans, a faded T-shirt, and no belt or jacket. My backpack was my purse.

Following the case manager's directions, I entered Paul's ward and asked about him. A male, military male nurse took me over to his bed and mentioned that they had reduced his drugs to wake him up. Paul was still unconscious but looked comfortable. They had removed the intubation tube, and he was now breathing on his own. He seemed more like himself without all the tubes and machines. All the bandages had been removed from his head. Again, I saw his shaved head with the craniotomy incision that extended from ear to ear over the top of his head. The staples were still there. Then I noticed an S-like scar that snaked down his neck. I was confused by its presence. I'd ask the doctor about it. The shrapnel wound, about an inch long, just below his left cheekbone, had been perfectly stitched, probably by a plastic surgeon. It was almost healed, but there was a clear depression under the scar where the metal projectile had shattered his cheek and skull. He looked peaceful.

❧

While Paul was still sleeping, I turned to a very young, clean-cut, handsome soldier in the next bed. His Mom, about my age, was by his side, looking overwhelmed. Both of his arms had been amputated just below the elbows, and new prosthetic limbs had been attached. He was trying his best to get them to work and, although frustrated, seemed very upbeat. When I asked how he was doing, he told me about an incendiary explosive device, IED explosion in Iraq that had caused his injuries. His focus was not on the injuries but on missing his buddies and wanting to get back to Iraq. His Mom said she was glad he was alive, but added in a soft voice, "So young to be encumbered." She avoided the word "disabled." I wished him a swift recovery.

The male nurse suddenly called out, "Mrs. Johnson. Paul was coming out of his coma. I watched him from the foot of his bed so he could see me and waited. He awoke but seemed disoriented. He looked directly at me and said nothing, then looked at the nurse and said in a loud voice, "God damn it, I'm hungry. I want some pizza and a cold beer. When can I get some f—ing food? I'm f—ing hungry!" Paul continued this out-of-character colloquial rant for a few moments. The nurse went over to calm and distract him. I was shocked by his profanity. He was not the easy-going, polite Paul I knew. He was completely focused on his hunger and still had not acknowledged me. The nurse laughed, turned to ask if he had been in the Navy. I shook my head no, hoping that this behavior was a result of the medication and not the injury.

After a few minutes, Paul calmed down. I went to his side, took his hand, and explained that he had been in the Canal Hotel bombing in Baghdad and had a brain injury requiring surgery. I added that he had been medically evacuated first to Landstuhl Hospital, then to

Walter Reed Hospital, where he was now. I also told him about the loss of sight in his left eye. I'm not sure it all sank in.

He gathered his thoughts and dispassionately recalled his memories immediately after the bombing. He described things vividly, and his memory of that day was very accurate. Then he went off on a tangent, saying that when he woke up, his dream was interrupted. He had been in the middle of these incredibly vivid, drug-induced, James Bond-like dreams of espionage and adventure. He had many dreams while in the medically induced coma, and they were all trying to escape his consciousness. I was so glad he had been entertained while I sat wondering if he'd live or die. The conversation was all about himself.

He showed no emotion at all during my entire visit. He had no reaction when I told him of his injuries. I'm not sure what I was expecting, but it was probably the guy I had married. No, he was not in that bed. I did not attempt to hug him. Soon, he was tired and dozed off, without his pizza and beer.

❧

I spoke to the ICU's chief neurosurgeon, who had already reviewed Paul's extensive files, which were almost two inches thick. He gave me details about how Paul had been medically evacuated by chopper to a military triage point near Baghdad. He was examined, sedated, and immediately intubated.

The doctor said that Paul had lost over thirty pounds while being fed through a tube into his stomach at Landstuhl. When I asked about the s-shaped scar on Paul's neck, he explained that whenever a person has shrapnel in his head, before they attempt to remove it, they make an incision and clamp off the affected carotid artery to the brain to prevent a bleed out, then they remove the shrapnel. "Yikes, he could have died," I thought. Paul received massive doses of antibiotics to help prevent pneumonia while being intubated for almost three weeks. Now, he was extremely weak and could no longer walk. He would be receiving physical therapy to train him to walk with sight in only one eye.

He indicated that the brain surgery he had in Kuwait was a technique he had taught his neurology students at Walter Reed. He was pleased with the results of his student's work. I had several questions about the brain injury and what we might expect in the future. I explained that Paul and I both wanted to continue our lives in Kenya if possible. He frankly said that the first year was the most critical, and neurological issues could arise. He did not encourage us to return to Kenya, but stressed that if we did, we would need to have enough cash on hand in case something went wrong and we needed to fly back to Walter Reed Hospital immediately. He did not elaborate on what might go wrong. I added to my list of things to do before I left, getting out ten thousand dollars in American Express Traveler's Checks, just in case.

The doctor had ordered a battery of physical and psychological tests, including motor skills and other sophisticated tests, to determine if there was any brain damage that affected mood, personality, memory, or problem-solving skills. Due to the loss of sight in his eye, he no longer had the depth perception necessary to walk, especially going downstairs. He would need extensive physical therapy to learn to walk again with monovision.

The next day, he was transferred from the ICU to the Neurology floor for further treatment. His appetite had always been good, but now he barely ate anything. He was exhausted, confined to a wheelchair, and became sullen and depressed. He had also lost some good friends in the bombing and was suffering from the entire tragedy. I could not imagine what he was going through. Nor did he share any of his thoughts. Paul was inside his body, but his thoughts and emotions were locked away deep in his soul. He slept most of the time, which I expected. Once awake, I would try to convince him to get in the wheelchair and would push him to physical therapy.

The days turned into one long fog, and I do not remember many specifics. It was clear that my job now was to get him off his butt and functioning back in the normal world. I felt he was fortunate. The only permanent damage appeared to be the loss of sight in his left eye. Maybe my gut had been right.

This pattern continued for days—extremely tired, sleeping most of the day, and refusing to eat. He was very quiet and did not want to do anything. I told the doctor that he seemed.

Okay, get over it, I said to myself. It was not like Paul to be so stuck. He needed to get out of his funk. I hauled him from the bed to the wheelchair and wheeled him into a beautiful outdoor courtyard. The gardens on the fourth floor were lovely, with flowering bushes, ample walkways, and benches. It was a great way to remove us from the hospital environment.

I'd sit on a bench, he would sit in his wheelchair, and we began discussions about what we wanted in the future. His mind was focused, and his speech was normal, with no more profanity. He wanted to stay in Kenya, and that was my first choice as well. Making that happen became my primary focus.

He did not express any feelings of sadness, regret, anger, or apathy. He was very serious during our discussions and never joked as he often did. The damage the bombing had done was not like an amputated limb. It was inside his brain. I did not pressure him, knowing he needed time to recuperate. I worried about his lack of appetite, so when I could, I'd bring him a pint of Häagen-Dazs ice cream, which he always loved and finished every bit.

By the end of each day, we were both exhausted. While he slept, I went to the gym to clear my head. I'd been sitting on my butt for days and days. I needed some exercise, then I could sleep better. The elliptical bike was a great distraction, and I zoned out after forty minutes. The hospital cafeteria was amazing — lots of selections, fast food, delicious entrees, a hearty soup-and-salad bar, and, of course, an ice cream bar. As a result, I started gaining a few pounds, sometimes enjoying steak, Italian, or Mexican dishes. I had been American-food-deprived while living in Africa. This was a temptation I rarely resisted. After all, I needed my strength. I'd drop by the cafeteria on my way to Fisher House for soup, salad, and maybe some ice cream, then head to my room.

I thought I would meet several family members at the hospital, but I never saw any at the cafeteria or even in the hallway. Then I realized that most family members were waiting for their injured soldier to come home once he was released from Walter Reed. I was comfortable being alone and was on an important mission.

❧

Back in my room one night, I got out Paul's credit card bills and contacted each company for information on the accumulated purchases. However, because my name was not on the card, I was not authorized to be given any information—another dead end.

A few close friends and coworkers began arriving to see Paul, and he soon became very engaged in discussing his experience. Several men from the IMF team at the Canal Hotel came to visit. From their discussions, I got a much more accurate picture of what happened immediately after the bomb struck the building. Paul was under contract to provide security to the IMF personnel, so immediately after the blast, he tried to stand up and attend to his clients. But he had a ten-foot pole in his head that convinced him to lie down and wait for the medics. Paul was clearly the most seriously wounded, so the soldiers placed him on a gurney and hauled him down two sets of stairs, being very careful to hold the ten-foot pole still impaled in his cheek firmly. The soldiers put his gurney on the grass outside and told him to wait for evacuation.

His associates described the shrapnel as a light piece of aluminum ceiling frame used to hold prefab ceiling tiles in place. Believe it or not, a small piece of the actual piece of shrapnel had been transported with his records on the gurney when he was evacuated to Walter Reed. It still had dried blood on it and became his talisman.

❧

For days, I functioned on autopilot, taking one day at a time. My full-time job was talking to doctors and specialists, trying to understand Paul's progress. There was an internet room with three computers for patients and relatives on each floor. At least once a day, I'd review my email and provide relatives and friends a progress report.

Doctors were everywhere in this military teaching hospital. Doctors on duty one day may not be there the next day. It was hard to tell who was in charge. At his first physical therapy session, he was told to stand up from his wheelchair. A tall, large, muscular therapist put a strong strap around Paul's chest, under his arms, and stood behind Paul for support. Then he told him to walk. Paul took only a few steps before he collapsed, exhausted. A few other soldiers, some single or double amputees, were working out while a therapist stood nearby to provide guidance and encouragement. I realized that this was a private place for the wounded to struggle to improve. They did not want an audience. As I walked out, I thanked God that Paul had received relatively minor injuries. Other young soldiers were struggling to walk with multiple prosthetic limbs that they would need for the rest of their lives. Others, with permanent spinal injuries, sat in wheelchairs. It was heartbreaking. The war was ongoing, but the news never showed the young soldiers' reality of the casualties of war.

❧

At last, Gloria came down from Connecticut to see us. We had known each other for over twenty-five years. She visited us in Germany in 1990, and we took her all over the country, sightseeing. It was so good to see her. She understood me and knew what I was going through. I shared my secret with her about his credit card betrayal, the impotence, lack of affection, and my uncertainty about trust in our marriage. She advised me to focus on today, and things would work out, one way or the other. It was good advice.

I continued to stay at Fisher House. My routine was to wake up by 6:30 a.m., shower, get dressed, go to the cafeteria, have breakfast, and then see Paul. Then I'd get him into the wheelchair to take him for a spin around the hospital. When he napped, I'd talk to doctors or use the internet, have lunch, and then go back to see him and bring him any news. He'd have Physical Therapy, PT, after lunch, then doze off again. I'd grab my gym bag and work out for a while. Finally, I'd end up back in the cafeteria for dinner, then back to my room to zone out in peace and quiet.

Paul took tests for intelligence, problem-solving, and personality, among others. A specialist would bring him a multi-page test and ask him to complete it. I tried a couple of problem-solving questions and didn't know the answers, but Paul had no problem at all. I was so relieved. A physical exam showed that his lower jaw, lips, and mouth were all numb, as well as the left side of his face.

Another problem was that he could not open his mouth very wide. At first, he had trouble chewing but soon got the hang of it. The muscles of the left eye looked normal. Only the optic nerve had been damaged. But after a couple of weeks, the eye muscles grew lethargic, turning the eyeball to the left and making it very noticeable. He was fitted with a large black eyepatch, which he started wearing everywhere. The patch allowed people to look at him without being distracted by his wandering eye. Now he looked like a pirate with a shaven head. There was no parrot on his shoulder, only because I'd left his parrot, Quique, in Kenya.

❧

Paul's IMF employer visited us at Walter Reed and explained that he had arranged for Paul to remain on full payroll until Paul returned to work full-time. The IMF would pay all his medical expenses. I felt the overwhelming urge to go up to him and give him a big hug, thanking him so much for his company's generosity. Instead, I started to cry, explaining that this would enable us to return to Kenya without financial worries. He then expressed, "Paul is an asset to the NGO world. We want him to recover and continue supporting his humanitarian efforts in Africa. The IMF will also provide Paul with a small furnished apartment near the Chevy Chase metro while he is still in DC for medical therapy. What a huge relief! My financial fears were set aside. At last, the future was looking a bit brighter. Paul needed time to heal and could do it in Kenya.

On the second anniversary of the 9/11 Terrorist Attack on the U.S., we were told that President George W. Bush and the First Lady, Barbara, would be visiting the wounded soldiers at Walter Reed in an expression of appreciation for their service. Paul was chosen to be in the group to see the President. A separate hospital wing was prepared and scanned by the Secret Service before his arrival. President Bush walked up to us and introduced himself and his wife, Barbara. We had a brief conversation with them. They were both very cordial and supportive of Paul's need to heal. Photos were taken, then would be signed by the President and sent to us.

35

After several weeks at Walter Reed, Paul's doctors agreed he could be released to receive follow-up outpatient treatment at a National Rehabilitation Hospital in Washington, DC. The National Rehab Center's mission was to assist patients to become independent enough to live a quality life. Walter Reed made all the arrangements for him to receive daily outpatient treatment. He packed his things, thanked his doctors and nurses, and was discharged.

Paul went for therapy every day. We moved into the one-bedroom furnished apartment provided by IMF management. The flat was in the Chevy Chase neighborhood, a nice part of town, close to the Washington Metro system, shopping, and a variety of restaurants.

Each day, we'd go arm in arm to steady him for his daily treatments at the National Rehabilitation Hospital via Metro. He could walk a short distance, then must catch his breath. He was slowly getting stronger but had problems with depth perception, especially on stairs or uneven ground. Sometimes he'd trip and fall, not seeing an uneven sidewalk or a subtle step down. He'd just curse under his breath, pick himself up, and continue.

Many mornings, after breakfast, we began walking through the streets of DC, taking the Metro to various places. September was a beautiful sunny time with warm days. The leaves were turning shades of yellow, red, orange, and brown. It was a perfect time to be outside.

My favorite destination was Rock Creek Park, where I put him through his paces. I would lead, and he would follow through the dirt trails and then off the trail, through the bushes, up hills, and eventually, through uneven, rocky terrain. I could see him getting stronger. It seemed like his emotions were muted. He didn't complain during our treks though the woods but never thanked me either. Once he regained leg strength, he quickly regained his balance. He treated it like a job and never complained, but he tired quickly.

His improvement allowed us to try various outdoor restaurants for lunch. We always loved Washington, and on weekends, if the weather was good, we walked along the Old Canal in Georgetown to enjoy nature. As time went on, he slowly got much stronger. However, the long afternoon naps would continue for months. His Mom and sister came to visit from Utah, and he was elated to see family.

Paul was getting stronger and more confident each day. Still getting tired after rehab sessions, he'd lie down for a long afternoon nap. He signed up for a special driver training course for people with monovision and proudly earned a new DC driver's license. That was a little scary to me.

His brain had been seriously injured. He had become serious, often very quiet, reading or watching a video. He had lost his quick wit. He was there physically, but his personality had changed. He never acted elated or relieved when he reached a physical milestone in his recovery.

❧

After a couple of weeks of living in the apartment, I told Paul about the bills I had found in his mail for over $35,000 in credit card debt. I showed him the statements. He expressed no memory of them. I told him I was devastated because he had kept this a secret from me.

I told him he lied to me by omission. He was irritated that I had brought up the whole thing. Finally, with no regret or emotion, he said, "I do not remember what the debt was for."

Paul offered me no comfort or reassurance. He did not apologize or feel sorry for hurting me by not telling me about them. His demeanor was flat, like it had been in the hospital. It was almost as if his emotions had been severed. He said flatly, without a bit of remorse, "It is my business and not yours." I replied, "It would have become my business if you had died in the bombing. It would have been my business if we had tried to buy a house and were turned down because of your credit."

It was now clear that he felt he could keep things from me. When I asked him to request past statements so we could find out, he agreed. His lack of remorse shocked me. It was as if I had told him he had broken my heart, and he had flatly replied, "Sorry to hear that, but not my problem." That was not the Paul I had fallen in love with. The statements could shed some light on the mystery.

Being with him twenty-four hours a day, I noticed how quiet and distant he was. All the closeness had died the previous year. We were in the same room but miles apart. He had survived a horrible terrorist attack, and his entire body was traumatized, not just his brain. I assumed this behavior was due to the trauma.

If I am sick or have a headache, I'm not in a good mood either. How much time would he need to recover and get back to work? Would he be the same old Paul I met in Germany, or someone else? He was different in so many subtle ways. It may take time for his easygoing personality to re-emerge. I was puzzled by this huge change in him, but I hoped my old Paul would return. All the doctors told me that I needed to be very patient. However, patience is not one of my accomplished virtues.

We had long talks about whether we should move back to Kenya or move back to the US. Kenya still called to us. We both wanted to try to make it work. Neither of us wanted to re-enter the rat race in Washington. Kenya was under our skin.

Paul was eager to return to work at least part-time to prove to his colleagues that the injury had not diminished his mental acuity. He spoke to Wayne and Howard in Nairobi by phone. They reassured him that he was welcome back as soon as he was able. We wanted to give it a try.

❧

After a couple of weeks in October, Paul was much improved, getting around very well on his own and still attending his daily rehab sessions. I felt confident he could manage on his own for another couple of weeks before he booked a flight back to Kenya.

Before I returned to Kenya, I needed some sanity in my life, if only for a few days. I called Gloria to see if I could visit. She welcomed me with open arms. I poured my heart out to her, not just about Paul's severe injury, but his impotence and the lack of any affection in our lives. She listened, then replied, "You just need to hang in there and see what the future holds." After a few days, I returned to DC and continued my flight home to Nairobi.

Paul would return in early November. His prognosis was good. The doctors estimated it would be about six months before he'd be fully recovered. They did not like the idea that he was leaving the country, but I remember his neurologist warning, "In the first year, anything could happen, and if it does, you should get him on a plane to Walter Reed immediately."

36

Landing in Nairobi, I was completely numb after two months on this rollercoaster. I had tried my best to suppress my negative feelings and continue to soldier on. My emotions were completely locked away inside my gut. I could not cry. I knew I had to take it a day at a time. Once I was with him again, I realized how deeply I loved him, and just wanted him to apologize for the pain he caused me and promise to be truthful in the future. But, he indignantly and emphatically refused, leaving a rift between us that he didn't see.

Returning home to Kenya was a soothing balm for my soul. I began to relax. There was still stress in my life, but at least I knew Paul would be fine. My gut had proven to be right! A small consolation.

In late November, I welcomed Paul, the survivor, back home with mixed emotions. At the Nairobi International Airport, I hugged him and said, "Welcome Home," recalling everything he had endured since the bombing only four months before.

He was still very thin, his beautiful, light-brown, curly hair now very gray, trying to poke through his shaved white scalp. Healed scars drew attention to the trauma he had suffered. Two red scars were very visible on his face—one across his nose at an angle, maybe from flying glass, and the other on his upper right cheek where the metal rod entered his skull. I now observed a closed, injured soul that communicated on a superficial level, with no feelings or emotions.

❧

He surprised me with his new monovision Maryland driver's license. Paul was still able to drive. That sounded a little scary, but Paul was a very careful driver, albeit a bit too fast for me. Rehab taught him to move his head back and forth to see the entire 180 degrees in front of him with only his right eye.

When he was back behind the wheel, I watched him a lot at first, but soon regained confidence. He was still a very safe driver, though I still screamed, "Watch out!" whenever I saw the potential for danger. That's just my gut telling me I didn't want to die.

❧

When he arrived home, the Kenya boys greeted him with love and relief. The dogs went crazy when they saw him. He finally felt at home. Yumiko, our Japanese neighbor, arranged a homecoming party for Paul with all our friends. There was relief in everyone's eyes when they saw Paul. He got lots of welcome-home hugs. It was a joyous occasion, but he tired quickly, excused himself, and returned to our home. It was obvious that he was traumatized.

Paul's recovery was slow, but the prognosis was good. He became consumed with his need to resume work, but worried that the stigma of a traumatic brain injury could hamper his future career opportunities. Perhaps his colleagues would regard him as having diminished intellectual capacity, as less capable, and as no longer his former self. I reminded him of all the extensive intelligence and problem-solving tests he had passed with flying colors at Walter Reed. Perception was reality to him. He would have to face it head-on.

❧

We still intended to remain in Kenya if we could manage financially. The IMF salary would make that possible. I was so relieved he had no medical bills from the Army. Military insurance paid for everything.

I assumed a background role, while Paul's new routine included spending hours on his laptop, watching videos, reading, and napping for hours.

Soon, the boys went back to boarding school, and we had privacy. Gone were the distractions of life with kids and the hired Kenya "mum" who cooked and cleaned for them.

Often, after breakfast, we took the dogs, Eiger and Sasha, for a walk in the vast tea plantation just a short way down our dirt road. Early morning coolness lingered, and the sun had not yet emerged from behind the Tigoni hills. This plantation spread over several acres, all on steep hills for good drainage. Each field was divided into large sections, separated by walking paths. Within each section, narrow and steep rows crisscrossed the terrain. Experienced Kenyan women were busy early each morning, handpicking the mature tea leaves. We greeted them from a distance with a wave. "*Jambo, Habari Yako?*" I greatly admired these hardworking Kenyan women, who seemed to be the strength of the country. They also chopped elephant grass along the road and hauled it back home on their backs to feed their one milk cow. They would sell vegetables on the sides of the road, while a baby slept in the kanga sling on her back. Others washed clothes in a nearby stream. Young children fetched water in gallon buckets and hauled it back home on top of their heads. Men, on the other hand, were always seen together, outside a small shop, chatting with their neighbors and friends, no doubt, about important business.

Okay, back to our morning walk. With Paul in the lead, we cut across tea sections, making our way through the rows of vibrant tea bushes that came up above my waist. It was useless to try to look for snakes. After a hard rain, sometimes I had to hold onto the branches to avoid sliding down the path. Our destination was a beautiful pond at the base of the valley. His balance had improved dramatically. I was pleased.

Eiger jumped into the water and waited for us to throw him sticks. He was obsessed, refusing to return the stick in his mouth, swimming in circles, and waiting for another stick to be thrown. It was a lovely, peaceful time in the middle of nature. After almost an hour of non-stop swimming, Eiger exhausted himself and swam to shore with six or eight sticks in his mouth and a big grin on his snout. We retraced our path up the hill to our log home, had lunch, and took a short nap. I felt blessed to be living in such a beautiful place. Time passed slowly, day by day.

❧

With more time on my hands and not much to do, I set out on a mission to improve the flower gardens. I created a low-maintenance cactus garden that could withstand the heat and adorned the garden with a variety of local volcanic rocks. Sometimes, I'd ask Paul to drive to the rift valley with me to collect really unusual volcanic rocks.

I loved reading books, so I found an old English-language used bookstore in Karen, choosing books to teach me about Kenya: *Out of Africa*, *Born Free*, *The Flame Trees of Thika*, *I Dreamed of* Africa, *The Constant Gardener*, and *West with the Night*. They told stories of the British of the old days who moved to Kenya and tried to survive in the untamed bush.

In these early days, I tried to move on, but Paul's betrayal was never far from my thoughts. He had broken our sacred bond of trust without remorse. I was torn about leaving him. I still loved Kenya and the kids. When I returned to Nairobi in October, I had a conversation with Nancy, Howard's wife, and confidentially told her about Paul's betrayal and the unexplained thirty-five thousand dollar credit card debt. She listened carefully and was very clear, "He needs you now. There will always be time to leave him if you choose to, but now is not the time." She understood that I was struggling and suggested I see Father D'Agostino, the Catholic priest, and the psychiatrist I had met at his Nyumbani Children's Home. Desperate for validation and some resolution for our relationship, I agreed and made an appointment to meet "Father Dag," as he was called.

❧

Father Dag cordially invited me into his Nairobi residence. After a brief explanation about Nancy's referral, I described my marriage: for the first ten years, a loving marriage; then his prostate cancer surgery and impotence, loss of intimacy, and all affection. I reviewed the terrorist bombing, Paul's head injury, and his current behavior. Finally, I told him of discovering his betrayal and the credit card bills he kept from me. I needed guidance from a professional to help me understand and deal with this reality.

Without acknowledging my suffering, Father Dag said the same thing Nancy had said: "You should not confront or pressure him until his brain injury fully heals, at least another year." That was his advice. Put my head in the sand and wait. I reluctantly agreed. What other option did I have?

He did not address my anger, confusion, or anguish in living with a person I no longer knew, or even the secret betrayal. He focused on what was necessary for Paul, without offering any advice to help me get through this. Maybe I should just be praying, but as you know, I don't just sit and wait for God's intervention. I felt worse now than before I saw him. The message was clear: wait for another year.

Given this new guidance, I set aside all the pain and worked on the present. As I dismissed the pain, it merely sank deeper. Every time we went to bed, and he turned away and would not snuggle, I felt the pain.

My new role as a dutiful, congenial wife included no benefit of conversation, affection, or intimacy, so it was an easy, superficial role to play. I continued as a caregiver and supporter. We were now roommates who respected each other. It became the mechanics of daily life. I knew down deep that I still loved Paul, but he was now a hollow, empty man. Oh, how I missed the man I married.

❧

Ever since I told Paul about his secret credit card debt, he had remained indifferent, having no memory or regret. He expressed irritation and impatience that the issue was still with me. Eventually, the credit card history statements came in the mail, and we opened them together. This was the moment of truth! All the purchases occurred in the Fall of 2001 after Paul had been diagnosed with prostate cancer and was out of work, waiting for surgery. The answer to the question was not a mistress or a bastard child somewhere. All the transactions were ATM withdrawals in Maryland, where the flight school was located. I saw month after month of cash withdrawals of seventy-five, or one hundred dollars, that continued until his surgery. Whenever he needed cash for his flying lessons, he just charged it. The statements showed that even after we moved to Kenya, he continued to charge the flights we took in and around Kenya, throughout that year. The balances kept growing for well over two years. He had been paying only a minimum balance each month.

With the evidence in front of him, he suddenly remembered spending it on his flying lessons. He added, "But I am not a bit sorry, because I had an entire year of flying around in Kenya. Now that I have lost my eye, I can no longer fly." Very true and truly selfish. He paid off all his credit card debt with part of the seventy-five thousand dollars insurance payout for the loss of one eye. In his mind, it was resolved. There was still no hint of remorse or compassion for how deeply I had been betrayed. He coldly reiterated, "It was not your business. It was my business." He wanted me to get over it. Zero balance = no foul.

❧

After hearing Father Dag's advice, I stepped back and tried to put myself in his shoes. When Paul took the flying lessons, he had been under enormous stress, facing an aggressive cancer diagnosis that threatened his manhood and possibly his life. He was unemployed with an uncertain future. He knew me well enough that if he had told me he needed more money for the lessons, I would have said it was not a good idea, given our precarious financial and current job situation. So, he did not bother to ask.

At the end of the day, I still felt conflicted, hurt, and marginalized. I knew I could not dismiss the fracture created in our marriage. As Nancy said, time would give me an answer, sooner or later.

❧

Shortly after Paul's return, I ran into Maryanne, Wayne's wife, at an afternoon party. She is a tall, thin, beautiful woman with lovely blonde hair and an adorable British accent. Maryanne is a white South African, born of British parents. She left home on her own at the age of sixteen and moved to Nairobi, Kenya, to build a new life. This confident, intelligent woman pulled herself up by her bootstraps and began a very successful career in journalism, a passion of hers. Her other passion was helping Kenyans.

She and I started talking off to the side, and I asked if she would be interested in having lunch sometime. We met for lunch and soon became best of friends. We have the very same birthday, so that we could be Cosmic sisters.

Years ago, Maryanne developed an NGO, named Sandia, in the highlands of Kenya, near Lake Victoria, that provided education and medical support to a remote Samburu village. Although originally from South Africa, she lived her entire adult life in Kenya.

At the drop of a hat or a good excuse, we would take off into the bush, in her Toyota 4x4, to check on her NGO and visit old friends. She introduced me to the real Kenyan bush country. We ate roasted goat, slept out under the stars, and had incredible adventures. Most importantly, we became very close friends and were able to share our current challenges in life.

When she established the Sandia NGO many years ago, she became friends with the Samburu elders, and they trusted her. Maryanne successfully negotiated the professional filming of the entire Samburu Male Circumcision Ceremony, which takes place every fifteen years. It was a way for the Samburu to preserve this time-honored tradition of their tribal culture.

At the end of the day, I still felt conflicted, hurt, and marginalized. I knew I could not dismiss the fracture in our marriage. Nancy said that time would give me an answer, but when?

37

A few years ago, I became friends with a Kenyan American woman from Colorado named Eunice. As a divorced mother, she had recently returned to Kenya, her birth home, with two teenagers and only two suitcases. She had been involved with a Christian church in Colorado. She had shared her dream with the congregation of returning to Kenya to build a Children's Home on her mother's two-acre property in the rural countryside, not far from our home in Tigoni. The church agreed to back her dream.

Eunice was a good-looking woman in her mid-thirties who had so much energy and enthusiasm that it was contagious. As a native of Kenya, with her outgoing, confident nature and fluency in Swahili, she opened doors to Kenya's Department of Child Services, DCS, local churches, and nearby communities. With the help of Father Dag and his *Nyumban*i Children's Home and the Kenya DCS, she was determined to open a new HIV/AIDS home for children. HIV was an overwhelming epidemic. HIV-positive newborns were often abandoned at the hospital by their very ill mothers, who were dying of AIDS. Before I could believe it, Eunice had rented a furnished apartment for her and her kids and was caring for two HIV/AIDS-positive infants. Father Dag taught her how to manage the challenge.

I knew HIV/AIDS was transmitted through unprotected sex and contaminated syringes. However, I also learned that only HIV contaminated bodily fluids, or the consumption of contaminated breast milk, can infect a healthy person. A healthy child getting infected by an HIV/AIDS child only occurs if the HIV/AIDS person gets a bloody injury that is accidentally absorbed into an open wound or the eyes of a healthy child. For this reason, no one in Africa ever stops to offer help when there's a car or motorcycle accident.

Slowly but surely, Eunice completed the construction of a large home on her mother's property north of Nairobi and named it Tumaini, meaning Hope in Swahili. She initially became the guardian of about fifteen needy children—infants, toddlers, and school-age children—who had been abandoned. I watched as her dream became a reality. These kids were adorable and well cared for, with big smiles on their faces. Eunice hired several local women to care for them as if they were their own.

She continued to network, meeting government officials, local leaders, churches, and private businesses as potential donors. I stopped by from time to time and brought the boys with me. The boys became friends with some of the children their age.

Eunice's home felt like a large family, and all the kids seemed quite happy. I was amazed at the amount of work entailed in running such a place. Her home was running very efficiently, with Eunice at the helm as super Mum.

There was formula to prepare. A nurse supervised the babies' care and feeding, including any HIV medication needed. Housekeepers cleaned every room and washed clothes and linens daily. A caretaker tended a small organic farm behind the house, with fresh veggies, several egg-laying chickens, four pigs that ate the leftovers, and two milk cows for fresh milk. There was a security guard 24/7 and a full-time driver. Last, but not least, a chief cook and his assistant prepared and cooked all the meals each day, plus snacks. It was a dream come true for Eunice.

❧

After spending some time at Tumaini, I recognized the need for documented rules, standards, and procedures to maintain a consistent high level of care in this facility. I suggested to Eunice that I could volunteer to document the procedures required to establish and maintain consistency. Tumaini was like the old nursery rhyme, written by Jane Cabrera, "There was an old woman who lived in a shoe. She had so many children she didn't know what to do." Eventually, there were between fifteen to twenty paid staff caring for fifty children, all HIV/AIDS-compromised. The home was established as an NGO, so it needed to run like a small business. Records must be kept on each child's health, social skills, problem areas, and school records. Each section of the children's home management needed to establish standards and procedures. At the time, everything was in Eunice's head, requiring everyone to come to her with questions. She agreed that she needed documentation but did not have the time to do it herself, so I agreed to help.

Several mornings, I'd pack up my laptop and drive to the Tumaini Children's Home. My boys always wanted to come with me to play with a few of the kids their own age while I worked.

I started with simple rules for the children and staff with signs in Swahili and English, placed in appropriate places: "Wash your Hands with soap before each meal"; "Wash your hands with soap after using the toilet"; "Close the door when you enter or exit the house"; "Put dirty clothes in the hamper." This was a basic set of rules for staff and children alike.

I finally found something worthwhile to do with my life. Eunice and I became friends, and she loved the boys. My day would start with a hot cup of Chai from the kitchen staff. Sometimes I would stay for a typical Kenyan lunch of *scuma Wiki* and *ugali*, cooked collard greens with onions and spices served with a cooked maize mixture resembling mashed potatoes. It was very tasty. While the Kenyans used the *ugali* as a spoon to scoop up the *scuma wiki*, I preferred a fork.

While Eunice handled management and outreach, I handled policies and procedures. If my boys were on school break, they would accompany me and play with the kids there. I was amazed at the amount of work entailed in running such a place. I worked in the office two or three mornings a week.

Most of the fundraising was provided by the sponsoring church in Colorado. Twice a year, donors from Colorado would travel to Kenya and spend a week or two painting, doing carpentry, getting to know the kids, and then going on safari before returning to the U.S. The home was a well-oiled machine full of happy kids.

38

After being home for only two months, Paul met with Wayne and Howard to request returning to work part-time. They agreed and gave him small assignments to work on an hourly basis. He jumped back into work and seemed happier.

By April, this strength was back, and Paul was itching to go back to work full-time. I understood how important this was to him professionally and for us financially. By now, he was a well-known hero for having survived the UN bombing, and he was good at telling these war stories.

He reached out to his NGO network and quickly landed an interview for a job in Amman, Jordan, with the International Organization for Migration, IOM. He was elated to receive an offer of a one-year term as a Special Security Training Instructor for the mandatory training of all UN/NGO staff. The downside was that the job was in the Middle East, in Amman, Jordan, supporting the UN effort in Iraq.

I was happy he had gotten an offer and encouraged him to go, but told him I was not willing to go to a Muslim country for only one year and leave our home, friends, and our Kenyan boys. I would rather stay in Kenya with the kids and continue my volunteer work with Eunice. He agreed that Amman would be very boring for me.

❧

Once he settled in Jordan, he called and asked me to come to Amman and check it out. I was excited and booked a flight to Amman for a week.

On weekends and evenings, Paul showed me around the desert city of Amman, built on seven small hills, called circles, or roundabouts, with the first circle being the middle of the old city, containing a large Roman amphitheater. The earliest evidence of settlement in Amman comes from a Neolithic site, where some of the oldest human statues ever found are dated to 7,250 BCE. Jordan was fascinating, but very hot and dry.

King Hussain, the King of Jordan, was educated in the West and remains a friend of the US. Jordan has become a modern Arab city and a major tourist destination. I noticed McDonald's, Kentucky Fried Chicken, shopping malls, and movie theaters, all frequented by locals. Excellent restaurants throughout the city offered a variety of cuisines. Our favorite hangout was the Sushi Bar at the Howard Johnson's Hotel on Thursday nights.

On the weekend, we drove over three hours south, through the desert, to the nearby Dead Sea, where numerous hotels and spas thrive.

Jordan is a very exotic country with a religious history going back to the time of Christ. In each Arab city, Muslim prayers are broadcast five times a day. Most Muslim men stop and pray. When driving, I'd see truck drivers pull over, get out their prayer rugs, and pray to Allah on the side of the road. Other men in the McDonald's parking lot did the same, without hesitation or self-consciousness. I was impressed with their faith in Islam, a religion I knew very little about.

❧

Paul was relieved and happy to be back in the NGO mix. He proudly introduced me to his co-workers, and everyone said, "Oh, you are Barbara. Paul talks about you all the time. I feel like I know you already." When I heard that, my heart soared with happiness and hope. Paul was honoring me as his wife, as he always had. It showed that he loved, respected, and was proud of me, as he always had been. Apparently, he felt the same way inside but was unable to express it to me. I watched as his outgoing, social personality returned.

I enjoyed my visit and was relieved to see Paul engaging with his new colleagues. At a dinner with his staff, he introduced me to a charming South African from the UN Iraq Mission, who was looking for someone with an Information Management background. Paul had given him my resume, and he wanted to interview me. Following my successful interview, we hoped I would receive an offer soon. It would be wonderful for me to get back to work again and end our physical separation.

If I accepted an offer, I'd need to find a good home for the Kenya kids. Eunice's house came to mind instantly. We'd continue to sponsor the boys in school and at the Tumaini, and I could travel to see them often. I returned to Tigoni eager to hear about a new job offer.

❧

During Christmas of 2004, I was at home with the boys and spoke to Paul on the phone, wishing him a Merry Christmas. Everything was fine. The next day, December 26, Boxing Day, the most enormous tsunami ever recorded hit Indonesia, Sri Lanka, and India. An earthquake with a magnitude of n9.1off the coast of Sumatra generated a giant wave that hit all coastlines in its wake, with relentless force and destruction. Over 200,000 people died.

Paul called immediately to say he had been asked to go to Jakarta to help in UN relief efforts. I felt helpless, saying, "What can I do? I'm just sitting here doing nothing." He said, "Buy a ticket and meet me in Dubai. I'm sure the office will put you to work. They need all the help they can get. You can stay in my hotel room."

We met in Dubai, and I spent two weeks at the IOM office in Jakarta, performing administrative duties to support personnel arriving in the area to assist.

Paul, on the other hand, was on the road, trying to get basic relief supplies to the affected areas along the coast. I did not see him much, but was in contact with him daily, and he described the problems of getting supplies over washed-out roads to the Banda Aceh area, the worst-hit area.

The IOM employees were glad I was there to help. Each evening, I walked from the office to the hotel several blocks away, passing by endless sidewalk cafes, each cooking something exotic. The city was cooler now, and neighbors came together socially. I walked all around the city and over to the protected port of Jakarta. The locals were charming, though I did not partake of the street food, fearing food poisoning.

❧

At the end of my two weeks, I got the opportunity to take a UN flight to Banda Aceh to see the devastation firsthand. Paul met me when I landed and showed me the destruction. Mass graves were being used to bury the dead and hopefully prevent disease.

A wide swath of beach had been wiped out, with nothing remaining except concrete foundations, adorned with colored tiles, in the sand. It was all that was left of an entire oceanfront community. I could make out the floor patterns of the various rooms, based on the different styles. The foundations were the only remains of a house and an entire family. Further inland, hills of debris sat motionless, deposited by the destructive wave. I saw people moving through the piles and piles of debris several feet high.

Mother Nature created an immense wave, hurling homes, cars, boats, churches, and people with its deadly force as it destroyed everything in its path, wiping out the beach and forcing debris and people far inland. Complete houses were broken into pieces, mixed with clothes, appliances, furniture, and everything that once made these houses a home. The mountains of debris, some up to five feet high, stretched on as we drove past. Single shoes, children's toys, and clothing, mixed with crushed appliances and vehicles, were all that remained. It was shocking.

❧

We saw men walking along the top of each debris field carrying long red poles, which were used to mark the location of one or more decomposing corpses revealed by the two-week-old stench of death. In another area, where the Aceh River reached the ocean, smashed fishing boats rested in the streets and on top of half-demolished structures. Stores were wiped out. This tsunami swept everything in its path inland, pushing debris up the river almost forty kilometers inland.

Amidst the horrible destruction locals were helping with the relief effort. It was an apocalyptic scene! English-speaking locals were eager to tell me the story of when the tsunami hit and the sad realization that family members had died in the tragedy.

I went to a narrow part of the beach that backed up to a nearby cliff. There, it was clear to see how high the tsunami came, halfway up the cliff, wiping out all the trees to a height of forty feet. A huge barge had been washed ashore, now leaning on its side in one piece like a beached whale. Cows roamed the streets. I saw a few trained Asian elephants that were helping remove downed trees. The entire scene was beyond human comprehension.

❧

Emotionally changed forever, I returned home and waited for my UN job offer, and waited, and waited. The wheels of the UN bureaucracy turned very slowly. I had given up, thinking I'd never become a professional again. I was resigned to stay in Kenya, while Paul traveled around the world supporting various humanitarian relief efforts. He would visit Kenya when he could. He seemed very happy again, doing the humanitarian work he loved. I missed him but adjusted to being alone. Over a year went by with no news, and we both thought my UN job offer would never happen.

Paul got his next assignment with the IOM, now in Sri Lanka. He called to ask if he should accept it or try to get another job in Amman. I told him to go ahead with his career. There was no reason to stall his career. I'd stay in Kenya with the kids, dogs, Maryanne, and Eunice.

Part Eight

39

After almost two years, I finally received a call and an email offering me a P3 professional position as a senior information management officer with the UN Iraq mission, UNAMI. The position was for a year, renewable.

This meant I'd have my career back, which I needed desperately. The offer named Baghdad as my duty assignment, which scared me shitless. After all this time, and now they wanted me to live in Baghdad. The Iraq War was ongoing. Terrorism had increased, and videos of several Americans being beheaded had been broadcast over the internet when the ransom demands had not been met. As an American, I knew I'd be a target if I were captured in the Green Zone. During the original interview, I was told I would be stationed at the UNAMI facility in Amman, Jordan. I would need to go to any UN Iraq facility on an as-needed basis for thirty days at a time. I called Chris, the manager who had interviewed me, and asked for clarification. He assured me that I would spend most of my time in Jordan, but would have to be willing to travel to Iraq if the job required it. That was my understanding, too. Okay, my stress level went back to normal.

❧

I wanted this job very much, but I knew there would be risks in Baghdad, even though I'd only be in the Green Zone for short periods. I was sixty-two years old, at a time in my life when I had raised two sons and was proud of them. I had an amazingly successful career and a wonderful marriage. Once again, I looked inside myself and realized that if I were killed, it would be okay. I had experienced a great life and was at peace. I was impressed with the job, but I needed more information before I felt comfortable signing on the dotted line.

The solution: I Googled *"beheading"* and watched in horror as a terrorist sawed an American's head off with a hacksaw, not just one mighty slash from a long, sharp sword. The bloody thing took less than two minutes. Okay, I said to myself, I could deal with that. Not too much suffering!

Elated, I accepted the offer with a start date of May 6, 2005. Was I crazy? No, I was fearless and lived life to the fullest. In the Spring of 2005, I finally received a signed one-year contract. It was a professional, diplomatic position as a senior IMO with the Security Section.

UNAMI's mission was to coordinate the humanitarian, political, and development efforts within the UN agencies in the midst of the ongoing Iraq War, with Coalition Forces occupying Iraq.

I was ecstatic. Finally, I was back on course to continue my career after three years of retirement. I felt fortunate and thankful that my skills and experience matched the UN Iraq requirements, despite the dangerous and volatile environment throughout Iraq. I knew it would be a fantastic adventure. Anyone in their right mind would never consider a position in such a war zone, but for me, it was the answer to my prayers. I realized too late that, by taking early retirement at fifty-five, I had unwittingly severed an enormous sense of myself by turning my back on a satisfying career to watch elephants. Paul's life-threatening injury and our future only served to exacerbate my need to become independent.

Paul, now a celebrity for surviving the bombing in Iraq, was working in Sri Lanka, with his career back on track.

I would eventually realize that we had put our marriage on the back burner and sought challenge, responsibility, and a professional environment to satisfy our desire to do something worthwhile with our lives. We had not done this on purpose, but of necessity. He seemed to be back to his old self, so I buried the issue of the debt and ds betrayal. He had been through enough and we both wanted to move on.

❧

With both commitment and courage, I embraced this once-in-a-lifetime opportunity. This assignment, so different from my career with the U.S. Government, drew on my strengths and IT expertise in a new, multi-my work environment in the Arab world.

Before that, I had only worked with U.S. citizens in the intelligence field with top secret clearances. I understood that it would be very different working with UN professionals from all over the world, with differing customs and diverse work ethics. I didn't realize the huge challenge it would become. Paul congratulated me, saying that he was proud I had finally gotten the opportunity, but saddened that he had moved away and we would continue to be physically separated.

I was only given a few weeks' notice before I was expected to arrive at UNAMI in Amman, Jordan. Things started moving very fast. I had mentioned to my sons that I had been hoping to work for the UN, and now it had become a reality. I explained to each of them why I needed to restart my career and why I was willing to work in such a dangerous environment. I explained that I felt comfortable, at this point in my life, going into a war zone and being in significant danger. I had raised two wonderful sons and had a fantastic career and marriage. Although I did not want to die, I was at peace with my life. It was just a risky stepping-stone I was willing to take to get my life and my career back.

I spoke to Eunice about accepting the Kenya boys into her children's home. She had grown to consider the boys as family and assured me they would be fine. I agreed to support them financially with lodging and private schooling.

Gathering my boys, Peter, Steven, and Albert, at the kitchen table, I explained why I must go back to work and leave Kenya. Extremely upset, their first reaction was to run away back to the street life. The boy's grades were not great, but they were trying very hard.

Over the next couple of weeks, we had many heart-to-heart conversations about the reality of my leaving Kenya, and they began to understand that I must take this job. I told them it would break my heart if they returned to the street as beggars, after all the progress we had made. As weeks passed, they gradually acquiesced. Thank God.

I gave notice to the landlord of our home in Tigoni and put the car and the furniture up for sale. I had moved so many times during my life that it was easy. Ads went up on bulletin boards, and I contacted the Kenya Wildlife Service to obtain a permit to transport the three parrots, including the two African greys, as endangered species under CITES regulations. Transporting our dog, Eiger, was easy in comparison. Paul agreed to return to help me. I needed to move to Amman first and get settled in a furnished apartment before the animals could be shipped.

❧

My Kenya wardrobe consisted of several pairs of lightweight, breathable cargo pants with zippers above the knee, allowing long pants to be quickly converted into shorts. I accented this with casual jungle-print shirts and an occasional safari vest, and blended into the bush like an old white Kenyan. With this new diplomatic job, I'd have to dress up a bit and wear something other than flip-flops. Unsure of the acceptable business clothing I would need, I decided to buy suitable clothing in Amman. I still had a couple of suits from the old career days that would suffice.

This became the ultimate adventure of my life. Before I knew it, I was on a jet plane to Amman, Jordan. My excitement was palpable.

I thanked God for this opportunity. I was full of confidence, anticipation, and hope. I was going to live and work in a strange Arab country. It would be nothing like Germany or Kenya, that's for sure.

❧

Upon arrival in Amman, I was welcomed at the airport by a UN representative. After checking into a small hotel, I was taken to the compound to meet and greet my colleagues in the Amman office. I completed check-in, received my identification card and diplomatic passport, and was then given time to find an apartment and get settled. Within a few days, I found a very nice, furnished three-bedroom apartment that accepted pets. A friendly Palestinian family owned it.

The quiet neighborhood consisted of three- and four-story homes with flat roofs and small, fenced yards, each with ample fruit trees.

Olive trees lined the one-way street. My apartment was only two blocks from the five-star Four Seasons Hotel. The three-story building next door was the Jordan Interpol office, the International Police facility in Jordan. A young Jordanian officer in his blue uniform served as a gate guard. They were very courteous. I felt very safe having protection nearby.

After signing the lease, I was given my apartment keys and settled into my new home. The Muslim call to prayer started. It reminded me of the movie *Exodus* I had seen as a teenager. It added a sense of the exotic and a bit of mystery to this foreign land.

I had moved from my home in the Kenyan highlands, surrounded by tea plantations, to a large city in the middle of the desert. My new view was a mixture of light tan, dry sand and small rocks, and an assortment of two-to three-story stucco homes painted white. Limestone buildings, with an occasional palm tree or verdant olive tree lining the sidewalk, added a tiny bit of color to the landscape.

My apartment was furnished with typical Arab furnishings—ornate gold-velvet sofas and thick draperies. I had an air-conditioning window unit to cool the living room, and old-fashioned radiators in each room to keep them toasty warm in the winter. Surprisingly, it would drop below freezing in the winter, and sometimes a dusting of snow would occur. I had good Wi-Fi, but the television stations were all Arabic. I had already gotten used to reading instead of watching television in the evening.

❧

After two weeks, the pet shipment was scheduled to arrive along with a few household goods and, of course, my African masks collection. Paul arranged for Mohammed, a Jordanian he had worked with, to help me through Jordan's customs and immigration with the animals. He spoke English and Arabic.

The next morning, Mohammed and I headed to the international cargo building of Queen Alia International Airport, outside Amman. I had all the official certificates and permits. I had learned that many Arabs consider dogs and cats dirty. Although they serve a security purpose, they are usually not permitted in the house. It was strange to me. Arabs were not aware of the love and devotion each animal brings to their lives.

A huge U-shaped airplane hangar, open on both ends to the heat, served as the customs building at the back of the airport. Even in the early morning, it was hot and stuffy, with no breeze or air conditioning. After reviewing all my paperwork, the customs officials told Mohammed we must first go into the city, twenty kilometers away, to see the head of the Jordanian Department of Agriculture about the parrots. If they had indicated a potential problem to Mohammed, he said nothing to me. I thought it was unusual, but we had to leave the pets in their cages, hoping to return soon.

When we arrived at the Department of Agriculture facility, Mohammed explained to the official that I was working for the UN and was importing three parrots from Kenya. The clerk disappeared, and in came a lovely, short, stout woman wearing a black hijab that covered everything but her face. She spoke a bit of English and explained to Mohammed that we had obtained permission to export the birds from Kenya but had not obtained a permit to import them into Jordan. Oh shit! She appeared alarmed that the birds had already arrived from Kenya, explaining that no permits were currently available to import live birds due to the avian flu. I told her Kenya did not have a problem with Avian flu, but she promptly went to her computer and brought up a list of countries affected by the virus, including Kenya. I was very distraught and implored her, "What can I do?" She explained that the birds would have to be tested by an official veterinarian and quarantined in my home for a month while awaiting the results. I explained that none of the birds were sick and had been kept in cages at home, but she replied that they could have been virus carriers with no symptoms. If they tested positive, they would be put down. That was it.

❧

I totally lost it and started crying. Our feathered friends were part of our family for more than ten years, and we loved them. Paul's blue crown conure named Quique would say, "What'cha doing? Give me a kiss. You are a brat. Give me a break!" My quieter African gray, Cassidy, that I'd raised as a featherless baby with an eye dropper, talked very clearly. He would call, "Paul, Paul," using my voice. In the U.S., we used to hike with them, with clipped flight feathers, often in the summer. Our third bird, named Grumbles, was a rescued African gray with a broken foot. He did not talk much, but he would grumble like a lion when frightened. They were our flock. I was trapped in a Catch-22. I had imported the birds into the country illegally, and there was no way I could return them to Kenya. I continued crying softly. This compassionate woman, who, I realized, was responsible for approving all agricultural imports, tried to calm me, saying they were probably healthy and that I shouldn't worry. At that point, I evoked the assistance of God to ensure the tests would be negative.

I had to stay on hold for a while because I don't call God that much. Eventually, I left a voice mail message asking God for his help, and again, God probably thought to himself, "Barbara who? Wolfe? Johnson? I never hear any prayers from her, unless she is in trouble, but she is a good, honest member of my flock, so to speak. So, I'll help her out again." Perhaps I should have called God now and then to say, "Hi, I'm doing fine, and thanks for the great UN job."

After a silent prayer, she wished me good luck. The next stop was the office of the Chief Jordanian Veterinarian to ask him to inspect the birds at the cargo building at the airport. It wasn't easy to find his office, but when we finally reached it, he was out to lunch. We waited in the blazing sun. When he finally returned, he had no transportation. He got in our vehicle, and we got caught in city traffic, bumper-to-bumper. It was late afternoon when we returned to the cargo building.

❧

By this time, the weather was in the high nineties, and the cargo building was unbelievably hot. The birds and the dog were panting in their little cages. I approached them and offered reassurance. I felt so bad that they were still stuck in their small transport cages. I gave the birds some fresh water and a bit of food, but was not allowed to release Eiger on a leash to do his business.

Mohammed and the veterinarian began a lengthy, loud, heated discussion with the customs officials. I stood off to the side, understanding nothing. After what seemed like an hour of loud bickering, the officials agreed they would release the birds, not to me, but to the vet. The vet would accompany us to my apartment to inspect the quarantine area. However, they said, it was 4:30 p.m. and too late to process the necessary paperwork. We'd have to come back in the morning.

That's when I lost it! I was aware that this Muslim country is a male-dominated culture. The officials had dismissed me and talked only to Mohammed. But enough was enough! I was tired, hot, and genuinely concerned about my birds. I was a member of the UN with a diplomatic passport. And I was not going to leave the cargo area without the animals. Surely, they did not want an international incident over a few birds. I was going to break through this damn patriarchal society, NOW!

❧

I walked over to the group of men, showed my diplomatic passport, and stated very calmly and assertively, with Mohammed translating, "I will NOT leave the cargo building until I have these birds. My dog can tough it out overnight, but tropical birds are very sensitive. Surely, you all realize that these tropical endangered birds have been under extreme stress for over thirty-six hours. The temperatures drop at night in the cargo hangar, becoming very cold and causing them to become very sick." As Mohammed translated, the officials looked startled. I stepped back as louder discussions ensued. After another ten stressful minutes of heated Arabic negotiations, the belligerent customs officials relented. The birds and Eiger were released to the vet. The bird cages and large dog crate were put in the back of the van. Mohammed, the veterinarian, and I left the airport, post haste, for my apartment as the sun was setting.

❧

Upon arrival at my apartment, the vet took fecal samples from each cage and said he could inspect them at any time. I agreed. What a relief. I thanked everyone for their extraordinary effort, *shukran,* paid Mohammed generously for his success, and wished them a warm goodbye, *Mae alsalama*. Thank God. I had gotten the birds safe at home, at least for now. I heaved a long sigh of relief. My animals were home safe and sound. First, I removed Eiger from his cage and took him for a short walk around the block to do his business. He was very curious, smelling all the new scents. Then he was startled, barking and lunging at a tall Arab man walking toward us, wearing a long white *hijab*, robe. It freaked Eiger out. I sighed again, thinking we'd all need to adjust to this culture.

I got the birds out of their small wooden travel containers and put them in their very own cages in the back bedroom, which had lots of light from the windows. They seemed tired but rallied when they saw their own cages with familiar toys, fresh water, and food. It would take a month to get the test results back, and all the tests were negative.

Thank you so much, God. You came through again. My birds were now safe in Jordan, while the global avian flu epidemic continues to this day

40

The Jordanian people were reserved but cordial and welcoming. My Palestinian landlord and his family, who lived in the building, were kind and helpful. The husband spoke English, which made things much easier. Finally, I was settled in my apartment and began to feel comfortable in this Arab country.

I was soon getting the lay of the land, or should I say desert. The UN provided bus transport for staff members each morning and evening, so I did not need to buy a vehicle. On the weekends, taxis were convenient and inexpensive. Trying to learn Arabic and communicate with drivers and shopkeepers was a challenge, but everyone was patient.

There were many Westerners in Jordan, even more now because of the Iraq War. I learned there are even some Christian neighborhoods in Amman where people live peacefully beside their Arab neighbors. What a concept!

Outside my apartment was a small liquor store next to a small grocery store and a tiny souvlaki and falafel carry-out. Muslims do not drink alcohol, but I was able to buy a few bottles of wine for special occasions, like getting home from work.

My upstairs neighbor, Celine, was a single woman from Australia, a bit younger than I. She also worked for the UN and had been with them in various countries for many years. She and I became good friends, and she helped me adjust to the workplace norms. It was also lovely to have a new friend to do things with socially, who could also help me navigate the culture with my assertive nature, without stepping on toes or egos. I was back at work and loving the challenge.

❧

During my career, if I needed, let's say, a particular travel form from the admin office, I would email a request to the responsible person, and the form would be in my inbox the following morning. However, I soon learned that, when dealing in this new international worker environment, much more face-to-face explaining, cajoling, and kissing ass were required in trying to agree on when I could expect the request to be completed.

Sometimes, it was like pulling teeth to get any response, and it was difficult for me to adjust to what I considered a lackadaisical work ethic. I was not used to having to develop a personal relationship with a colleague to get the damn form I needed.

❧

As a new employee, I was required to complete a Safety and Security Course before I could travel to Iraq. The purpose of the course was to make UN staff members aware of the numerous dangers in Iraq and how to mitigate dangerous situations, including enemy fire, rockets, and other weapons, and how to stay calm during hostile checkpoints when navigating a vehicle in and out of mine fields. The most crucial training was what to do if you are kidnapped by terrorists and taken hostage.

There were fifteen staff members and contractors, four women and eleven men, in our class. We were issued radios and taught how to use them. "This is Charlie Seven, over," meaning this is C 7, my personal UN call sign, to the UN radio operator. I was getting a taste of what it's like in a combat zone. We were all psyched! I still use those alphabet call signs when I spell my name or email over the phone: "My name is Wolfe (whiskey Oscar, lima, foxtrot, echo)."

My Personal Protection Equipment, PPE, i.e., body armor, was issued on the first day of employment and included a well-used navy-blue metal combat helmet and a very heavy, lead-lined bulletproof vest that fit, extra small.

After three days of lectures and passing all the written tests, the last two days were practical exercises on a Jordanian military base in the desert outside the city.

❧

We were divided into three groups, five to each armored vehicle. Simulations included real-life situations in our bulletproof SUV on how to deal with checkpoints with angry Arab guards, yelling and trying to intimidate us. Then we traveled over a sandy desert road and were fired upon. Rifle fire and mortars were set off nearby. Hostage simulations were the most frightening, with Jordanian military dressed as angry terrorists, yelling in Arabic, pointing automatic weapons at us, and pounding on the windows, ordering us to get out of the vehicle, our only safe place.

Even though I knew it was only training and not a real scenario, my heart started pounding when the rockets and AK-47s began shooting. The terrorist actors in Arab garb started shouting in Arabic to get out of the vehicle. I thought they might be able to break into our armored vehicle and drag us away.

During the land mine exercise, our designated student driver drove our vehicle into an area marked by signs indicating land mines. "We had been taught to stay on the tire tracks on the road and not deviate from them. However, this young driver got very flustered and said, "I cannot go forward, so I am going to turn around."

I shouted at him, "No, you are not, because you may kill us all. You will slowly back the vehicle up on the same road; there is no other alternative." Perhaps I was pushy, but in real life, I didn't want to die!

None of the other passengers said a word. Does that say something about me?

Most of us passed the course. We got an authentic taste of the realities and many risks in Iraq. It woke me up to the danger, but rather than scare me, it made me vigilant and prepared me for life-threatening situations. Now, I was able to focus on my job and the tasks I had been given.

❧

My boss, Chris, said he'd like me to go into Baghdad for a week to understand the operations and security requirements in Iraq.

Wow, there was no grass growing under my feet. Well, Jordan didn't have grass anyway, just white chalky dirt and endless sand, but I digress. I can honestly say I was not scared. "Baba was going into a war zone! My travel plans were approved by the UN headquarters in New York City, air reservations were made to fly from Marka Airport in Amman, Jordan, to the Baghdad International Airport, BIAP, in Iraq, through the U.S. State Department/military forces using their trusted workhorse, C-130 Hercules. I was like a little kid, so excited about this new adventure. I had hired a mature Jamaican woman as a housekeeper. She had lived in Jordan for many years and agreed to come twice a day and feed the animals and walk Eiger while I was out of the country.

I had been working for the UN for about a month and knew only a few people at UNAMI. My colleagues in the security section were friendly and very helpful. I also met admin folks in human resources, training, logistics, and IT.

In my usual professional persona, I am friendly, but always in a business context. I was the oldest member of the mission, and I felt like a different duck. Most of the professionals were between twenty-one and fifty, except the head of mission, who was probably my age.

I was a loner and was not the outgoing, gregarious life of the party. Most professional diplomats were career professionals in political and humanitarian areas. I had nothing in common with them. They were cordial but kept to themselves. I certainly was not going to befriend a male staffer. I was married and wanted no confusion. I had heard that mission life could be lonely, leading to affairs. My IT background didn't align with that of the humanitarian or political experts, so I was out of place and kept my own counsel.

❧

Travel day arrived, and I was picked up outside my apartment early that morning by the UN logistics staff. I was driven with several other staff members to a small airport on the far side of Amman. I was not required to wear or access my PPE in Amman, but was required to wear PPE during any Iraq transport, flights, UN vehicles, or State Department buses between Baghdad International Airport, BIAP, and the Green Zone. It became much easier to wear it everywhere in the airport. At Marca, we were processed in, our luggage checked, and were given an air voucher, not a ticket. Then we waited and waited and waited in the airport lounge.

I'll explain why: the Coalition Forces were at war with Iraq, so terrorist incidents were common. The State Department was responsible for the transport of all Coalition-related forces and U.S. diplomats in and out of the Theatre of Operations in Baghdad. No flight time was ever scheduled until real-time U.S. intelligence indicated that the route was safe. For several hours, we munched on snacks, drank water, went to the bathroom, read, and waited for our flight.

At last, our flight was announced, and we walked onto the tarmac to the C-130 with hot engines running. Seeing the Air Force officers in their sharp jumpsuits gave me confidence. The U.S. had my back.

I got to know our military in 1976 when I worked at Fort Bragg, where the 82nd Airborne Division used these bloated, guppy-looking prop planes for paratroop training. In the 1990s, Paul and I had also flown on a C-130 during our Christmas break for a vacation. These planes were cold and extremely noisy, but very reliable.

❧

I took a jump seat along the fuselage and buckled up. As with most military planes, there were no movies, refreshments, or a bathroom. Only a male stand-up urinal was available. What about all the water we just drank?

The three-hour flight was uneventful. I could not read because there were no overhead reading lights. The roar of the props was deafening. After about two and a half hours in the air, we started our descent into BIAP. The pilot informed us that we would be performing a sudden spiral landing, to avoid any enemy artillery fire. This was a maneuver from altitude, suddenly turning the plane into a steep downward spiral, which made it more difficult for us to become enemy targets as we landed. I was fine, but some passengers became sick. After we landed safely, the rear cargo door opened. Intense, hot, dry air hit us like we were walking into a 130º Faran height, a furnace. Welcome to Baghdad.

The BIAP is quite large. The U.S. military had secured and occupied only one side of the airport, with the runways in the middle. Commercial flights were still ongoing, on the commercial side.

After getting our bags, our logistics team herded us to the shady side of a building and told us to "hang out' and wait for a chopper to take us into the Green Zone. They passed out bottles of water and showed us the nearest bathroom. It was late afternoon, and I was hoping a chopper would arrive soon. The heat was getting to me. I hunkered down and people-watched, remembering to hydrate continuously.

An hour later, off in the distance, we saw a massive cloud of sand approaching us, not at altitude but at ground level. It was a great, tan-colored sandstorm, blocking out the last of the sunset, moving rapidly along the ground, directly toward us. It arrived quickly, with fierce winds driving sand into all our exposed orifices. A few experienced staff members told us, newbies, to cover our eyes, ears, and mouths. Is that why the Arabs wore those white-and-red, or black-and-white, checked fabrics that looked like bath towels?

Someone handed out more water and warned us again not to get dehydrated. Thanks so much! After another hour, we got the news that choppers cannot fly in a sandstorm or after dark, so we were stuck at the BIAP for the night, dozing off sitting on our sandy luggage, with no dinner or breakfast. I had a couple of granola bars in my backpack, which became dinner.

❧

By 5:00 a.m. the next morning, the skies cleared, and about thirty of us waited in line for the Black Hawk military chopper ride to the Green Zone. This Blackhawk ride was a first for me, and I was excited, although a bit concerned about falling out of the open doors next to our seats. "Buckle your seatbelt tight," I said to myself. Only about six people with their luggage were allowed on each flight. Once we were strapped in, and the pilot got clearance, he started the engine, dipped the nose, and off we went, flying very low over the Red Zone to the Green Zone of Baghdad. We flew quickly at tree-top level to avoid enemy fire while passing neighborhoods of small, one-story white stucco homes with small yards and concrete walls. Maybe one or two straggly palms stood in the sun as weary sentries.

Within a few minutes, we crossed over the muddy Euphrates River and landed at a small, paved chopper base in the Green Zone. Logistics personnel were there to pick us up and take us to our living compound. All N vehicles were bulletproof white Toyota SUVs. We were briefed every time we left one location, such as the UN housing compound. To go to another location, such as another office in the Green Zone, we were required to wear our PPE and keep the doors and windows locked.

I was sweaty, dusty, gritty, hungry, and exhausted, but so elated by the experience. I know Paul was jealous. He had never been in a war zone.

I watched in awe as we drove through the Green Zone, passing demolished buildings, ornate arches, and roundabouts with elaborate sculptures.

Twelve-foot concrete walls protected all coalition forces' compounds. Driving by, all you could see were twelve-foot walls on either side of the road. Security checkpoints and facility entrances had armed guards with machine guns on alert. This was a war zone, just like on CNN.

❧

After going through a checkpoint, we pulled up to one of the only high-rise buildings in Baghdad. Once a luxurious eighteen-story Al Rasheed Hotel, built by Saddam Hussein in 1982. Coalition Forces now occupied the Al Rasheed. The guests included coalition personnel, U.S. military personnel, UN personnel, journalists, media personnel, and visiting dignitaries.

The ostentatious lobby, made of white marble, with ornate gold chandeliers and large, white marble columns, had seen better days. I waited in line at the hotel desk to get my room key and pinched myself. I am really in Baghdad? Boy, will I have stories to tell. The elevator took me to the seventh floor. A security guard checked my UN identification card and wished me a good evening. I entered my home for the next week.

My room was also white marble, with a dirty, dark red carpet and drapes. The Al Rasheed had once been a grand five-star hotel, yet had fallen into disrepair many years ago. The entire room, as well as the marble bath, had seen better days. I suspected it had not been thoroughly cleaned in years. A few lights worked. It was a sad testimonial to a once-prosperous era in Iraq. I was told to keep the drapes closed at night for security.

After unpacking and having a hot shower, I went to the lobby, where I found a large cafeteria run by Haliburton, a U.S. company working for the Coalition Forces. The selections were mouth-watering, and I was starving. I scarfed down scrambled eggs, ham, and sausage, in an Arab country, with English muffins, orange juice, and coffee. It was an all-you-can-eat buffet, free for identification cardholders. A few Brits and Aussie military personnel in desert uniform were also living there, as well as visiting diplomats. U.S. military personnel were housed in small posts near the Green Zone.

Although truly exhausted, I was stimulated by this fantastic adventure. With my badge and PPE, I felt welcome and respected. I also felt very safe in the presence of the military.

In Iraq, I could take off the PPE only when I was inside a UN office compound, but had to keep it close by in case of emergency, most likely incoming rocket fire from the Red Zone into the Green Zone, over the narrow Euphrates River. Usually, they were poor shots, but a few times, they hit our compound, killing and injuring staff. Loud sirens would go off, saying, "Incoming, Incoming! Put on your PPE! Shelter in place!" We would grab our PPE and dive under a desk, conference table, or bed, away from the windows, until we heard the "All Clear."

I learned that the Green Zone ,or safe zone, was occupied by the Coalition Provisional Authority, including the United States, the United Kingdom, Australia, Italy, Spain, and Poland. This Green Zone, an almost four-square-mile island, was a relatively safe zone, surrounded by the Iraqi enemy's 'Red Zone. 'The Green Zone was in the center of Baghdad, along the Euphrates River, and included many former government buildings, including Saddam's lavish palace, which had become the U.S. military's operational headquarters.

The Green Zone had been bombed and demolished. Ornate archways had been damaged. Other buildings still standing now housed numerous contractors—Brown and Root, Halliburton, and others—who provided security and personnel services to the Coalition Forces. An AAFES Exchange, or PX, as it was called, had been built nearby. The PX offered clothing, toiletries, snacks, souvenirs, and a variety of necessities. This secure complex included a Burger King and a Pizza Hut to make soldiers feel almost at home. A few local vendor shops sold Persian rugs and souvenirs.

It was such an eclectic mix of off-duty humanity. Off-duty canine teams milled around with their trained bomb dogs sniffing for car bombs. I always sought them out to talk to them about their training. Each dog had an air conditioning unit in his kennel to keep him cool when not working in the sun. They had a strict schedule of very limited duty hours. I was impressed. There were a few German Shepherds, but most were short-haired, tan, agile Belgian Malinois.

After seven days in Baghdad discussing Information management requirements and challenges with senior security personnel, I realized the unique security needs of this mission. I was doing something worthwhile, and it felt good to be back at work, doing my best.

❧

After my short introduction to Iraq, I packed up my gear for the return flight to Jordan. Any authorized personnel exiting Iraq, once approved for travel on a particular flight, congregated at a staging area within the Green Zone in the early evening. Once again, young, armed State Department personnel were responsible for the security of the Red Zone transport from the Green Zone to the BIAP. Each of us was logged in and briefed on what to expect. Return transport would not be by chopper but by specially built armored buses called Rhinos, built in South Africa. We waited for hours before the State personnel granted clearance to travel, usually in the middle of the night. Once the command to load was given, like cattle, we boarded our assigned Rhino.

Armed U.S. military Humvees provided forward and aft security, while overhead assets were available if required due to a hostile attack or an Improvised Explosive Device, IED in the roadway. It was usually a thirty-minute ride, unless the convoy was told to stop until further security clearance was obtained. It was all very professional, and I felt safe, especially surrounded by several military personnel seated near me. Our luggage would be transported separately in a truck. We were only allowed a backpack on the Rhino.

Any armed personnel, including military and UN personnel, were told to holster their weapons for the duration of the transport and to defer to the U.S. State armed personnel in charge. Once we were loaded into the Rhino, the State person in charge of each vehicle briefed us on emergency procedures in the event of an attack or explosion. The State personnel were in charge of all security for the duration of the trip to the BIAP. Regardless of military training, individuals were to stand down and let the State personnel handle any hostile situation. Only State personnel were authorized to use their weapons.

If a Rhino came under attack or became disabled, another Rhino would be summoned from the Green Zone. State personnel would carefully transfer each person out of the disabled Rhino into the new adjoined Rhino, usually through a hatch in the roof. I was sure military personnel sitting near me would help an old lady in body armor through the hatch in the roof, before I peed in my pants.

At times, the Rhino would be told to stop in transit and wait for security clearance. Authorization to continue was given once the route was secure. This was a serious combat environment. We were in the Red Zone, all the way to the BIAP.

I reflected on the situation. This could be dicey, but I remained optimistic and did not panic. The journey went without incident. After about twenty minutes, we took a left onto the dirt road to the BIAP. The Rhinos dropped us off at U.S. military facilities that included a chow hall, bathrooms, a resting area with televisions, books, and bunk facilities. We gathered our luggage, were issued a bunker number for sleeping quarters, and were told when to gather for the morning briefing for our flight to Amman.

Finally, in the middle of the night, I went off to get a late dinner/early breakfast. The sleeping quarters I found were long, hangar-like tan tents inflated by huge air conditioners, with Army cots lined up in rows, with pillows and blankets available. Port-a-Potties and shower facilities were nearby. Sleep came quickly, with refreshing cool air and the drone of the air conditioning motors. I set my watch alarm so I would not miss the morning flight briefing. It had been a smooth military operation, though navigating in the dark without street signs on often muddy, rutted roads was a challenge. Next time, I'd bring a flashlight. After a few trips, I got the hang of it and eventually became a veteran who even knew how to find the PX on base.

41

I cannot tell you how wonderful I felt to be given this opportunity. It was such an amazing, off-the-chart, exciting adventure in a war zone. Most of my work was done outside Iraq, in the safer environment of the UN office in Amman.

Only a small contingent of critical personnel was permitted to travel to Iraq sites in Baghdad, Erbil, or Kuwait to perform their duties. Their stay in Iraq was limited to only thirty days due to the stress. When I went to Iraq, I always stayed in the Green Zone and had no requirement to venture into the unsecured Red Zones. Most of the political, humanitarian, and security personnel often went on Missions outside the Green Zone to meet and coordinate with Iraqi government officials, schools, and hospitals.

After the thirty days in Iraq, an immediate seven-day rest and relaxation, R&R, was required to compensate for the extreme stress caused by being in the war zone environment. Staff looked forward to this R&R at the end of each duty in Iraq. I would usually go to the Dead Sea, to Sharm El Sheikh, or take a longer vacation to see Paul, the Kenya boys, or my family in the U.S.

After working for the UN for over two years, I was attended a stress management course by our resident psychologist, when suddenly sirens went off, and we heard rockets detonating very close, making the ground shake. We were used to the sound and the public announcements, *"Take cover, Put on your PPE, shelter in place."* The instructor shouted that she was canceling her talk, as we all laughed, put on our PPE, and got under the conference table.

We had developed a *laissez-faire* attitude about our ever-present danger, assuming it would not touch us. Very naïve, but I suppose it's how the body copes.

❧

On weekends in Amman or on R&R, the staff often chilled out at resort hotels at the Dead Sea, only an hour away, while others would travel to the Jordanian ruins of Petra, the Wadi Rum desert, or go diving at Aqaba on the Jordanian side of the Red Sea, or Sharma El-Sheikh in Egypt, across the Red Sea. I visited all those spots, but my favorites were diving in the Red Sea with Paul, going on a three-night camel safari in the Wadi Rum Desert in southern Jordan, and camping in Bedouin tents with Maryanne and her daughter, my good friends from Kenya.

Paul was now working in Sri Lanka. We stayed in touch by email and an occasional satellite phone call, but we were miles apart in many ways. He was enjoying his humanitarian work, feeling healthy again. I was embarking on a new career, alone in the Middle East.

❧

I was assigned as a Senior Information Management Officer, to the UNAMI Security Section, reporting directly to the section chief. It was a new position, created to improve the section's ability to perform its duties with the latest technology, given the danger and instability in Iraq. My section's mission was to protect all UN professional staff members wherever they entered the Red Zone, which encompassed most of Iraq, for political, humanitarian, or security purposes. Any visit by UN personnel, outside the Green Zone, into the Red Zone was called a mission. The Red Zone was very dangerous, so the mission received full protection from Coalition Forces, usually in Humvees.

For each UN mission, Army Humvees would drive into our compound, ready for deployment. I felt very secure as I greeted the young army personnel in desert fatigues as I walked across to the cafeteria for lunch. It felt like I was back at Fort Bragg. Unfortunately, I knew that some of these young men and women would return home with severe injuries, disabilities, and emotional trauma, as I had seen at Walter Reed Hospital. Others would not return alive.

❧

A new staff living compound was located about two kilometers from our office compound. All personnel used only fully armored vehicles and white Toyota SUVs. The living compound comprised a complex of about seventy-five trailers, one for each professional staff member, arranged in a complex labyrinth, one next to the other in rows.

Trailer numbers were not in any order, so it was easy to get lost in the pitch-dark trailer maze, especially in the middle of the night after riding a chopper into the Green Zone. Soon enough, I learned my way around.

Each UN compound was enclosed within a twelve-foot-thick concrete wall. The entrance/exit had a secure checkpoint with armed guards twenty-four hours a day, where Identification cards were checked, and each vehicle was scanned for potential bombs. Hoods and trunks were searched as well. Sometimes, military bomb dogs aided the process.

The housing complex, my home away from home, included a fantastic cafeteria offering a wide variety of American food, as much as I could eat or take back to my room. Water bottles were available everywhere. There was a well-equipped gym I often used in the evening to unwind, and a game room with a ping-pong table that I never used. My trailer included a single bed, desk, television, and bathroom, all with Wi-Fi, heat, and air conditioning.

The U.S. military had taken over Saddam Hussein's Palace. This senior military staff enclave offered many perks to official personnel, including a large swimming pool complex and a well-equipped workout room. I signed up for yoga classes there, always led by a ripped, young army soldier. Namaste!

I got to know most of the women staff members in my section, who were qualified in personal security protection. These were young, good-looking, experienced, gun-toting security officers, with prior military or police experience, from all over the world. Sometimes they arranged a Sunday spa day in the Green Zone and invited me a few times. We went to an Iraqi home in the zone, in our armed vehicle, of course, and drank champagne while listening to music and having our nails painted. It was a way to let our hair down and have fun.

One of my closest friends, Vicky, was a UN nurse from New Zealand. She was also a part-time roommate who was assigned to Baghdad regularly. She stored her stuff at my place, and when she had time off, she'd stay with me or repack and travel somewhere on R&R. We had lots of fun.

❧

During weekends, most staff slept late in their air-conditioned trailers. After a leisurely lunch, many, including me, went into the office, since there was not much else to do.

❧

Let me describe a bit about my job. I was assigned as a Senior Information Management Officer, to the UNAMI Security Section, reporting directly to the section chief. It was a new position, created to improve the section's ability to perform its duties with the latest technology, given the danger and instability in Iraq. My section's mission was to protect all UN professional staff members wherever they entered the Red Zone, which encompassed most of Iraq, for political, humanitarian, or security purposes. Any visit by UN personnel, outside the Green Zone, into the Red Zone was called a mission. The Red Zone was very dangerous, so the mission received full protection from Coalition Forces, usually in Humvees.

For each mission, Army Humvees would drive into our compound, ready for deployment. I felt very secure as I greeted the young army personnel in desert fatigues as I walked across to the cafeteria for lunch. It felt like I was back at Fort Bragg. Unfortunately, I knew that some of these young men and women would return home with severe injuries, disabilities, and emotional trauma, as I had seen at Walter Reed Hospital. Others would not return alive.

❧

My primary task was to design a secure web-based system using commercial off-the-shelf software. It was quite a challenge not just to define the requirements, but also to turn them into a comprehensive procurement document to be approved by UN Headquarters, and then to turn the approved document into a Request for Proposal, RFP for international bidding.

The complex, cumbersome, snail-paced UNHQ management bureaucracy had to approve any expenditure, no matter how important. I went to UNHQ in New York City and briefed the Safety and Security powers-that-be on the procurements required and the importance of the system. I realized now why it took one and a half years for me to get a job offer.

In this male-dominated culture, I tried my best to go from a confident, assertive businesswoman to a quiet, non-confrontational, yet intelligent woman. I tried to find my place, but I was a different duck swimming in strange waters, with other cultures trying to work together, all with different work ethics. However, I refused to be the blushing, uncertain woman who deferred to men at all costs, and demurred if challenged. Yuck, that was impossible for me! My female co-workers gave me some good advice, which made things a bit easier, but I am who I am.

❧

Amman, the Capital of Jordan, is at an elevation of two thousand feet. The weather is hot and dry, in the 80s in the summer and 40s in the winter. I've witnessed snow falling on the olive trees lining the streets in winter.

A great perk was the ability for professional staff to sign out a UN vehicle for the weekend. When I was able to get a vehicle, I'd usually plan on going to the Dead Sea Marriott Resort, less than an hour away, with a friend for a day of sun, swimming, covering my body with the famous therapeutic Dead Sea mud, and floating in the buoyant water.

Swimming there can be dangerous because the water's high salinity can irritate your eyes, so everyone stays close to shore. UN personnel had a special rate of twenty-five dollars a day to use the spa. It was a hard life working in a war zone, and we deserved our beachside spa days.

I learned to love hummus, souvlaki, and falafel on naan bread from the neighborhood take-out shop. A three-story mall nearby had both Western and Arab shops. Supermarkets had most things I needed, but not the Cheez-Its I love. The olive display case contained a wide variety, and a small room held all kinds of nuts and dried fruits. My favorite was dried mangoes.

❧

Hotels, malls, department stores, supermarkets, and other public establishments had one distinct difference. Due to the 2005 Al Qaeda bombings of hotels in Amman, tight security was always in effect. Anyone entering a large public building, such as a mall, hotel, or supermarket, was required to place handbags, briefcases, and similar items on a metal detector conveyor belt and walk through a body metal detector. Other than that, life in Amman was normal. I did not need my PPE until I traveled to Iraq.

❧

Time went by quickly, and I got into a routine once again, married but still living alone. I was happily independent, capable, and not interested in any male companionship. I steered clear of all social get-togethers.

Whether in Amman or Iraq, I went to the gym, read, and watched television in the evening. In Amman, I had my pets to come home to. I was content with my life and happy to be back in such an unusual, challenging career. As Eiger grew older, I noticed him slowing down, not wanting to complete our usual walking route. Otherwise, he seemed fine and was excellent company. The neighborhood respected us when I took him for his walks.

42

I finally arranged a seven-day vacation for Paul and I to be together doing what we loved. It was a liveaboard diving vacation in the Maldives, a group of islands in the middle of the Indian Ocean. We were both advanced divers but had not been on a long dive trip since his accident.

This vacation was significant, and we were looking forward to getting together and doing what we loved. The boat supported about twenty divers from all over the world. After long flights, we found our dive boat and took off from the Maldives Harbor, headed for the open sea. The director and dive master briefed us on rules and regulations, dive and mealtimes, and safe dive practices. We prepared our gear for the first dive. Paul had forgotten to pack part of his equipment and had to rent what was available on the boat. It would be about a ninety-foot dive to the bottom. Our initial jump-off point was only forty feet deep with excellent visibility.

I held back so the impatient divers could get in the water first. Paul deflated his Buoyancy compensator, BC, jumped in, gave an okay signal, and descended to the bottom to wait for me. I jumped right after, deflated my BC, and swam down toward him. Approaching forty feet, I inflated my BC a bit to allow me to swim above the bottom. As I approached, Paul looked very agitated and angry. He was banging his BC valve on a nearby rock. He had plenty of air, but he was unable to inflate his BC. There is a handy inflation valve on the BC, but we had not been diving in a while, and in a panic, had forgotten about it.

As I neared him, I realized he was panicking. Other divers had taken off with the dive master in the lead. I looked up to make sure the boat was still there, but it could take off for the dive pick-up point, leaving us stranded. I motioned for us to surface and return to the boat with me, but he refused, growing more agitated.

Then a female divemaster saw Paul struggling, she swam over, took him by the arm, and guided both of us up to the boat. Once safely onboard, Paul tried to explain what had happened. I realized it had been a close call, especially if the boat had left without us.

After resting for a few moments, she told Paul to relax and sit this one out. She invited me to continue my dive, and we both jumped back into the water and had a thrilling dive at 90 feet, seeing a huge eel, many colorful fish, and the carcass of a large albatross floating near the bottom. At the end of our allotted time at depth, we hung on the anchor line for our three-minute decompression stop and ascended to the boat.

She later took me aside and told me very seriously that Paul was an unsafe diver and that I should not rely on him as a buddy. She would ensure that I had a qualified divemaster looking after us during our remaining dives on this trip. It shocked me, but I understood that his panic could have caused our death. It seemed the bombing had affected him in ways I could not comprehend. However, once his equipment was changed, Paul did fine on the other dives. It is easy to be fine when all your equipment is working, but panicking underwater, when things go wrong, is dangerous. I kept a close eye on him, and we finished off the week with a sea mount dive. I was sad when I realized we would never dive again.

Later, I thought about the incident and tried to understand why Paul lost control when he realized he was in a crisis. Then I remember a time in Kenya, shortly after we had arrived and moved into our rental house. Paul drove into our compound after dark one night. Eiger ran to catch up to his car, and Paul ran into him. I had watched him drive in and saw the entire thing. Eiger was lying on the ground, obviously hurt, but Paul was ranting and raving, shouting, "Why me? Why did this happen to me?" He ignored Eiger and focused only on himself.

Noticing Eiger's leg was damaged, I shouted at Paul to help me put him in the car, then jumped in to calm Eiger. I immediately told Paul to call Sarina, the local vet. Finally, he stopped his self-flagellation guilt trip and called the vet. If I had not been there, I don't know what would have transpired. I am the one who becomes controlled and unemotional in a crisis. Paul, on the other hand, just lost it and was useless. It was scary! This happened long before the bombing. That was just Paul.

I was very sad about losing our incredible diving hobby. It had been an excellent sport we had grown to love. We dove in Roatán, Hawaii, Bermuda, the Cayman Islands, the Red Sea, and finally the Maldives. My trusted buddy was no longer there to keep us safe. He was not even there to keep himself safe

43

I was enjoying my challenging UN assignment when Paul received his next contract in Panama City, Panama. I visited him and helped him pick out a small apartment in Old Panama neighborhood. He also visited me when he could. We were happy with the arrangement. Neither of us insisted that the other modify his or her career to accommodate the other. We respected each other's needs and tried to make it work, long-distance.

I was in the middle of system design and the procurement of critical items needed by the mission when management asked me to continue my assignment for a fourth year, and I accepted.

My section chief, a remarkable Australian, rotated after a normal three-year assignment, and Ivan, a new Russian chief, about my age, arrived.

I scheduled time to brief Ivan on my assignment, but he abruptly told me he was not interested. "You will now report to the training officer, Joe, your new boss." I knew Joe. He was a good training officer but knew nothing about information management systems. He called me into his office and, without even asking to be briefed on my responsibilities, insisted that weekly status reports and all memos go through him, then to the recipients. Joe was now a roadblock to my effectiveness.

Exasperated, I made a case to Ivan that I should be reporting to him, but he would not budge. I soon realized this environment was a personal Cold War all over again, Russia vs. USA, and that I would not win. As time went on, I became increasingly frustrated and ignored. Then, one weekend, I was sexually harassed in the public PX common area by Joe, my new boss. I also had a witness.

❧

I had had enough of his shit and sought advice from my closest colleagues in Baghdad about the incident, to corroborate my story if needed, and then called Paul to explain what happened. He agreed that I did not have to put up with that shit and suggested that I turn in my resignation and retirement notice. "It's time for us both to retire," he said, and I agreed.

I filed a formal sexual harassment complaint, then turned in my termination notice. After the word got out about my sexual harassment complaint, several other professional women from the security section also filed complaints against their coworkers, who would harass them, knocking on their trailer in the middle of the night, and threaten them. I heard later that I had started a wave of sexual harassment exposure. The UN was happy to see me leave.

44

I had had enough of the UN rat race and was proud to resign. The slate was clean, and I looked forward to being back with Paul and carving out a new life called retirement. Paul and I talked on the phone at length about what retirement meant and where it would be. We agreed that Kenya was our first choice. The Kenyan boys were there, as were many friends, and Paul had the UN network Paul could use.

I contacted Maryanne, my best friend in Nairobi. As soon as she heard that I was coming to Nairobi to find a retirement home, she offered her home as a place to stay. So many good memories returned when I arrived. She welcomed me like a sister. However, she cautioned that things had changed in the five years I had been away. Inflation was rampant. Security was very marginal. Plus, corruption was at an all-time high. Maryanne had even added a steel safe room to her house and had been confined there for five days during a local tribal uprising. It did not sound hopeful!

I set off to see what kind of home we could rent and quickly learned that housing had more than doubled. We could not afford to retire with inflation like this. What a disappointment. Then I had to explain to the boys that I would not be moving after all. I returned to

Jordan. That wasn't easy, but they were in their twenties now and realized I had my own life. I promised to keep in touch over social media and visit them.

❧

Our second choice was the Pacific Coast of Costa Rica. We had traveled there from the U.S. in 1990 and fell in love with what I called the Tropical Switzerland, with mountains, rainforests, volcanoes, the Pacific Coast, and sandy beaches. The jungle was home to wild animals such as jaguars, ocelots, several types of monkeys, sloths, and tropical birds like toucans. It is a friendly, stable country with plenty of police but no military, and it is a friend of the U.S. Because it lies near the equator in Central America, it is considered tropical, with only two seasons. The high season for tourism is December through May, during the dry season, which is sunny and in the high nineties at the beaches. The low season runs from May to December, when clouds roll in and the rainy season begins. The temperature in the low season is about ten degrees lower. The Pacific Coast provides refreshing ocean breezes and lots of fresh air. In many cases, no heat or air conditioning is required. San José, the Capital, is a large modern city that lies in the mountains at over thirty-five thousand feet.

Situated on the earthquake's Ring of Fire, Costa Rica's charm includes many waterfalls, volcanoes, and hot springs. In this seismic zone, there are frequent mild earthquakes that rarely cause damage.

❧

Returning to the U.S. was never an option for us after living so many years overseas. Whenever we visited the U.S. while living overseas, each town or city seemed like a cookie-cutter of the next, thanks to all the franchise shops that had taken over. Shopping areas were the same—Home Depot, Macy's, Lowe's, Marshalls, TJ Maxx, and franchise restaurants like Ruby Tuesdays, Chili's, Burger King, McDonald's, Kentucky Fried Chicken, or Waffle House, and Denny's.

Paul was still busy at work, but he encouraged me to explore for a place to live anyway. I booked a flight and a rental car and soon arrived in the tropical heat of San José, the Capital of Costa Rica. I headed out of the city to the South Pacific coast near Jaco.

Our goal was to rent a furnished house for at least six to twelve months to determine whether the environment and the lifestyle were what we expected and wanted long-term. After only a day or two of visiting several real estate offices in the area, I realized there were no rentals except for weekly beach rentals in Jaco, where the rent was one thousand dollars a week. That was discouraging. I never thought I'd have any trouble finding a house to rent, but I learned that most Gringos buy land first and then build their dream home. I continued my drive south along the coast to Dominical. During the two-hour drive through a few small towns, I encountered vast palm plantations that went on for miles along both sides of the road. Then, I spotted a small community of shingled houses built in the 1950s to house all the plantation workers and their families. The palms produced palm oil, which was processed and exported worldwide.

Dominical is a very small, laid-back surfing destination on the southern Pacific Coast for young adventurers and old hippies on a tight budget. Mature trees line the main drag of Dominical, which stretches for only three or four blocks. Along the small beach, accommodations and popular surf lessons were always available. An assortment of restaurants and bars open to the sea breezes tempt visitors with a Tico breakfast, fish tacos, or the old standard, a giant cheeseburger with all the trimmings. A variety of colorful souvenir shops set up on the beach entice tourists. Popular surfer rentals consisted of a bunk bed with a sheet and a ceiling fan. If you wanted to splurge, hot water was extra.

Realizing that beach towns were not the place to look for a house to rent, I headed east into some beautiful rolling hills with two-lane switchbacks. Then I arrived in Platanillo, a very small town with a Catholic Church and a small Tico bar with a small restaurant, named Carolina's, next door. Next to the Catholic Church was a community center with a soccer field. Across the street was a small local convenience store offering everything from potato chips of all kinds, milk, beer, wine, and liquor, plumbing supplies, rope for catching cattle, and, of course, all kinds of ice cream bars.

Just outside of town, I found a small, nondescript hotel with a restaurant. I was going to do some serious searching, but, of course, I knew no Spanish. But Paul was a fluent Spanish speaker. After lunch, I grabbed the local advertising rags to find realty offices. I called a few offices and either got a Tico who didn't speak any English or a Tico who barely understood me, but said, "No rental homes."

I reported my frustration to Paul that evening. He encouraged me to talk to locals, so that night I asked a bartender at the hotel whom I should contact about long-term home rentals, and he gave me the name of JJ Realtors, near Platanillo, just up the road. I suppose I had been expecting a home market like in the States with lots of variety everywhere, available to rent or buy at different prices. Before turning in, I had a little talk with myself and told myself I had to be patient and not expect to find endless lovely rentals. It looked like the country and the customs were evolving. I was in a lush rural area with rolling hills of cattle land. The cattle industry was thriving here. There were no townhouses or planned communities anywhere but in Jaco or near San José. I ratcheted back my enthusiasm. Maybe I would not find anything on this trip, but at least it would be an adventure.

❧

I woke early and had a typical breakfast of scrambled eggs with ham, an ample serving of gallo pinto, beans and rice, with pineapple and mango slices, and delicious Costa Rican coffee. I was now energized, got in my car, and found JJ's office in the little town of Platanillo, four blocks long. He was a young Tico who spoke perfect English after living in the U.S. He began by saying, "You have come to a very rural cattle town where the locals are friendly and helpful. Several Gringos have built homes and settled here. I think you would enjoy it."

I explained, "My husband and I are Americans. We want to move to Costa Rica to retire. We have chosen the South Pacific as our first choice and are interested in renting a furnished home for at least six months to a year. We need to understand the social culture, the climate, and experience the cost of living, as well as the availability of medical and dental facilities. In short, we want to be sure we'll be happy here for the rest of our lives."

JJ asked, "What do you want to pay for rent?"

I had no idea what the market was like, but deciding to go low, I said, "About seven hundred dollars a month."

Without taking a breath, he said, "I have no rentals at all. People own their homes, and there is no rental market. Usually, people come down here and want to build their own eclectic dream home from scratch."

I could understand that, but during our trips, we had found several lovely homes. They were closer to the suburbs of San José, and not in Platanillo, three and a half hours from the Capital. I thought for a second, and then asked, "Do you know of any homes for sale that had been on the market for a long time and perhaps the owner might consider a rental contract for six months to a year, or until the home was sold?"

I leaned back in my chair to give him time to think. After a few moments, a light came on in his mind. He reached into his desk drawer and pulled out an embossed flier showing a gorgeous home with traditional tile roofs, beautiful gardens, a pool, and a guesthouse.

He handed me the flyer and started telling me about the finca, but I didn't hear a word he said. I kept looking at this beautiful home with an expansive lawn and gardens, cradled by huge mango trees. Wow, I thought. I have died and gone to heaven, but did not even smile to indicate my delight. He said the rent was much higher, fifteen hundred dollars a month, well above the seven hundred dollars I had quoted. I read through it quickly and learned that the property included twenty-two acres. I wanted to shout to the heavens, "This is it!" This is it! It's perfect." But instead, I slowly passed the flyer back to him and replied, "Oh well, it is quite high, but could we go see it anyway? It will give me an idea of what home construction is like."

"Sure," he said, and escorted me to his truck. He explained, "I only have a gate key. I'll have to get house keys from the owner's caretaker, John, just down the road."

"That's fine. At least I'll get an idea," I responded.

❧

After a five-minute drive down a small two-lane dirt road, he stopped at a black gate and unlocked it. The gate opened to a magnificent, verdant vista of a tropical wonderland, with a beautiful white house at its center. He slowly drove down the curved driveway and parked next to the house. This was overwhelming. Huge, majestic trees provided a bit of shade here and there. This 180-degree vista included a view of the Pacific and gentle rolling hills. Close by, an ample front yard sloped gently to a large pool with a lovely, blue-painted guest house. A variety of flowering trees provided ample privacy and tranquility. I was mesmerized by the gentle breeze coming off the Pacific. I didn't need to look any further. This was a dream come true, much more than I had ever imagined in my mind's eye. And even a swimming pool!

I peeked in the windows and noticed the home was fully furnished with bamboo furniture and pictures on the walls. The flier indicated there were two bedrooms and two baths, a large, shaded veranda in front, with an amazing, vaulted ceiling with large wooden beams in the central part of the house. The living room/dining/kitchen area was all open and airy. Three sliding glass doors at the front opened onto the spacious tiled veranda, which overlooked the lawns, gardens, pool, and guest house. Did I mention that it was turn-key, furnished, and immaculate? Oh My God!

I thought I would spontaneously combust right there, trying to keep my amazement to myself behind a serious, but very impressed expression. Pure joy coursed through my veins at finding this treasure. JJ added, "There are mango and orange orchards to the right, and the property had a constant spring-fed stream along one of its boundaries."

Talk about tranquility and beauty! I was hooked. The sales price on the flyer was seven hundred and fifty thousand dollars, entirely out of our orbit, but we could rent for six to twelve months while we looked around. As we drove away, I expressed to JJ, "This is an incredibly beautiful home. Thank you so much for taking the time to show me this property. I'll mention it to my husband this evening."

JJ offered, "I'll contact John and see if I can get the keys for you to see the inside of the house tomorrow."

I immediately phoned Paul and told him I had found our dream home, and sent the photos I had taken. He was awestruck and agreed we could afford a six-month lease. I scratched my head. Could I be moving from a trailer in Iraq to this beautiful property, even for a while?

I met JJ and John the next day at the property. John was a friendly retired cop from Florida who had married a Tica, and they lived just down the street. He knew the house well and showed me around. I was sold. JJ did not have any rental agreements on hand, so John made an appointment with his attorney, who drew up a six-month rental contract, May through December, with an option to buy. It was now April. The owners always came down for six months, December through April 2010.

❧

The deal was done! John insisted I move out of the cheesy hotel I was staying at and into a small house on his property. I needed to open a bank account to quickly wire the deposit and the first month's rent, and to get the lay of the land. I agreed and met his lovely wife, Maria. They drove me all around the area, then drove up a small mountain to a larger town, San Isidro de El General, where almost everything could be found, even a Subway Restaurant. They also introduced me to some of their gringo friends in the area. By the end of the week, we had become fast friends. I could not wait to move to Platanillo.

45

The anticipation of retiring and being together in our dream home was exciting. There were several retired gringos, westerners living in our little town, from the U.S., Canada, and even Europe.

At last, Paul and I were settling down, at least in the same time zone as our families, which made it easier to keep in touch. Our kids with their families made trips to visit us and see our new place. They were blown away by the beauty and the location of our farm, with its fantastic view of the Pacific. They enjoyed the nearby beaches, surfing, zip-line adventures, horseback riding through the forest to beautiful waterfalls, and, of course, a relaxing swim at sunset.

❧

Everyone was very welcoming. Ticos were very helpful and kind. Paul was fluent in Spanish, but I was hopeless with languages and constantly listened to Spanish compact discs in the car. Soon, we had a friendly group of friends and socialized often. There were no good restaurants nearby, so we'd organize dinner at someone's house. Paul and I were very happy and content. The next step was to search for a permanent home to buy or build.

Costa Rica is a tropical paradise. The temperature was typically seventy degrees in the early morning, with a high of eighty-five degrees in the shade. It cooled off by dusk, reaching a nightly low of sixty-five degrees. Screened windows and sliding doors were always open, with soft sea breezes bringing a cooling effect. At night, while watching television, I would close two of the three front sliding doors, leaving only one open for the dogs to get out. Sometimes we had a stray fruit bat visit us during the night and literally 'hung out' around our ceiling lamps, creating quite a disgusting spray of guano by morning. I began to prefer the rainy season we were living in. It was usually cloudy and cooler with rain in the evenings. Powerful thunderstorms are common at night. I've always loved gardening, but this was not in the States, in the temperate zone. It was the tropics, and it was totally different. Tropical flowering trees and bushes around the property grew like weeds and had to be trimmed regularly. The area around the house, which I call the compound, had many large, mature trees along the perimeter. A giant Spanish cedar tree towered over the driveway, and two large mango trees shaded the gated entrance. There was a delicious Valencia orange orchard just down the path from the house. I love the fresh orange juice and usually give many oranges to neighbors because we couldn't eat them all. I have planted several other fruit trees, like lime, avocado, and banana, which should bear fruit in the future.

❧

When we were living in Nairobi, we had met an American who had started raising and training protection dogs, primarily for the military special forces and police departments. The breeds include Dutch Shepherds, Belgian Malinois, and a few German Shepherds. After watching a demonstration of their intelligence, expert training, and exuberance, I was hooked. They mentioned having a sister organization in Costa Rica, so I called and arranged a visit to Guanacaste in the north. I was not interested in the protection side of the training, but hoped I could work with the puppies to socialize them before the hardcore obedience training and attack work began. We needed a new dog. Eiger died at the age of twelve and was buried in the Jordanian hills. He was a devoted companion to both of us.

We drove six hours to the Guanacaste Peninsula, to the small beach town of Nosara on the Pacific coast, to meet Brandon, an energetic, enthusiastic young American man. He moved from the U.S. to Costa Rica to surf, fell in love, married a young, beautiful local woman, and started his dog-training business.

Brandon welcomed us, showed us his training area, and then gave us a demonstration of their unbelievable obedience training. Dutch Shepherds are similar in size to German Shepherds, but their short coats are brindled, with black and brown stripes that give them a unique, tiger-like appearance. Brandon's dogs were beautiful, friendly, and showed total obedience. They were alert and always focused on him. I could tell they were having fun too. I was impressed with the training technique, which did not use treats or discipline but instead relied on simple encouragement and constant praise, or, as Brandon put it, direction, correction, praise." Paul and I were convinced we had come to the right place. We wanted a good companion but also needed home security. A sign on the front gate would announce *Perro Bravo,* Attack Dog, to deter the occasional petty crime that exists in the country.

Brandon shared that this training technique originated years ago in Germany. Issue a command in German, and the dog obeyed immediately, without question or coaxing. These dogs loved to please their master and never begged for food or treats. The terms *good sitz*" or *"good platz"* and a pat on the head were enough to make them smile.

❧

That night, over dinner, we agreed that this was the right kind of dog for us. We were excited to know we'd receive a fully trained female. Brandon did not have the right dog for us locally, but agreed to contact his business partner in Canada, Baden Canines, to see what he could do.

In less than a month, we learned that our dog, Brisa, would be arriving from Canada in a week. On this trip, we would meet our new dog and then undergo the complex, four-day training required to interact with and handle Brisa, our new family member. She was beautiful and very friendly. After getting to know her and leading her around a bit on the leash, Brandon told us to take her back to our hotel to start the bonding process. He loaned us a kennel to keep her in at night.

The next morning, we met Brandon, and he started by having Brisa and me go through simple walk, sit, down, and stay commands in German. Brisa was amazing, and I was pleased by her precise movements. After about an hour, Brandon approached me, with a little smile on his face, and asked, You let her sleep with you, didn't you, instead of leaving her in her crate?"

I said, No, she was in her crate all night." He remarked, "I have never seen a dog bond so quickly to anyone." I was psyched. We were a team, and I became the alpha. Paul and I took turns with Brisa, learning techniques and understanding her signals, while Brisa thought to herself, I already know all this stuff." Her intelligence and instant obedience were phenomenal. I had never seen a dog so responsive, without ever expecting a treat. After four days of training, we headed home with Brisa, our protection dog.

Once home, Paul and I took Brisa for walks every morning, and we met new neighbors, Sonja and Fritz. Paul just walked up to their gate and introduced us. They were from Holland and had a large horse ranch with at least ten horses. We got to know each other, and she invited me to go riding with her. I had not been on a horse for many years, so she gave me an older, gentle female named Ginger. I loved riding. I was back in the saddle after my childhood riding experience. I found horseback riding was like riding a bicycle. It all came back to mind, but my muscles had lost that memory, and it took time for my body to adjust. After several weeks, I was galloping up a small hill, laughing with pure joy.

John and Maria introduced us to other friends, Nancy and James, from Atlanta, and Lily, a single retired nurse from Minnesota. Nancy and I often got together with Sonja and Lily for lunch. One day, she asked me to pet-sit a Jack Russell rescue named Hatti while she and James went to the States. I agreed but told her, "Paul will fall in love with Hatti, and you will never get her back." I was right! Paul fell in love. Now it was Brisa and Hatti running the farm.

Nancy and I often went on adventures in San José, to hot springs and craft shows. She was a southern belle from Georgia. She was a widow who had recently remarried and moved to Costa Rica with her new husband, James. She was a kind, gentle soul, very humble and religious. Her hobby was rescuing abandoned dogs and taking them to her veterinarian for an examination, including immunizations and neutering. Then she'd find them good homes. She was a delightful, loving person, and we became good friends.

46

We were loving life in Costa Rica as the months flew by. December was fast approaching. We had not found any homes we really liked. A couple of homes we reviewed had been built for a very tall couple, so I could not reach the top shelves of the kitchen and bath cabinets. The stairs were constructed eight inches tall, instead of the world standard of seven inches. Try going up and down those stairs with a load of laundry, I would have broken my neck. Another house had a pond in the middle of the living room, creating an inviting, cool place for our dogs to lounge, perhaps roll over, then walk through the house dripping wet. Moving on, the next house was cute inside, but felt more like a prison than a house, with heavy black burglar bars covering all the windows and doors. JJ was right. Each was a little unique.

Paul had established a corporation, a limited liability corporation, LLC, for himself as a private contractor. He got a contract taking him all over the world. Sometimes he was gone for several weeks. I continued meeting with realtors within fifty kilometers of Platanillo to find a nice building lot for sale in a safe, private area. I went looking for lots on the sides of mountains, drove through creeks, pineapple farms, and cattle ranches, but nothing felt like the right place. I also began to understand the complexities of building a home in a third-world country." Was there access to water and electricity, or did you need to drill a well? There are earthquake building codes and required soil samples to ensure your house or pool does not slide down the hill in a downpour. Proper drainage was a major concern during the tropical rainy season, as torrential downpours left the land saturated—a landslide waiting to happen. This was uncharted territory, and the more we looked, the more horror stories I heard of people getting scammed, contractors that didn't know what they were doing, or the new solar system never worked. Some contractors just ran out of "building" money and left.

We looked and looked, but nothing had our name on it. By early November, I knew we'd have to find another rental. The house's owners had already asked us whether we wanted to make an offer to buy. I knew it was far beyond our financial means. I said, "No, we love it, but it is out of our price range." It was time to find another rental and move out.

I found a nice, small furnished house in a secure neighborhood with a small pool, just down the road from Platanillo. We would not have bought it, but as a rental, it was fine—a little quirky, with a garage door instead of a front door—but at a lower rent. We signed a six-month lease. The home was vacant, so I was allowed to move things in as soon as we had signed the lease and paid the first month's rent.

Then one day, I opened the gate, returning home after moving another load of our stuff to the new rental. I pulled in and stopped in the driveway, looking at the vista: the gentle rolling hills, the Pacific Ocean, and the beautiful house we had grown to love. I had put emotional roots down and really loved this place. This beautiful place has been my home for six months. I would really miss it. Later, I was having coffee at Maria's and mentioned to her my sadness about having to move. I explained how much I regretted having to move out of the wonderful house we had grown to love. She said, "Barbara, I have known the owners for years. They need to sell. Call Sharon and make her an offer?" I replied, "I would be insulting her. There is a huge difference between her asking price and my offer." Maria replied, "Talk directly to Sharon, no one else. Maybe she will accept. It's worth a try. I took her advice and sent her an email explaining how much we loved the property she had built. After some haggling, our offer was accepted. It was over our budget, but we did not have to build a house from scratch. I was ecstatic, and Paul was very pleased as well. This is going to be our home. Thanks so much, Maria, you made it happen!

❧

We scrounged all our available money, and then some, and closed in January 2010. Then we had to pack up our stuff in the new rental and move it all back, but this time into our very own home. It was a task of pure love. We were so blessed.

Our first project was to put up a six-foot chain-link fence around the house and pool area so the dogs could run free. The police had visited us more than twice to tell us that Brisa was barking at the children as they passed on their way to school. Word had gotten out that we had a protection, i.e., an attack dog, and I could not blame them. He ordered us to tie Brisa up. If there were another complaint, he'd confiscate her. We hired a contractor to build a long, sturdy, six-foot chain-link fence around the entire living area. He also added two small dog kennels, adjoining the bodega by the driveway, a place to secure the dogs when workers were on the property. It was a worthwhile investment.

❧

I continued horseback riding with Sonja, all the while, in the back of my mind, thinking I should have my own horse. I had wanted a horse all my life. Why not? After all, I had a farm with lots of pasture. A local cattleman named Olher took us to see a stallion named Baru, a beautiful, black-and-white-painted quarter horse. When I test-rode him, he was gentle and responsive. Yes, he was just what I wanted. We bought him and had him transported to the farm. Baru was so calm and gentle, not bothered by the big trucks passing by.

❧

The first time I took Baru out riding with Sonja, he was very quiet and obeyed my signals. We turned down a nearby seldom-used dirt road and continued a leisurely walk. Then, Sonja asked, "Do you want to try to canter up this hill with Baru?" I had done it many times with her horses, so I said, "Sure." When I gave him the signal to canter, he immediately responded, but with each stride, he bucked both back legs in the air, causing me to be thrown forward onto his neck, losing any control of the reins. He was like a bucking bronco, and the faster he cantered, the quicker I was thrust forward, gripping his neck, and unable to pull him back. I was scared to death and focused on not being thrown over his head, where he could stampede over me. When we finally arrived at the top, he slowed to a walk. I promptly stopped him and dismounted, shaking like a leaf. I was finally safe and burst into tears from sheer terror.

Sonja tried to minimize the incident, saying, "He seemed really happy to be cantering, but you know, he is a stallion." She wanted me to know that he was not a malicious, out-of-control runaway horse.

"Yes, I understand." She hooked up a lead to his bridle and to her saddle on the other end, and I agreed to get back on and return home with her. I knew he had to be castrated, or I'd never ride him again.

The vet came to our house and castrated him on our front lawn. That solved the problem, but it would be quite a while before I trusted him. Baru should not be alone. He needs a companion," Sonja said.

She sold me the first horse she bought years ago, Rosy, an older, pure white mare, who would be a good companion for Baru. We could also ride her. With two horses on our farm, I had a lot to learn, so I employed David, one of Sonja's workers, to divide the open land into pastures, using teak trees found near our quebrada

❧

Ticos say, Without animals, a pasture will turn back into a jungle in no time." With all the pasture we had, we needed to keep the grass down, or it would attract poisonous snakes that could quickly kill a horse or a cow.

I proposed to Paul, "Let's buy a few young cows that will serve as lawn mowers in the pasture. There is a spring-fed *quebrada* creek they can use for fresh water. He indicated it was probably a good idea, but he was not interested in picking them out. The following week, I went to the cattle auction with Olher, who spoke perfect English. With his help, I bought five small, weaned female cows to be our lawnmowers. Once they were grown, I could breed them and have more calves, and that is what I did. The cows kept the grass down, got fresh water from the creek, and fertilized the land. The cows became very friendly, and I felt safe walking in the pasture with a small stick, petting their foreheads and around their horns, and giving them bananas.

Then of course, a new corral had to be built to shelter the animals. Olher did the construction and used the timber from our abundant forest. The existing cow grass was not that nourishing for horses. So, the next thing on the list was to gradually plant horse grass seed at the start of the rainy season and fence off the pastures so we could rotate the animals from one pasture to the next, and so forth. Once I divided up all the available pasture, I ended up with eight pastures, leaving forested areas for the wild animals. I was becoming a rancher and a conservationist.

❧

I loved the tropical terrain in Costa Rica and the Ticos' Pura Vida attitude. The Costa Rican government had developed a comprehensive program for protecting their precious natural resources to include the mountains, active volcanoes, lush forests, jungle, and vast oceans on both sides of the country, but especially the wild animals, panthers, ocelots, numerous kinds of monkeys, anteaters, and tapir, an unusual genetic cross between a horse and an elephant. Wild birds filled the skies. Long-billed toucans were very vocal each morning and evening around the house. Scarlet macaws inhabited the warmer coastal areas around Jaco. Amazon parrots flew over our *finca* in noisy flocks looking for the best-tasting fruit and nuts.

47

Things had been so chaotic moving to Costa Rica, and I really missed my sons and their families back in the U.S. Things were quiet around the ranch, and I decided to visit them over Christmas. Paul agreed to stay and look after things. Our friends in Platanillo always took turns having holiday festivities, and Paul was invited to their home for Christmas dinner.

I was relaxing after Christmas with my family in Illinois. A text arrived from one of my friends letting me know that Paul had been very drunk at their Christmas party. That was not unexpected. He had been drinking more often.

❧

A few days later I got a call, I'll never forget. Paul called in the late morning, very distressed, to tell me he could not find Brisa anywhere. "What!" I exclaimed. He repeated, "I have not been able to find Brisa this morning." My mind raced. I looked at my watch, and it was 11:00 a.m. That is impossible! I was in shock and disbelief. I took a slow breath, trying to stay calm and help him. I asked, "Did you feed her this morning?" After a few moments, he admitted in a flustered tone,

"I can't remember." That was when I lost it. She was my devoted, loving dog. She could not be 'lost' in the fenced compound.

The neighbor's email immediately came to mind, about his recent drinking, and bluntly asked Paul, "Had you been drinking?" He, of course, said, "No," when I knew he always drank in the evening. It was wrong of me. I panicked. Paul said he'd keep looking and hung up. I had never had a dog as intelligent, obedient, and devoted. We were so close. She followed me everywhere and was the most loving and obedient dog I had ever had.

An hour later, he called and told me he had found her floating dead in the pool. It made no sense, because soon after we brought her home, I had trained her to jump in the pool on command and would turn her around to face the steps and say, "Out." She knew how and where to get to the steps if she accidentally fell in.

He took her body to our veterinarian, who told him there had recently been reports of four other dogs drowning in pools due to cane toad attacks. Oh, my God, now I understood. I just froze, visualizing the horror of her death. The poor girl had tried to rinse out her mouth in the pool and probably went into convulsions. The loss of her left me with an emptiness I cannot explain or attempt to heal.

❧

Our dogs never bothered the occasional toad that would show up on our veranda at night. However, these cane toads have a hazardous side. When confronted by an animal, they spray a hallucinogenic chemical into the dog s mouth. This causes the dog to froth at the mouth, trying to expel the chemical; eventually, they can lose consciousness, and often seizures occur. We had been informed about this by neighbors. I had been told how to treat it, but Brisa and Hatti had never bothered cane toads.

Paul was devastated and felt helpless. I was as well. She was our baby and our protector. She was dead, after only two years with us, and such a wonderful part of my life. He asked where he should bury her. I thought for a moment and remembered how the turkey vultures fly all around, soaring on thermals as they hunt for prey. I wanted a symbol of Brisa's life to continue. I told Paul to take her body down to the pasture, down the hill out of sight, and leave her there, unburied. The vultures would come and take her, giving them nourishment. In the future, whenever I see vultures flying above the house, I d think of Brisa, the best dog I've ever had.

When I returned, we went down to the place where he had laid her down, and there was nothing left, no bones, not even a bit of fur. She had returned to the earth. We both sat and cried, holding each other. I apologized to Paul for lashing out and blaming him. He loved her too.

❧

Things were even more difficult between us after Brisa s death, but we maintained our daily routines as a sign that things were fine. Each afternoon, we'd pour glasses of wine and walk down to the pool area to sit and watch the beautiful sunset. One evening, Paul had already settled with his glass of wine in a chair by the pool. It was a bit cooler and refreshing, now that the day's hot sun was descending toward the horizon.

Since the air was cooling down, our rescued long-haired sheepdog, Chico, and our large black lab, Thunder, began playing tag, running full speed and chasing each other around the pool near the guest house. Holding a full glass of wine, I walked toward the pool, keeping an eye on the rambunctious dogs. Finally, they had a bit of fun after a really hot day. I was almost to the pool when Chico instantly switched directions and slammed into my left knee at a full run. I yelped in pain, so did he. Time slowed. The intense pain in my knee was overwhelming. I stood there dizzy, unable to utter a word. Ever so slowly, I fell on my butt in shock. I sat in the grass, unable to speak for a few moments, hoping the pain would subside. Paul finally saw me and came over, asking, "What happened?" and helped me up.

After several minutes, the pain subsided. I tried walking and was surprised to find that if I leaned on my right knee, I could walk without any pain. Okay, it's not broken, I thought to myself. The pain subsided, and we continued our ritual as the sun set over the

Pacific. I could even walk back to the house if I leaned to the right. I figured I d be fine. What a relief; it would be okay if I pampered it for a few days.

My knee never swelled, so I continued with my normal day and even went for a walk in the pasture. I mentioned to Nancy that I still had pain if I walked a certain way. She insisted I get an ultrasound, saying it could be a meniscus tear in my knee. I took her advice and went the next day. The ultrasound confirmed a meniscus tear. I knew I'd probably need surgery eventually, because Paul had had both knees repaired after years of running marathons. I got the name of a trauma surgeon, Dr. Gomez, at CIMA, who had done his residency at Boston Hospital. The doctor spoke perfect English, and when I called to make an appointment, he asked me to have an MRI of my knee before my appointment.

A week after the collision with the Chico, Paul and I drove to San José, got the MRI, and then drove to CIMA one of the best private hospitals in Costa Rica. I had learned not to rely on the country's socialized medical system.

Dr. Gomez greeted me warmly. I turned and saw a young, tall, very handsome Costa Rican. He requested the MRI, saying he d look at it and then call me into his office.

❧

After a few moments, his door opened, and without any formality, he declared, You have a broken leg and should not be walking on it. Come into my office," as he leaned down and helped me hobble on my right leg into his office. He explained to Paul and me that I had fractured my left tibia on the outer side of my knee, where the dog hit me. The weight-bearing portion of the tibia had been shattered, with many bone fragments remaining. There is also meniscus damage. He then explained, "The problem is that you have been walking on the leg for over a week, and scar tissue has started to form. You will need surgery to repair the damage immediately. A titanium plate with pins will be inserted to support the tibia. Damage to the cusp of the tibia must be repaired and strengthened. To do that,

I may have to take some bone from your hip. After surgery, I will provide you with a removable cast, but you cannot put any weight on that leg for four months. You can use crutches or a wheelchair. Physical therapy, PT will begin one day after surgery at CIMA, and that will continue for four months."

Oh my God, this is very serious. I had never broken a bone in my life, and because our dog was running around playing in the yard, I had a severe fracture that required a plate and pins. Yikes!

What now? Paul and I looked at each other in shock. We explained to Dr. Gomez that we had reservations about going back to the U.S. in a week for Thanksgiving. He explained, "I don't care where you have the surgery done, but it should be done as soon as possible, and you should plan to be off your foot for four months.

Over a cappuccino in the hospital cafe we discussed the options. I could return to the U.S. and have surgery under Medicare, but none of my family or his had a home that was conducive to living on one floor in crutches or with a wheelchair. We quickly realized that the best place for my recovery was at home in Platanillo.

We returned to Dr. Gomez's office and asked him to perform the surgery. He scheduled me for surgery the next day.

❧

I was sixty-five, so I needed a general physician at CIMA to determine I was healthy enough for surgery. I was immediately sent for blood tests, a chest x-ray, and an EKG. Then, he warned me that I must buy crutches right away and not put any weight on my left leg. In parting, he said, "Sorry, but nothing to eat or drink tonight or in the a.m."

I awoke from the anesthesia, feeling a bit drugged. Dr. Gomez soon visited and told me the surgery had gone very well. He had inserted a titanium plate along the side of my tibia and showed me the long, sutured incision along the side of my leg. He had also repaired the meniscus. A removable cast would be my closest friend for four months, and he stated that it must stay on unless I was having physical therapy or taking a shower. I stayed in the hospital for two more days, started physical therapy, and was released. The adventure had just begun.

Getting in and out of our SUV was very painful with the leg brace. Dr Gomez explained to me what a serious break it was, and that I must stay completely off the leg and avoid falling if I wanted to recover fully. He explained, Think of your tibia as a wine glass that has shattered. I thought to myself, “Had he heard about the accident with the wine glass?”

He continued, “I have done my best to glue it back together, but it is very unstable until the bone grows back, and if you put any weight on it or fall, I will never be able to repair the damage completely so that you will have future problems.” It was a very sobering reality, since I rode horses all the time.

❧

The PT schedule was very demanding, three times a week at CIMA, a three to four-hour drive each way from Platanillo. We tried it the following week and had to get a special disability room at the hotel. It was very uncomfortable in the car, then in and out of the vehicle for the appointment, eating out, and the return drive, which was over three hours. If I had to pee, it was a nightmare going to a gas station and having Paul help me drop my drawers. It was too much pain for the whole therapy ordeal. After my appointment, Paul asked to speak with the PT department head. She introduced herself, and Paul tried to explain the problem: “The long travel time to CIMA, overnight in a hotel, eating out, in and out of the vehicle constantly, was too painful and exhausting. We cannot afford to stay in a hotel for three nights every week, for the three required appointments each week for the next four months. He explained further, “We live in Platanillo, almost four hours away from CIMA.” He then asked, “Is there possibly another therapy center she could use in San Isidro, only thirty minutes away?”

She looked at us with compassion and explained that this surgery and PT treatment were part of a state-of-the-art program designed by Dr. Gomez, and that another physical therapist would not be trained to do it. She smiled, then explained she had a therapist working for her who lived in San Isidro. She said she would try to arrange for the therapist to work three days a week for us. In the end, she was able to get this therapist to come to our house on her days off, stay in the guest house for three nights, and eat with us. She gave me three days of intense therapy, eventually in the swimming pool. It was a perfect solution.

❧

When we finally got home, and Paul helped me into bed with the crutches, I realized I could not rely on them for safety. With three exuberant dogs at home, I knew crutches would not protect me from falling. The tile floors can be slippery in the rainy season. I decided to use a wheelchair for four months to ensure I kept my knee protected. After all, I still had horses to ride.

The wheelchair was comfortable. I could park the chair behind me and, while standing on my good leg, cook dinner, wash dishes, and even brush my teeth. The dogs even gave me space to maneuver around the house and onto the veranda.

The chair was more difficult for Paul, though, because whenever we went somewhere, he d have to pull the car up to the side of the house, help me from the chair to the car, then put the chair in the back. As a result, we didn’t go out to eat much.

For the first few weeks, I was the most comfortable in bed, where I could prop my brace on a pillow to keep the swelling down. The downside was having to call Paul,” when I needed something. He quickly became very testy, yelling loudly, What?” from the front of the house. I knew it was difficult for him, but I had nursed him back to health after the bombing, taking him for walks in his wheelchair all over Walter Reed, bringing him ice cream, feeding him, and making sure he got the proper care when he was hospitalized.

❧

After a couple of months into my convalescence, we both admitted to each other that our marriage had crumbled into a pile of hopeless desperation. Paul offered, “I will stay until you are back on your feet, then we'll separate, and I'll go back to the US." I agreed. It was a relief for both of us.

The next morning was weird because Paul had our separation already planned out. He invited me for breakfast to present his plan. Over coffee, he started, "I know you love the finca and living in Costa Rica, so you should keep the finca. I will take four other properties we had accumulated during our marriage, our international timeshare, the Roatan land, and the Paritta land investments."

The division worked out equitably for both of us. It was a done deal. Our Costa Rican attorney prepared legal documents and new wills. Neither of us ever spoke of divorce, so I asked him if he minded if we stayed married because I needed his international military medical insurance. He agreed, chuckling, "I doubt I will ever want to remarry."

At least we had cleared the air and could now look forward to a new life, apart. I knew it was for the best, but the pain of being together for thirty-two years was an emptiness I could not fill.

48

Neil and his daughter, Anastacia, came down on vacation to build me a chicken coop. We had water run to the coop, and I soon had chickens laying eggs every day, ducks, and eventually, a cute pair of geese. Then, of course, I needed to build a pond for the ducks and geese. I d go down each morning to feed them. Soon, there were baby ducks and cute baby geese following their momma, all in a row. Being a farmer brought me even closer to the wonders of nature. At sixty-five, I was still learning about farming and ranching, and it challenged me.

Paul had a few consulting jobs, and he would go overseas and then return weeks or months later. He seemed to enjoy them. I started volunteering at an animal rescue center on Saturday. It was fun, and I met more Gringos. I also joined the newly organized Pérez Zeledon International Women's Club in San Isidro. I met several lovely retired Gringa ladies, and we d sometimes meet for lunch and play cards.

A friend, Dale, taught me how to pick up a wild sloth in the road without getting clawed and move him to the other side, near a tree he could climb. This knowledge came in handy when Paul and I came upon a sloth crossing a major highway. Paul positioned the car at an angle in the road and put on his hazard lights so oncoming cars would notice him. I got out and picked up the little guy. Paul began directing traffic to stop cars. The drivers saw what I was doing and pulled over with their hazard lights on. Many got out to watch. I walked slowly to the other side and realized there was no large tree nearby, so I carried him through some tall grass, hoping there were no snakes. I finally arrived at a large tree, and he grabbed on. Then he slowly turned his head toward me, smiled a genuine smile, and reached out his three-toed hand in a gesture of thanks." I felt blessed to be able to help.

The neighborhood had cute wild white-faced monkeys and larger, very loud howler monkeys that love fruits and nuts in our trees. I found some almond seedlings along the beach and reforested them around our property. The common white-nosed coatimundi, called *pazote*, is a terrestrial animal the size of a raccoon that climbs trees and fences.

Retirement in Costa Rica was uplifting. The beauty of nature and tranquility surrounded us. It was truly paradise, but we also knew it was not a first-world country. We came to expect long lines at the bank or the municipality, and almost daily electric outages. Waterline breaks caused water to be shut off until repairs were completed. Road closures due to landslides, downed trees, vehicle accidents, or road improvements are a common occurrence. I could be stuck in a traffic backup from perhaps thirty to forty minutes, up to six hours if there was a fatal accident. However, the Costa Rican municipality was very responsive. I always had extra water in the car and a fruit bar, just in case.

❧

Eventually, another silent elephant entered the room, observing both of us. I was busy feeding chickens, riding horses, going to lunch with a friend, gardening, and reading good Kindle books I downloaded to my phone.

Paul always made coffee in the morning, then would sit on the veranda all day watching videos on his laptop. I'd get my coffee and be busy on the farm all day. I'd make lunch and dinner, then we would have a glass of wine and play cards before retiring, each to his own side of the king-sized bed.

49

After four long months and a new x-ray, I was given a clean bill of health. The brace came off, but Dr. Gomez suggested I use a cane for a while to stabilize my walking on the uneven ground in Costa Rica. I felt great and both my legs were very strong. With the extensive PT, I did not lose any muscle mass in either leg. Dr. Gomez said, "Not yet, but eventually, perhaps you could start riding Baru again." Yes, I will!

At last, I was back on my feet at home, getting back into my new routine without a wheelchair. Then, suddenly, I got a shocking email from Eunice, my friend in Kenya, who ran Tumaini, where my Kenyan boys were living. She explained that Albert, now twenty-two years old, started complaining of severe leg pain. After numerous trips to various doctors, with no results, she finally took him to a hospital in Nairobi. After a battery of tests, they diagnosed him with leukemia. He was now hospitalized and had begun chemotherapy. She also indicated that she was planning a fundraiser, but she did not have the money for his treatment, which would cost thousands of dollars. There is no socialized medicine in Kenya, and most Kenyans have no insurance, unless they have professional jobs.

I was a bit skeptical of her letter, and called her to get more details, but got the same story. I had always had an odd feeling about Eunice. During my time with the UN, I often traveled to see the boys. Eunice and I agreed to meet at her home, but when I arrived after a long flight, she had disappeared with an odd excuse. It was bizarre to me, then troubling, and finally suspicious. The boys did not understand her behavior either. I wondered if she was being honest with me.

I was very worried about Albert's illness and hoped it was not as serious as she had claimed. My leg had healed, and finally I could walk with extreme care. I flew to Nairobi for about ten days to investigate Albert's diagnosis.

Africans often try to scam *muzungus*, whites, because they have money. It had happened to me before, so I was wary. I would never send her the thirty-five thousand dollars she said she needed for this round of chemotherapy. I needed to go to Nairobi to see Albert, talk to the doctors, tour the facilities, and review the actual test results to determine whether it was real.

Finally I called my good friend Maryanne in Nairobi, and she graciously invited me to stay with her while I sorted things out.

Paul understood what I had to do and agreed to stay at the finca until I was back from Kenya." We still had plans to separate. Nothing had changed. In fact, I was pretty fed up with his impatience and lack of compassion during my four-month recovery. He wanted to leave and return to the U.S. to be with his children. We agreed that he would pack up all his stuff while I was in Kenya and leave as soon as I returned.

❧

My trip to Nairobi was long, but uneventful. I was free of the cast and felt strong, but I took my cane to help me navigate. I drove straight to Maryanne's house and was welcomed like a long-lost sister. She was very warm and understanding. She and I became very close when I lived in Kenya. It was so good to see her and connect with an old friend.

I arranged to meet Eunice, and she took me to see Albert in a small hospital setting. He was lying in bed, and gave me that big smile of his, and said, Hello, Mum, you came." I said, Of course I came," and gave him a big hug. He was no longer a child but a tall, handsome twenty-two-year-old man who had been studying to become a minister. He explained about his pain and the medication he was on. I could tell he was very weak, but he still had that radiant smile of love.

The next day, Eunice and I went to see the doctor who was treating him. He spoke English very well and explained the type of leukemia Albert had, the extensive treatment involved, and the uncertain prognosis. Steven, my other Kenyan boy, was there at the hospital, and I was so glad he was supporting his brother. Peter, the oldest boy, was working and could not get away to visit us. It disappointed me.

Before my trip, I had contacted an oncologist in the U.S. I explained my dilemma of being in Costa Rica and learning that a relative in Kenya was diagnosed with leukemia. She was invaluable, discussed the best treatment for his type of leukemia and the names of the chemotherapy drugs involved. The doctor confirmed that he was getting the best treatment. The reality was dire. I confirmed that he was mortally ill. Eunice had been telling me the truth. I paid the current bill for the first round of treatment. After each treatment, there would be a three to four-week break, then he would return to the hospital for another round of chemo.

I had only been in Kenya a week when Albert finished his first round of chemo and was released from the hospital. He looked very thin yet had that wonderful smile and was anxious to go home to Tumaini, where he lived. I asked Eunice if I could stay at the Tumaini, and she gave me a small, cluttered room in her quarters to sleep.

❧

Albert was feeling better, but would get weak and tired quickly. I wanted to spend some time with him, so I suggested visiting where we used to live in Tigoni. The caretaker of our old log home allowed us to look inside and reminisce. We then visited an old Kenyan neighbor who welcomed us. After only two hours, he was exhausted and asked to return to Tumaini. He was the same courageous boy I met that day at Westlands. He had worked so hard to become a certified Christian minister and was on the cusp of launching a career. My heart ached as I wrestled with the severity of his illness.

Albert introduced me to his girlfriend, who visited Tumaini. I could tell they were very much in love. He wanted to be with her all the time and forget his troubles. He seemed stable for the time being, so I booked my return flight home.

I knew treatment would be expensive, but I had savings. Eunice had a fundraiser for Albert after I left, but only five hundred dollars was raised. I realized the financial responsibility was mine, but that didn't matter. What mattered was his health.

Attempting to plan for his future, Eunice and I had started researching the possibility of a bone marrow transplant if the chemo treatment failed. Through his doctors and the Internet, we learned that countries like India and China had bone marrow and stem cell transplant facilities that cost significantly less than in the United States or even in Kenya. We were investigating every alternative.

❧

Bringing the boys to Costa Rica had never been an option. This country is white, with a few blacks on the Caribbean coast. Since the boys were black, they would be discriminated against at every turn. I had not seen any blacks until I visited the Caribbean coast. In addition, they were not my legal sons or related to me. In Costa Rica, they'd have no medical care or a work visa. They would be tourists, allowed to enter for only ninety days. They would be stuck in a foreign environment without friends and familiar surroundings, isolated in a white community. If I had been in the States, it would have been a bit easier.

I headed for home with hope, realizing the damning prognosis looming in the distance. Albert agreed to keep me posted using WhatsApp. Every few days, I d get a call, and he seemed fine. He could not yet return to his ministry instruction and was a bit lost, just waiting for his subsequent treatment. I could tell he was clinging to his girlfriend, and I assumed they had been intimate.

❧

Then Albert called to tell me that Eunice had thrown him out of her home for having sex with his girlfriend. Albert had packed up and moved in with a good friend who also grew up in Tumaini. I was glad he had a place to stay. Over time, I could tell he was unsettled and hated having to be dependent on others, a prisoner to his disease, unable to work and earn a living. That frustration grew. He seemed too proud to be completely reliant on others for his food, shelter, and transportation, yet he was too weak to work. He became very despondent and had no support system at a time when he needed to be loved and cared for. I sent him money so he could contribute to the family he was staying with, but I knew he was proud and uncomfortable in his situation.

Then he started saying he was feeling very well and had decided to discontinue his chemo, get a job, and find a place to live with his girlfriend. I begged him not to, that he needed to get well first. He said he believed God would help him. I didn't have an answer to that. Each time he called, he reiterated his new plan, insisting God would provide. I spoke to his street brother, Steven, and he told me that Albert was determined to ignore his illness and move on with his life. He would listen to no one.

After a few weeks, Steven called to tell me Albert had become very sick and had been admitted to the hospital again. I spoke to Albert, but he refused any further chemotherapy treatment. It was now in God s hands, and he was comfortable with his decision. A few weeks later, Steven called to tell me Albert had passed away. It was not a big surprise, but it was still a shock. I wanted to honor Albert's wishes, but it didn't fill the emptiness and grief in my heart for the young Kenyan boy I had loved and raised as my own. I missed comforting him before his death, but he had the strength of God with him.

I looked back on his story. Albert had lived a tough life, been abused and rejected by his stepfather at a very young age. He finally escaped and spent two years on the streets with Peter and Steven, where I found them and took them in. He was then rejected by Eunice, whom he had considered a loving Kenyan Mum for years.

He lived his strong belief in God and put his life in God's hands. He is now at peace with God. I'll always love and admire him for his total faith. He was a fantastic person, and I am proud to have been a part of his young life. I have a handsome photo of him in my living room.

Later, I was contacted by the church in Colorado that supported Tumaini and was told she had been fired from her position as manager for her mismanagement and misappropriation of funds. The inconsistencies and drama made more sense. I knew something had been off.

❧

It was 2013. I was now alone, after being with Paul for over thirty-two years. I grieved our loss. On the one hand, there was a huge void in my life; on the other hand, I had been alone for much of my life and had good friends who supported me.

I was still grieving a ghost I had fallen in love with, and now he was gone. I could not get my head around it. I understood the reality but not the logic of our invincible love.

50

Upon my return home, I wished Paul a happy new life and saw the taxi pull away on his way to the airport and a new life. I was devastated and hugged him fiercely. Our happy 24/7 retirement had crumbled into living as unhappy roommates, and neither of us could endure the hypocrisy it had become. He was no longer the person I had married. We were now legally separated and had divided our joint assets as Paul wished. Dr. Gomez gave me the okay to ride Baru but warned me to take it easy and listen to my leg. For the first couple of weeks, Sonja and I took it slow, then we cantered, and finally galloped. My leg never bothered me. It was strong and solid. I sent my doctor a photo of me on Baru, and he was very proud of my recovery. Twice a week, Sonja and I galloped through the beautiful fields, through forests occasionally crossing streams. Baru still wanted to win a race and would suddenly get more horsepower when Sonja tried to pass me. We'd always have a great conversation during our ride, and I loved the exercise. After our ride, we'd stop at my house or hers for coffee, sitting on my veranda gazing out at the Pacific.

I smiled that I had fully recovered from my broken leg. Nancy, Sonja, Lily, and I continued to get together and have lunch at least once a month. I continued gardening and started collecting orchids. There are many wild orchids in Costa Rica that I found on fallen limbs, and others I bought. Gardening was a passion I had since I was a kid, helping my father. Gardening in Costa Rica was a learning curve because, in this tropical climate, there were only wet and dry seasons. The temperate climate in the States, with its four seasons, no longer applied.

Sonja was invaluable. I learned that during *menguante,* the waning Moon cycle, I could trim bushes during the rainy season and stick the trimmings in the ground, and they would grow. Since I had many bushes, I started giving my neighbors cuttings for their home.

Neil came down to visit with his girlfriend, Kelly, and my granddaughter, Anastacia, Stacia, for short. We had a great time, and Stacia loved seeing the horses and collecting eggs every morning. Neil decided to make Stacia a tree house in an old mango tree that looked out over the Pacific. She was eleven years old and loved it. Neil is a great cook, so we d have fresh tuna or shrimp. Or I d cook my old standards—meatloaf, chicken parmesan, or spaghetti.

❧

One afternoon, Nancy called and invited us to her house to see her new kids, baby goats. We jumped at the chance, piled into the car, and spent a couple of hours with Nancy explaining and demonstrating how to milk a goat. We each tried, and finally, Stacia got the hang of it. Nancy took me aside before we left and said she would be at my corral very early the next morning to pick up the cute little stray dog I had found and had been feeding. She continued, Don t tell James, my husband, because he doesn't like me spending money on stray dogs. I have an appointment with the vet tomorrow morning, and I will get him examined, wormed, and fixed. I already have a home for him."

The next morning, I drove by the corral and noticed that Nancy had picked up the dog along with the little sack he used as a bed. Later that morning, around 10 a.m., James called and asked, "Do you know where Nancy is? I told him, "No, I had tried to call her, but she didn't answer, which was not unusual for Nancy." He said, "I tried to reach her, and she does not answer." I was keeping her secret. He called again around noon, very worried. He said she should have been home for lunch, and still no word. I was worried about it now, too, and told him her secret. There was evidence she had picked up the stray dog in my corral, then was headed to San Isidro to the veterinarian's office. He immediately called the vet, but she had never arrived. By then, both James and I knew something was wrong. He and a friend were headed to San Isidro to see if their truck was disabled on the side of the road.

❧

I sped down to the corral again and looked all around the road for anything out of the ordinary, like skid marks or disturbed brush, but found nothing out of place. About five p.m., James called, frantic, "We found nothing along the road to San Isidro. I have notified the police that she is missing." It was now dusk. I called Maria, my neighbor, and asked her if she would drive down the dirt road by the corral, and I d hold the flashlight while looking for her vehicle. It was obvious Nancy had had an accident. We went very slowly, shining the flashlight into the bushes, and I was yelling "Nancy!" and blowing my whistle. We found nothing and heard nothing, so we got out of the car and continued walking along the road, looking for any sign of a disturbance.

A neighbor, Johan, heard that Nancy was missing, and he appeared on the roadway, looking as well. The road after my property was dense with bamboo and foliage. The property was overgrown and unused, but as we shined the flashlight along the barbed wire, Johan noticed a slight break in the wire. I had walked that road often with my dogs and saw that a new barbed-wire fence had recently been installed. We looked at each other, and Jerry said, "This is where she went off the road and down into the deep ravine." We could not see anything. We shone our lights straight down the drop-off, into nothing but jungle, but it was the only possibility. My heart sank. Oh my God, she has been in that hot truck for over twelve hours.

I immediately called James, and he rushed to the scene with a friend who had a long rope in his trunk. They tied the rope to Maria s vehicle and slowly descended about over eighty feet into the pitch dark, where they found the truck. It had fallen to the bottom of the ravine, overturned, then slid on its roof until it was out of sight. They yelled up to us that Nancy was inside and conscious.

Thank God, I thought, but wondered why she had not heard me calling her name and using a whistle to alert her when I was searching for her that afternoon. Why hadn't she gotten out of the vehicle?

❧

Johan called 911 and asked for a Red Cross ambulance and a rescue crew. We stood there in the dark, waiting and waiting and still waiting. James came up from below and took some water down to Nancy, and she told him she could not move to get out of the vehicle. We called 911 again and were told that the rescue fire truck was broken, so the ambulance crew had to divert to pick up the rescue equipment before they could arrive on the scene. They were now on their way. After standing in the darkness for another fifteen minutes, we saw the ambulance's bright red lights in the distance and heard the siren.

The Red Cross team, with only a few flashlights, attached a rope from a rescue gurney to the vehicle's bumper. Two rescue personnel rappelled down, broke the vehicle's windows, and removed her, strapping her securely to the gurney. They yelled up to us to pull on the rope, and with all the muscle power available, we pulled, and slowly she was guided up, and the gurney was laid in the middle of the dirt road. This was like a tragic action movie that was real life. My heart sank when I saw her.

I rushed over and kneeled by her side. She whispered very softly, I heard you calling me, but I was too weak to yell back." I could tell by her quiet whispering that her lungs had been compromised. Very softly, she explained what had happened. "I got the dog and settled her in the car and was trying to turn the truck around to go to the veterinarian, when suddenly the front wheels gave way, and the truck fell straight down to the bottom."

She was not wearing her seatbelt, so she had tumbled around inside the truck. She took a few breaths and continued, I was pinned upside-down on the dashboard and could not move at all. I have a lot of pain in my neck and think it is broken. The windows were up, and when the engine stalled, the air conditioner cut off. I was stuck there in that position all day in the horrible heat, praying to God for a miracle."

After a brief pause, she continued, "I knew I was seriously injured because I could not move my arms or legs, but I continued praying the entire day." She then added, I know I am dying. I can tell. My organs are shutting down, and that is why I could not yell. But I have made peace with the Lord." She might be right. She was a wise woman. What could I say in response?

Nancy and I had talked about what we wanted in case of a medical emergency. Neither of us wanted to go to the local socialized medical hospital because of all the horror stories we had heard. I explained to her that the ambulance would only take injured patients to the nearest local socialized hospital, in San Isidro. Once the Emergency Room, ER doctors performed triage to stabilize her, we would discharge her, and she would be transported in a private ambulance to CIMA Hospital in San José. A private ambulance had been ordered and was waiting to meet us at the emergency room. She nodded in understanding. Then she slowly repeated to me, I know that I am dying. I have been praying the whole time and have made peace with the Lord." I kissed her head and stood up.

❧

Why had they not put her in the ambulance? I saw James in the back of the ambulance, exhausted and in shock. Rescue personnel stood around, taking no action, as if their job was done. I approached James and asked why the ambulance had not loaded her and left. He responded without emotion that the driver refused to move until he had her cedula, Costa Rican identification and residency card, or passport. That was ridiculous. Her purse was in the truck at the bottom of the ravine.

I lost it and started yelling at the Red Cross personnel to get her to the hospital. Maria approached me and advised me to cool it, that yelling would not help. James just sat there. At last, the rescue personnel rappelled down again and, after another ten minutes, brought her purse, along with the sweet little dog that had been in the truck the entire time. I had forgotten about the little guy, but he seemed fine, wagging his tail, happy to be finally out of the truck. They loaded Nancy into the ambulance and drove off to San Isidro with sirens blaring. Maria dropped me off at my house, and I followed the ambulance in my car.

Sally, one of Nancy s close friends, met us at the hospital. Only one of us was allowed in the emergency room with Nancy. Sally spoke fluent Spanish, so James said she should accompany Nancy. James and I sat down in the waiting room and waited. It was around 10 p.m. Nancy was still conscious and in terrible pain. She had been trapped in the hot vehicle for over fifteen hours. My heart went out to her! We waited silently for hours, eventually drifting off.

❧

When I awoke, I asked James if he had gotten any news. He had not! We went back to the information desk and saw Sally. She said they had done an x-ray of her neck, and the doctor said, "She is fine." I retorted, She is not fine. She is paralyzed from the neck down." The private ambulance driver was still waiting to take her to CIMA in San José, three or four hours away. But they continued keeping her, but had not given her anything for pain. The driver advised James that he should insist on giving her pain medication and then refuse further treatment and release her immediately. The nurse commented that the records would not be ready for at least four hours. James said he would pick them up later and signed the discharge form. A nurse finally gave her a shot for her pain. Nancy asked me to take off her neck brace because it was hurting her so much. I started rubbing the place where it was chafing. The ambulance emergency medical technician told her, Just wait until we are in the ambulance, and I'll take it off." I turned to him and said, No, you won t. I don t care what the doctor said; Nancy has a broken neck and is now paralyzed from the neck down. Leave it in place!" "Of course," he replied sheepishly.

Outside, the sun was starting to rise at five a.m. They loaded her into the ambulance and left for San José. As soon as I got home, I called my doctor, Dr. Gomez at CIMA, and explained the accident and the need to be prepared to receive Nancy at their emergency room. He assured me they would have a neurologist, an orthopedic specialist, and other specialists on stand-by. I thanked him and then tried to sleep. My overwhelming feeling was that if, in fact, Nancy had broken her neck and was permanently paralyzed, she would not want to live as a paraplegic. She was too full of life. Nancy had a deep faith, and I m sure she and God had discussed the issue while she was trapped in the crushed vehicle at the bottom of the ravine. Time would tell.

❧

James called later that morning to tell me the doctors were waiting at the ER as soon as the ambulance pulled up. They immediately intubated her, putting her in a medicated coma, while they ran the necessary tests. James mentioned how painful the trip over the mountain was for her, with winding turns all the way up and then back down. She was strapped down, but the swaying still jarred her whole body. Every sway made the trip excruciating. She also told him she was dying. James had gotten a hotel room close to the hospital, and friends had come to bring him some clothes and provide support and comfort.

The next day, I drove to see Nancy in the CIMA Neurological ICU. James met me and took me in to see her. She looked peaceful. There were machines and monitors everywhere. James said her kidneys had started shutting down, so they had put her on dialysis. She was in critical condition. Doctors were trying to keep her alive at this point. He left me alone with her, and I talked gently to her. I placed my mother s rosary on her white sheet near her kidneys. James entered, frowning and asking, "What is that?" I explained, and he nodded and left. I drove home thinking she had probably been right, she was dying. If we had only found Nancy that morning before the heat of the day, could there have been a better outcome? I m sure she would have had a better chance of survival, but she also knew God was with her.

❧

I recalled the medical trauma course I completed while working in Baghdad, a few years before. The UN wanted every staff member to be qualified to perform emergency trauma assistance in case of an emergency. They had stressed that the *"Golden Hour"* was critical in providing critical treatment before shock set in. We learned how to evaluate the situation quickly, give the ABCs of treatment–Airway, Breathing, and Circulation–perform CPR, stop bleeding, monitor circulation, then administer intravenous fluids, and set broken bones. I never had to practice my new skill.

Three days later, James called to tell me her organs had failed and she had passed away. I thought I was prepared, but I was not. She was one of my best friends, and she was gone. Such a bright shining light, with her southern accent and her quick wit, she loved everyone, and everyone loved her. About a week later, I was sitting on the veranda having my morning coffee. Suddenly, a hummingbird flew two feet in front of my face and just hovered for several seconds, and then flew to the side and hovered some more. When it returned and hovered by my face again, I knew and said, "Nancy, is that you? I love you!" and she flew off. I was finally at peace that she was okay, but the loss of her friendship took its toll on me. I had lost Paul, then Albert, and now Nancy. A very nice memorial service was held about a month later, and friends from all over came to pay their respects. Life goes on, but it was never the same without her.

51

I found it hard to get my head around Nancy s tragic accident and untimely death. The accident was a horrible fact I could not dispute; I had witnessed the inadequate emergency services available in this rural area of Costa Rica. That, combined with my witnessing Nancy's emergency room misdiagnosis, saying 'she was fine' and having no awareness of her paralysis from the neck down, most likely caused by a broken neck. It shook me to my core, and I felt very vulnerable.

I had heard horror stories of expatriate patients inadequately cared for by the Costa Rica socialized medicine system, patients dying uncared for in hospital hallways without water or food. A neighbor of mine went into the hospital to get a cyst removed from his colon, but they perforated his colon, and he became septic. After two more emergency surgeries, followed by a heart attack and weeks of recovery, he miraculously survived with a colostomy bag that would accompany him for the rest of his life.

❧

I had been an eyewitness to the entire emergency rescue and hospital emergency care Nancy received, and was horrified. Friends with adequate resources or international insurance, accustomed to private medical care, chose to utilize private medical facilities; the most renowned were two private hospitals in San José. Nancy and I were advocates of the private services and avoided the social medical care available to us as residents.

I was living alone in a third-world country, so I chose to go private for my medical needs. I had an internal medicine doctor at CIMA and had yearly check-ups for high blood pressure. I also decided to get colonoscopies done at CIMA. The next time I was due, I took advice from friends who said this local clinic did colonoscopies regularly and was not as expensive, so I went there. My third colonoscopy was performed back at CIMA, and that doctor removed polyps that had been present for more than three years and had been missed by the other doctor. Shit, I could have gotten cancer for trying to save money.

I learned of the importance of the "Golden Hour" in trauma situations while in Iraq with the UN. Something had to be done to preserve the *"Golden Hour"* and bridge the gap between the 911 call and the ambulance's eventual arrival by offering a volunteer program that provides near-real-time trauma support. I was not sure how to do it, but I had to try. No one should lie in a ditch alone, bleeding for thirty or forty minutes until an ambulance arrives. The *"Golden Hour"* of care was critical.

Red Cross emergency services in San Isidro had only three ambulances, which may all be occupied, leaving them to respond to other accidents across the canton, delaying arrival by one to three hours. Once on the scene, you add on the rescue and the stabilization process, and scene triage. Transport to the victim somewhere in Platanillo consisted of rural dirt roads with no road signs. In the beautiful hilly terrain, cell coverage may not be immediately available to call 911.

The available International Red Cross first aid services consisted of clearing the airway, performing CPR, trying to stop bleeding, splinting prominent broken bones, stabilizing the patient on a gurney, and transporting the patient to the nearest socialized hospital.

❧

Grief is a fantastic motivator. I needed to do some research. First, I went to the Red Cross office in San Isidro and talked to the personnel in charge. They explained that all emergency services were staffed entirely by volunteers, trained only in rescue operations, Red Cross first aid, and CPR. The Red Cross volunteers were not emergency medical technicians, EMTs, certified like their private counterparts, who could administer oxygen or start an intravenous saline drip line.

The Red Cross offered to provide an official Red Cross First Aid and CPR course to private personnel for two hundred dollars per person. That was a positive, but on the brighter side, I knew there were private ambulance services with trained EMTs available. Private hospitals in San José, CIMA, and Clínica Biblica were renowned for excellent care provided by U.S.-trained Costa Rican doctors. A volunteer response capability did not exist. Limited private-sector emergency medical response services existed but were not readily available. A 911 call for emergency services activates only the socialized medical system. Red Cross volunteers responded, and the patient was taken to the nearest socialized hospital. It was only after the socialized hospital triage was complete that a patient could refuse further treatment and arrange a private ambulance or helicopter to a private hospital.

❧

Because of my trauma training in Iraq, I knew more could be done. The *"Golden Hour"* of trauma treatment is paramount. I focused on how I could develop a community-based, non-profit group that could bridge the gap between the accident and the arrival of Red Cross emergency response personnel.

First, I needed to see if such a service already existed. There was no need to reinvent the wheel. I talked to people I d met throughout Costa Rica, but found no such initiative. Then I spoke to Tico's friends to find out if there was any town-level or town-owned structure in place for Platanillo, and learned each town had an association with a board of directors that reported to the municipality. The purpose of the association was to address the community's needs with the approval and support of the Costa Rica municipality. My proposal needed to be approved and supported by the community as a joint Gringo/Tico project, or it would surely fail.

I finally had enough information to propose a solution and was excited, with many ideas in my head. My career was in project design and implementation of computer systems. This effort did not include computers, but it was a project, and I felt I could cobble together a cooperative effort that would benefit the community. Using my old skills as a systems engineer, I drafted a concept of operations document describing how the project would work and turned it into a PowerPoint presentation. I then vetted the idea with a few interested friends and neighbors to get their feedback. Everyone thought it was a great idea, but none had the time to make it a reality. My biggest personal stumbling block was my lack of fluency in Spanish. I could converse about day-to-day matters, but briefing and convincing the Platanillo Board of Directors would be a challenge, especially in a male-dominated society. I was also Gringa and needed to be taken seriously.

I decided to meet first with well-known members of the community, i.e., respected men and women who could stand with me and first support the concept of improved emergency services to the Red Cross officials, and then convince the Platanillo Association that it was a worthwhile effort for their community. So I recruited my local realtor, JJ, who had shown me my house, and a nearby restaurant owner, Edwin. They were local Ticos who also spoke fluent English and were respected in the community. I briefed them on my idea, and they immediately saw the benefit to the community and agreed to help me as translators. We were now ready to present the concept to the Platanillo Association.

❧

Members of the association gathered and held their regular agenda of local business, all in Spanish, which I did not understand.

Then it was my turn. I was introduced and gave the presentation in English with JJ and Edwin translating as I went along. I started by explaining Nancy's tragic fatal accident a few months before, and explaining the Golden Hour of response. I proposed forming a group of volunteers, Gringos and Ticos, working under the guidance of the association, as a subcommittee with the name of SOS Platanillo. The mission was to *Bridge the gap*" between the 911 call and the arrival of the Red Cross ambulance. Our volunteers would be trained in Red Cross first aid and CPR, and would provide immediate first aid, reassurance, and communication with 911 officials about the victim's condition. They would give directions, then wait with the injured until the ambulance arrived.

Residents were encouraged to become SOS Platanillo volunteers and to sign up for a one-year commitment in exchange for certification in Red Cross First Aid. The Red Cross would train each candidate in first aid and CPR at SOS Platanillo's expense. Upon completion of the course, the volunteer would receive a backpack of first aid materials. They would act as SOS first responders available 24/7, providing critical care and comfort until the Red Cross ambulance arrived.

Anyone who observed an accident, in or around Platanillo, would first call 911 to get the Red Cross response team activated, then the observer would call the official SOS central call number, and a volunteer would be dispatched immediately to the scene to provide first aid and reassurance that help was on the way. All of this depended on fluent Spanish speakers, although sometimes accidents involved tourists, and English was essential as well. The association was excited about the idea and agreed to work with us on the details.

❧

Next, I scheduled a meeting with the Red Cross and briefed them on the idea. I needed their buy-in. I was hoping that the Red Cross would do the training for free, but they made it clear that each course would cost two hundred dollars, which meant significant fundraising, which I knew nothing about. They stated that 911 must be the first emergency call made, and then the SOS Call center's central phone number could be called. The SOS Call Center would call the volunteer nearest the accident, and the volunteer would grab their first-aid backpack and rush to the scene on their motorbike. He could contact 911 to relay the patient's condition and any other important information.

Many neighbors were interested in the project, and I hoped to get assistance with its planning and execution. There was acceptance, and many new ideas were proposed, but no one had extra time to turn the concept into reality. I felt helpless because of my lack of Spanish skills and realized I needed someone fluent in Spanish who shared my passion for helping the community. I selected my Gringo neighbor, Philip, a retired Danish expat who lived nearby. He was excited about the project and agreed to participate.

Next was fundraising, sponsored by the association. Johan and his partner, Tim, were instrumental in coordinating the effort, and we raised enough money to hold a Red Cross first-aid class. We were off and running. Flyers and stickers were distributed to residents to let them know the SOS Platanillo emergency response" was coming soon.

SOS Platanillo was off to a great start; we had a trained team, procedures in place, and local outreach to ensure residents understood what to do in an emergency. I was ready to turn over the reins and title as SOS president to Philip, and he willingly accepted. He became the SOS focal point between the Red Cross and our association.

It still exists today, supporting the community. I am very proud of my project. Later, a nearby remote town, further up in the mountains, adopted our project model and now has its own SOS Las Tumbas, supporting its rural community. They are doing great work.

Part Nine

52

I had lost my marriage, then Albert died, and now Nancy. Each separate tragedy had hit me deeply. I felt as if I were on a boat with no rudder. I was lethargic, and while I usually pushed myself to get out and take the dogs to the beach, meet a friend for lunch, or do some gardening, I found myself just staying home, napping, or just reading for hours.

The most significant impact was losing Paul, the love of my life. I never imagined living without him. I was almost seventy. I loved the farm and living in Costa Rica, but it was different knowing Paul was out of my life. I was disappointed, upset, unsettled, brokenhearted, but there was nothing I could do to change anything. I could not call Nancy to talk about my day, nor could I arrange an outing to San José for shopping. She was gone too.

After Paul left, the neighbors looked at me differently. I was single and was the odd person out. After several months, the old couples we used to socialize with didn't include me as often. I considered selling the farm and returning to the States to be near my sons. But after a bit of soul-searching, I realized it was a bad idea. I loved my farm, my animals, Costa Rica s beautiful environment, and having friends around me.

❧

I had learned a lesson watching Gloria, a dear friend of mine. She had become unhappy after her husband died suddenly while living in Naples, Florida. She then sold her home and moved to a lovely three-bedroom condominium, but was still unhappy. I urged her to move to a beautiful independent living retirement home, and she did, but she never socialized with anyone and finally picked up and moved in her 1980s to live with an old friend in Maryland. She hated the new location and convinced her only son to take her in. She was never happy there either. Her misery and health problems always followed her.

I did not want that to happen to me. Finally, I kicked myself in the butt and decided I needed to reach out and try harder to make new friends. My sons had their lives and didn't need to have me nearby to worry about. I had raised them to be independent, and they were both successful. Thankfully, I was healthy and loved my animals. I needed to try my best to adjust to this solo lifestyle, and I did call my sons more often and was comforted.

If that was not enough, my best friend Sonja reluctantly shared that, due to her health issues, she was unable to keep the farm going. She and Fritz decided to sell their farm and move back to Europe. I understood, but it left a huge hole that has not been filled. We were good friends, riding buddies, almost every week we would play cards, drink wine, eat snacks, while solving the world s problems or at least Platanillo s issues.

❧

After a few months, I recognized my funk as depression and realized I needed some help. I contacted a psychologist, who lived an hour down the coast in Ohochal. Lynn was a petite woman with blond hair and a genuinely compassionate smile. She had retired in the U.S. as a psychologist and moved to Costa Rica, working only part-time and seeing her clients back home via Skype. I explained my situation and had several sessions with her discussing how to get out of my funk. One day, she said, "Barbara, you just need some friends, and I am going to introduce you to some of my friends. The first one is a wonderful, older woman named Ruthie, who has been a practicing Buddhist since 1970. She held Buddha talks every Friday in Ohochal. "I'll go to the next talk and introduce you," she said. Another group of friends also gets together every Saturday morning for breakfast at the Baker Bean Restaurant in Uvita, and you are welcome to join us."

She was right. I began going to the Buddha group talks every Friday and got to be good friends with Ruthie, the Buddha guru, and her friends. She was in her nineties, but her knowledge, intelligence, and compassion are amazing. A widow for many years, she came to Costa Rica alone and settled here. She was a fantastic inspiration. She had quite a following and always has good advice that can be applied to our daily lives.

I had never studied Buddhism, and she explained that it is not a religion but a philosophy and a way of life. I learned the Eight-Fold Path, and discussions began to sink in. I found myself looking inward. If I became upset or angry about something, I d stop and analyze why I was angry and whether it was worth all the effort and stress. Sometimes it was easier to put the anger in my palm and blow it away like a feather caught in the wind. It did not work in all cases, but often became a magic release. Over time, I became a better, more introspective, and more compassionate person.

I also drove to the Saturday breakfasts, which lasted all morning, with a friendly group of Gringos, and we d discuss a variety of topics. Lynn and Ruthie were also there. I became part of their group and was beginning to feel like Baba was once again accepted.

Ruthie knew I had to drive fifty kilometers each way to the Buddha Talk on Friday and then back on Saturday for breakfast, so she graciously invited me to stay overnight after her talk, and we d go to the Saturday breakfast the next morning. I agreed, and as a result, we became very close, talking and sharing stories of our lives into the night. Eventually, we became best friends.

❧

Over the past few years, several friends who were familiar with my career as a single Mom, travels to Europe, meeting Paul, and our history and adventures, would remark, “You have had such an interesting life, you should write a memoir.” After several people mentioned it, I began to consider it. At least I could leave a legacy for my grandchildren.

Then, one morning, while having coffee on her veranda, I mentioned to Ruthie that I was thinking of writing a memoir. She was delighted and said it was a fantastic idea. She majored in journalism and worked as an editor at Vogue magazine after college. During my career, I have written many technical documents concerning specific government computer projects, including requirements and design specifications, as well as operational training and user manuals. I had two technical documents I had written, published by the government, but I had never written anything for myself and had never even considered journaling.

I decided I would do it. As a total novice, I reached out for advice and assistance, and I joined a small, local writers’ group for guidance. Each of us was trying to write a book about our lives. We d meet once a month for lunch and review a chapter of a member s work.

I remember the comments from a few members on my early chapters. “Barbara, you are not writing a letter, ‘I did this, then I went there and the blah blah, blah.’ Tell us how you felt when you did this, or how you reacted, and describe how you dealt with those feelings. Share your feelings!” Easier said than done for a technical writer.

❧

Slowly, I revised many chapters and slowly learned to look inside myself, at that time in my life, and bring my feelings to life. It was not in my nature to talk about feelings, so I was breaking through new emotional ground and exposing feelings I didn’t know I had.

The whole process became cathartic as I wrote about difficult periods in my life, and I gained new insights into myself. I acknowledged the pain and humiliation in my first marriage and the adverse effect it had on my love life. I had locked painful emotions away. I looked forward to each new chapter, to cleanse my soul and provide me an opportunity to heal.

Ruthie was always interested in my writing, so I started bringing my laptop with me on the weekends and reading aloud to her. At Ruthie's age, she was going blind, so hearing my story gave her a window into my soul. Sometimes she stopped me to offer advice, ask questions to clarify a point, or provide a description. She readily agreed that I needed to express more feelings, but it was hard for me to do. Eventually, I learned to release my emotions onto the page and began enjoying expressing them. There were times during my writing when I d have an epiphany, not realizing what had happened because I had been consumed by it. As I sit finishing my book years later, it is a labor of love and exploration.

Looking back,

Ruthie has become my very best friend. She is an extraordinary woman whose wit and intelligence shine through our talks. She has been going blind gradually for a few years now. She can no longer drive and needs rides everywhere. She manages to navigate inside her house, and all her neighbors love her and gladly take her shopping or to the doctor. Occasionally, if she needs an appointment in San José, I'll bring her to my house to spend the night and take her to the doctor the next day. Chico, my male dog, always finds Ruthie and sleeps with her. She loves dogs and was flattered. We have developed a wonderful friendship over the years.

I sit here today, proofreading my manuscript one last time before sending it to my publisher. It continues to be a labor of love. Ruthie is still encouraging me to "just finish it, it's a good book, you need to stop and get it published." She is looking forward to seeing it in print, our joint accomplishment.

53

In early 2020, a strange new, very contagious virus named COVID-19 encompassed the globe like a lethal cloud. It could not be stopped. International travel, but the virus spread before we knew it, bringing serious illness, death, and destruction to the inhabitants of our Earth. It quickly became an unstoppable pandemic, and we knew nothing that could stop it. Everyone stayed home and watched on television as news reported rising hospitalizations, and the death toll rose in cities around the world. This enemy was new, and we had no defense except to wear a mask over our nose and mouth and wash our hands often.

Costa Rica promptly shut down its borders. Public beaches were even closed. Retirees stayed home, but workers had to continue work, always wearing a mask. Clients were required to wash their hands upon arrival, wear a mask, and always stand or sit three meters apart when in lines or on buses and taxis.

I limited my shopping to one day a week. In any public area, wearing masks and washing hands were mandatory before entering any building—a bank, church, grocery store, or other business facility. Everyone wore masks in public.

❧

Some friends and neighbors in the area did not believe COVID was that serious, but were forced to wear masks and wash their hands when entering businesses. After what seemed like forever, many people, including me, received the Pfizer vaccine offered by Costa Rica's clinics, and life became manageable, though still restrictive.

Once a vaccine was announced, some became suspicious of the brand-new vaccine that was rushed to market, thinking it had not been tested enough. How much testing is enough when the population of the world is dying, day after day? Some believed conspiracy theories that this was a plan to control the population.

As a result, friends and neighbors became fractured, fearing the deadly disease we could not see. There were the "vaxers," people who had been vaccinated, and "non-vaxers," those who refused the vaccine. Finally, in May 2023, after three long years of fear, isolation, loss of life, and jobs, the U.S. declared the COVID-19 pandemic was officially over as a public health emergency.

❧

I continued riding Baru during the pandemic, but it wasn't as enjoyable without Sonja. The beautiful trails were not the same. I missed the friendly dialogue with Sonja and the sharing we had, and I realized it would never be the same. After a long rainy season when I did not ride, I decided at seventy-six that I would discontinue riding. Baru was looking older, so I put us both out to pasture" to enjoy the rolling hills and gentle breezes.

My sons' father, Big Neil, died after several strokes, leaving them to take care of his estate. Neil had asked me, "What would I do if you suddenly died or were hospitalized and unconscious? I know nothing about the farm or your expenses, and I cannot speak Spanish." I casually said, The easiest thing would be to call Paul. I am sure he could come back to Costa Rica to help them navigate the law here and perhaps stay at the farm until you sort out what to do." Neil then said, You are still married?" I said, Yes, but formally separated." He pointed out that if Paul suddenly died, his heirs could try to claim half of my farm, even though Paul and I had legally divided our assets in 2013 and I legally owned the farm myself. He was right, and although I didn't think they would do such a thing, I needed to remove any potential loophole. I traveled to Illinois, where I was a resident, to obtain a formal divorce. Paul was agreeable, so I contacted an attorney and got all the papers signed. I am now divorced.

54

Paul left the U.S. and settled in Portugal to get his residency. It was a popular retirement destination. I had not heard from him in some time, so after the New Year of 2023, I sent him an email wishing him a happy New Year. He responded that he was pleased because he had just received his Portuguese residency and was looking forward to settling down.

I boldly asked if his invitation to visit him was still open. I was thinking of traveling to Spain to see Sonja and wanted to know whether I could also visit him. He said very enthusiastically, That sounds great. When do you plan to travel?" I replied, "It will probably be in the late spring or early summer when it's warmer." I was elated about his response and thought it would be nice to put the past behind us and just be traveling buddies as we had once been.

In early April, I was notified by his younger daughter via email that Paul had passed away on the fifth of April while living in Portugal. There was no autopsy, and the cause of death was vague, saying only that police thought it was probably a heart attack. Apparently, he had died alone in his flat, and the police found him a few days later. What a shock. He was dead! I felt tremendous loss and confusion.

❧

It was a long, hot summer. I was trying to get my head around the fact that Paul was dead. Being divorced was one thing, but his death was another level of shock and grief.

I needed to stay busy and not get into a funk, so I went on a cleaning spree, going through closets, dressers, and drawers to pass the time. In the back of a dresser drawer, I stumbled upon a small, red cardboard box, the kind used to store bank checks. My eyes widened, and my heart stopped beating for an instant! This little box contained micro-cassette tapes that Paul had sent me whenever we were apart for long periods. His voice was on those tapes.

This box contained Paul s voice, back when things were every day, and we were crazy in love. For the past ten years, I'd been wrestling with the question of What happened to make his personality change so dramatically?" "What had caused it?" "Could I have done anything to pull him out of it and get my loving husband back?"

I needed to hear his voice again. This was an intimate link to our past, when we were happily married. I searched for my cassette recorder but found it ruined by corrosive batteries left inside. Shit!

Epilogue

Thoughts went to my book. I had been distracted and made little progress during COVID-19, and although I denied it, I had hit writer s block and had to jump-start my efforts. Friends and family were curious and asked how it was going. I became embarrassed that I had not been able to draft the ending. I still enjoyed writing, but the final part of my story, the autumn of my life, left me wondering how I d end it. I decided to get away from everything for a month and finish my book.

Meanwhile, over the summer, Paul s Sister-in-law, Joan, whom I had known for years, told me about this cute cottage they purchased in Ruidoso, New Mexico. She described the area, including wild horses, habituated deer, and elk all around town, and said I would love it. I agreed to rent the place for October. Joan and Don agreed to meet me at the cottage and show me around before they left for home in California. I booked a flight, rented a car, and was there to meet me.

☙

It was a perfect time to get away by myself and have an adventure. I had never been to that part of the country. Once I arrived, I unpacked and made myself at home. The cottage was fully furnished and cozy. I got into a routine of fixing coffee, then breakfast, and working on my book for hours. Deer often came into the yard to feed on sunflower seeds from the bird feeder. They were so habituated that they would lie in the sun and nap in the yard.

Sometimes I d go out for lunch, then check out the small-town stores, especially the flea markets and antique stores. New Mexico is known for its beautiful turquoise, and I drooled over the jewelry, but I was in a phase of my life when I didn't dress up anymore. Ruidoso is a lovely, forested mountain town at seven thousand feet. It was about seventy degrees Fahrenheit and sunny during the day and the forties at night. This had been Native American country, and I had always admired how they respected and cared for nature and the environment. At the same time, we killed them and decimated their buffalo and tribal land. Although there was a lot to see, I stayed focused on my writing and quickly got into a groove, making good progress. I spoke to Ruthie occasionally, and she continued to encourage me.

❧

Amazon was a lifesaver. The old mini-cassette recorders are now obsolete, but I was able to buy a refurbished one and have it sent to the cottage. When it arrived, I checked to make sure it worked. The tapes were cryptically labelled, and I was not sure which one to start with.

The first tape was from August 2001, just before 9/11. Paul was finishing up his six-month assignment in the Democratic Republic of Congo, his first job for IRC. We always shared tapes when we were apart for long periods. One tape would contain about a week of newsy dialogue, sharing our daily lives, just like conversations we would typically have every evening at home over dinner, or later, naked, sharing a nice hot jacuzzi.

❧

I pressed "PLAY" and his familiar voice came alive. My heart was filled with overwhelming love. The honest Paul was alive, telling me, I love you, baby," that he could not wait to share a pint of Häagen-Dazs Cookies and Cream ice cream with me in bed. He shared his love of Congo, the isolation, and some frustrations with the UN bureaucracy, refugee shipments, or payroll for staff being delayed when a plane was delayed. He said he had started running again to stay in shape. He felt alive and happy. His six-month assignment was up in another week, and he was reflecting on the fantastic adventure, telling me, I could not think of working in an office ever again, after being in Congo." Paul had grown to love the Congo and their people. He mentioned taking a final walk around the small town of Lukalala, nestled on the Congo river, to say goodbye." While doing a bit of introspection, he shared that he wanted to be his best self, a good person who stayed in shape and would come back to me soon. I love you," he said.

He expressed his excitement about his next assignment as Deputy Director to the IRC Mission in Uganda in September. He said, We will be swamped when I return, getting my medical paperwork done, packing up the clothes and essentials we will need in Africa."

My heart soared as I listened to his voice. He was my old Paul" I knew so well—confident, intelligent, open with his feelings, caring, and, best of all, loving. His voice took me back to August of 2001, when I kept working in Virginia and waited for him to come home and start our grand adventure. A time before 9/11, the prostate cancer diagnosis, before the UN bombing. A time when we were very much in love and shared every part of our day, the successes, challenges, frustrations, and doubts.

I went back to a time when we were both happy, deeply in love, looking forward to a once-in-a-lifetime adventure in Africa. His voice washed over me, removing the doubt I had been dragging through my life since the bombing and his critical head injury. I felt validated. I had not been crazy. The real Paul" was talking to me and loved me as deeply as I loved him. After all the years of doubt about what had happened to the real Paul," I was uplifted and finally free, with his love protecting me.

Perhaps I'll never know why he changed, but it no longer matters. I am wrapped in his love, forever. We were unique and thought we were indestructible, but we were merely human beings who tried our best. Once we separated, we reconciled three different times.

Each time, Paul moved back to Costa Rica, but the mold had shattered and could not be repaired. No matter how hard we tried, the love and devotion we had shared for years were just a fond memory.

I finished the two tapes, then picked up the phone to talk to Ruthie in Costa Rica. She had been worried about how I would react to hearing Paul s voice. When I started describing my reaction, she interrupted and said, Barbara, you sound happy. Your voice is light-hearted, and I've never heard you as happy as you are right now."

I laughed and said, That is because I m still very much in love with my dead husband."

Acknowledgements

Many thanks to the following friends: Jan Hart, Tao Watts, Sheelagh Richards, and the Costa Rica Writers' Group for their encouragement, support, and feedback. A very special thanks to my granddaughter Anastacia Wolfe for teaching me how to "*show and not tell*"—what a difference it made. To my dear friends Bernadette Castner, Maria Cambronero, Cathy Mata, Roberta De Forest, and others for their encouragement and for asking, "Is it finished yet?" A final thanks to my editor, Adelia Richie, who taught me that I was not finished when I showed her what I thought was my completed draft. Your continuous helpfulness inspired me.

About the Author

Barbara Wolfe-Johnson has lived in many countries and has held positions with numerous United States government agencies, federal contractors, and non-profit foundations. She is the widow of the late Paul Johnson, and her two sons live in the United States. She lives on a small ranch outside the town of Planatillo near the Pacific coast in south-central Costa Rica.

The author and her late husband Paul Johnson

www.ingramcontent.com/pod-product-compliance
Lightning Source LLC
LaVergne TN
LVHW020652110826
845149LV00012B/1968

* 9 7 8 1 9 6 5 3 4 2 1 1 4 *